MARITAL AND FAMILY THERAPY

MARITAL AND FAMILY THERAPY
New Perspectives In Theory, Research and Practice

Edited by

Dennis A. Bagarozzi, Ph.D.
University of Georgia
School of Social Work
Athens, Georgia

Anthony P. Jurich, Ph.D.
Kansas State University
Manhattan, Kansas

Robert W. Jackson, Ph.D.
University of Vermont
Burlington, Vermont

HUMAN SCIENCES PRESS, INC.
72 Fifth Avenue
NEW YORK, NY 10011

Printed in the United States of America
23456789 987654321

Library of Congress Cataloging in Publication Data
Main entry under title:

Marital and family therapy.

    Includes index.
    1. Family psychotherapy.   2. Marital psychotherapy.
I. Bagarozzi, Dennis A.   II. Jurich, Anthony P.
III. Jackson, Robert W., 1936-
RC488.5M355   616.89'156   82-2994
ISBN 0-89885-069-X   AACR2

This book is dedicated to our families and friends who have been constant sources of encouragement and support in our work and in our lives: Judy, Dennis Jr. and Elizabeth Bagarozzi; Peter, Clara, Pete, Joan and Steven Jurich; Chris Jackson and Richard Kerckhoff.

ACKNOWLEDGEMENTS

We would like to express our sincere thanks and appreciation to the secretarial staff of the Research Office, Department of Family and Child Development, Kansas State University: Marcia Allen, Betsy Donnelly, and Linda Jensen, who patiently typed and retyped the edited manuscripts. We also wish to express our special appreciation to Judith I. Bagarozzi, M.S. who took precious time from her busy schedule to help us meet our deadlines by typing selected chapters and proofreading several manuscripts. Her help has been invaluable.

CONTENTS

CONTRIBUTORS

DENNIS A. BAGAROZZI, PhD
Assistant Professor
School of Social Work
University of Georgia
Athens, Georgia

Private Practice:
Atlanta and Athens, Georgia

RAMON G. CORRALES, PhD
Director of Family Services
Counseling Center for Human Development
Kansas City, Missouri

PAUL F. DELL, PhD
Director of Clinical and
Theoretical Studies
Colonial Institute
Newport News, Virginia

ALAN S. GURMAN, PhD
Professor of Psychiatry and
    Director, Outpatient Clinic
Department of Psychiatry
University of Wisconsin Medical School
Madison, Wisconsin

ROBERT W. JACKSON, PhD
Associate Director and Extension Home Economics Coordinator
School of Home Economics
University of Vermont
Burlington, Vermont

ANTHONY P. JURICH, PhD
Associate Professor of Family and Child Development
Department of Family and Child Development
Kansas State University
Manhattan, Kansas

FLORENCE W. KASLOW, PhD
Director
Florida Couples and Family Institute
West Palm Beach, Florida

DAVID P. KNISKERN, PsyD
Associate Professor of Psychiatry
Department of Psychiatry
University of Cincinnati College of Medicine
Cincinnati, Ohio

JANICE KOSTORYZ, MA
Research Specialist
Counseling Center for Human Development
Kansas City, Missouri

HAMILTON I. MCCUBBIN, PhD
Professor and Chair
Department of Family Social Science
University of Minnesota
St. Paul, Minnesota

MARILYN A. MCCUBBIN, RN
School of Public Health Nursing
University of Minnesota
St. Paul, Minnesota

DAVID H. OLSON, PhD
Professor of Family Studies

Department of Family Social Science
University of Minnesota
St. Paul, Minnesota

JOAN PATTERSON
Department of Family Social Science
University of Minnesota
St. Paul, Minnesota

LAURENCE RO-TROCK, PhD
Counseling Center for Human Development
Kansas City, Missouri

L. EDNA ROGERS, PhD
Associate Professor
Department of Communication
Cleveland State University
Cleveland, Ohio

CANDYCE S. RUSSELL PhD
Associate Professor of Family and Child Development
Department of Family and Child Development
Kansas State University
Manhattan, Kansas

LITA LINZER SCHWARTZ, PhD
Professor
Department of Educational Psychology
Pennsylvania State University
Ogontz Campus
Abington, Pennsylvania

BARBARA SMITH, OTR
Research Specialist
Counseling Center for Human Development
Kansas City, Missouri

HOWARD F. STEIN, PhD
Associate Professor of Medical-Psychiatric Anthropology
Department of Family Practice
   and Community Medicine and Dentistry

13

University of Oklahoma Health Sciences Center
Oklahoma City, Oklahoma

LANCE R. WILSON, PhD
Department of Family Social Science
University of Minnesota
St. Paul, Minnesota

PREFACE

Dennis A. Bagarozzi, Ph.D.

Most family therapists accept the premise that family behavior is lawfully determined and can be modified through well planned intervention. Pioneering family therapists such as Haley, Jackson, and Watzlawick recognized that one need not discover and treat the so called "causes" of dysfunctional family processes in order to correct them. Intervention, therefore, was aimed at modifying those factors that maintained dysfunctional patterns and jeopardized the growth and development of all family members. To accomplish this, however, a family therapist must know in some pragmatic sense what "effective" or "optimal" family functioning should be over the course of the family life cycle so that appropriate steps can be taken to help troubled families approximate this end. In order for a theory of family process and therapy to be valid, however, it must transcend ethnic, racial, sub-cultural, and cultural definitions of what is "normal," "acceptable," and "appropriate."

How one chooses to intervene in a developing family system is determined by one's theory of family process and development, how dysfunctional family patterns arise and are maintained, and how to bring about desired behavior changes within family systems.

In the first three chapters, the relationships among theory, assessment, treatment formulation, intervention, and evaluation are presented. Each chapter presents a variety of vantage points from which to view family functioning. The assessment procedures describe the family process from the family member's "inside" perspective as well as from the observer's "outside" perspective.

In Chapter 1, Russell and Olson discuss the empirical work that has been done concerning the development of the *Circumplex Model of Marital and Family Systems*. The treatment approach, which flows from the model, is decidedly "structural." Russell and Olson represent an applied scientific approach to the study of family systems. The scientific method of inquiry is readily seen in their descriptive accounts of family process, their presentation of clearly stated, testable hypotheses, which are derived from the model's major tenets, and the unbiased evaluation of the model's practical and clinical utility. The clinical uses of the *Family Adaptability and Cohesion Scale (FACES)*, also are presented, and the value of this instrument for making clinical assessments and devising treatment plans is demonstrated in a case presentation.

In Chapter 2, Rogers and Bagarozzi review the development of the *Relational Communication Coding System*. This behavioral coding system offers an "outsider's" perspective of marital interaction based on the seminal writings of systems theorists such as Bateson, Jackson, Sluzki, Watzlawick, and Weakland, and deals with the control dimensions of relationship processes (complementarity, symmetry, and parallel interaction patterns). The findings presented lend support to some of the central axioms of systems theory such as pattern redundancy, rigidity and flexibility, homeostasis, and the relationships between certain types of control patterns and marital satisfaction.

In the final section of Chapter 2, clinical implications are presented. Intervention to modify dysfunctional control patterns are discussed in terms of the type of changes that one might attempt to achieve with marital systems, for example, first order or second order change. The possibility that one's cognitive capacities can be linked to one's ability to make second order changes is introduced, and the clinical ramifications of such a possibility are discussed.

In Chapter 3, the development and standardization of the Spousal Inventory of Desired Changes and Relationship Barriers (SIDCARB) are traced. This instrument is designed to help clinicians gain some insight into each spouse's subjective "inside" view of the marriage from a social exchange perspective. Areas assessed are: degree of change desired, areas of inequitable exchanges, satisfaction, and commitment and barriers to separation and divorce. The clinical uses of the SIDCARB as an assessment aid and evaluative tool are presented in a case study of a severely distressed and chaotic relationship.

The model of treatment presented in this chapter grew out of work with couples and families who often were resistant, or openly refused, to become involved in any treatment approach that was "behavioral." As a result, a number of techniques were developed to deal with their initial resistance to overtly negotiating more satisfying and equitable behavioral exchanges. They should be valuable to the reader.

Section II is devoted to the descriptive aspects of scientific inquiry. A total of four chapters comprise this section, and each one deals with families who are experiencing severe crises. In Chapter 4, McCubbin et al. discuss their findings concerning the parental coping patterns and the dimensions of family life which contribute to the health and maintenance of children with cystic fibrosis. The coping strategies, which were found to be particularly helpful for this sample, are discussed in terms of the implications they suggest for working with such families. McCubbin and his colleagues offer a unique view of family crises. They see crisis as an opportunity to "promote" family well being. Problem solving strategies are singled out as particularly important in working with families under stress.

In Chapter 5, Corrales et al. deal with the crises associated with the birth of a severely handicapped child. The efforts of these researchers certainly have to be commended. Not only have they been able to describe the dynamics of these families, but they have given valuable insights into the special problems such families face. The descriptive accounts offered are derived from long hours of behavioral observations based on the standardized procedures developed by the "Timberlawn Group." The treatment procedures suggested by Corrales and his colleagues will prove invaluable for clinicians who work with the severely handicapped and their families.

Kaslow and Schwartz (Chapter 6) also have undertaken a pioneering descriptive study in an effort to gain some understanding of the contemporary religious cult phenomenon. Unlike previous investigators who have focused on the personality of the cult leader and the recruitment process, Kaslow and Schwartz have attempted to look at the relationship between family dynamics and cult membership. Although their findings are based on a small sample of ex-cult members, a picture of the cult member and his family emerges. Kaslow and Schwartz suggest treating such families by using a network approach. Through this modality, the ex-cult member is able to experience, in his own family, what he sought in the family of the cult.

In Chapter 7, Jurich discusses the treatment of families who have a suicidal member and stresses the importance of understanding the systemic nature of suicidal behavior. In evaluating the treatments of suicide attempters who were seen in individual and family therapy, Jurich found that family treatment group members improved significantly over the individual therapy group members on three sub-scale measures of the Tennessee Self-Concept Scale; total self-concept, self-satisfaction, and family self-concept. Jurich's findings underscore the importance of including family members or significant others in the treatment of suicidal individuals.

The third and final section is devoted to theoretical issues involving the practice of family therapy, dynamics of family pathology, and research into the therapeutic process itself. A total of three chapters comprise this section and provide the reader with much "food for thought."

In Chapter 8, Kniskern and Gurman present directions they believe family therapy research should take in the 1980s. Although they recognize the diversity of theories of family therapy, they are able to identify a number of salient issues and questions which are seen as being of central importance to all "schools" of family therapy as well as the continued advancement of the field.

Of the many research issues addressed, some, such as alternatives to the no treatment control group, criteria for evaluating effectiveness of treatment, specifying units of assessment in outcome research, and vantage points from which to evaluate therapeutic outcome, are given considerable attention. Finally, Kniskern and Gurman suggest that a component analysis of effective and essential ingredients be conducted for each "school" of therapy. As an example of how one might go about formulating research questions which are "school" specific, they use the "Structural-Strategic" school to illustrate their point.

In Chapter 9, Dell presents some valuable insights into some of the conundrums which one faces when attempting to unravel research findings concerning family theories of schizophrenia. After reviewing the major family theories of schizophrenia, Dell zeroes in on what he believes is a serious deficiency in the empirical literature: the fusion or confusion of two distinct and incompatible epistemologies concerning the nature of the schizophrenic process, one based on force, quantity, and characteristics, the other based on pattern, relationship, and qualities. The latter, however, constitutes what is truly innovative in family theories of schizophrenia, but which has been misunderstood by researchers and clinicians alike who interpret family theories of schizophrenia to mean simply "a different cause has been postulated."

Herein rests the confusion, because most family theories of schizophrenia present a totally different epistemology of mental disorder than do traditional medical theories of schizophrenia. Family theories are social in their philosophy and epistemology. Traditional theories of schizophrenia, on the other hand, explain schizophrenia in terms of cognitive deficiencies which reside within the individual; the social milieu's role in the process is seen as incidental. For family theorists, the active psychotic state that causes an individual to be hospitalized is thought to be an outcome of an escalating interactional process between the individual and his family members. Once the "patient" is labeled schizophrenic, he begins to fulfill a cultural role which is reinforced by his family, the medical profession, and legal system. From this interactive perspective, schizophrenia is seen as a process that brings the individual to the hospital rather than a disease entity which resides within the person.

Adopting an interactive view, however, has its own inherent problems, according to Dell, because the careful diagnosis that is required in order to conduct qualitative research is, in itself, part of the interactive process that is under investigation. Finding a way out of this paradox is one task with which clinical researchers will have to grapple.

In the final chapter, Stein, a medical-psychiatric anthropologist, makes what can be considered a meta-communicative statement regarding the family therapy field. Some of his observations certainly will spark controversy. These include the notions that family therapies of all varieties can be found universally and that family therapy as a set of distinct theoretical propositions and treatment modes is rooted in the American present but is a lineal descendent of individually oriented psychoanalytic investigation. For Stein, the greatest obstacles to realizing family therapy's holistic potential lies in its reliance on the culture-bound metaphors of the machine and the computer, plus its tendency to reify the family into a closed unit, organism, and level of abstraction which is separate from the people who constitute it and assign meaning to its relationship.

There is an interesting linkage between Dell's discussions of family theories of schizophrenia in Chapter 9 and Stein's observations. Both Dell and Stein view the family within the broader context of the society; however, Stein would expand the unit of assessment beyond the family system to the cultural system itself. He argues that diagnosis and explanation at the level of shared culture is essential in order to specify the roles played by both the symptomatic member and the pathogenic family in maintaining a societal homeostasis. In contrast to Dell, Stein warns that family therapy will over-focus on the family to the exclusion of sources of data which conflict with family therapy's central theme, such as intra-individual dynamics, unconscious motivation, etc. For family therapy to be considered truly holistic, for Stein, it must incorporate concepts of individual personality change and growth as well as address the dynamic interplay among the individual, his family, and the culture at large.

Although the reader may not agree with all of Stein's observations, interpretations, and suggestions, he or she will have been provoked into thinking differently about the families that present themselves for treatment or research.

Section I

DIAGNOSTIC AND ASSESSMENT AIDS

Chapter 1

CIRCUMPLEX MODEL OF MARITAL AND FAMILY SYSTEMS:
Review of Empirical Support and Elaboration of Therapeutic Process

Candyce S. Russell, Ph.D.
David H. Olson, Ph.D.

Introduction

Family therapists such as Watzlawick, Beavin, and Jackson (1977) have had a major impact on the mental health profession by reframing the meaning of symptoms. The focus has shifted from the *individual* to the context of his or her intimate relationship *system*. In order that that dramatic perceptual shift be maintained, it is important to have conceptual models which highlight relevant system variables and relationship types.

The Circumplex Model of Marital and Family Systems, introduced in this chapter, is designed to both sensitize observers to clinically useful information (assessment) and to organize that information into relevant treatment goals. It was derived from a thorough review of both the clinical and empirical family process literatures, where two themes were found to recur. One of these themes involves reconciling simultaneous pushes toward both separateness and togetherness (cohesion dimension). The second theme involves the relationship system's ability to respond to developmental or situational stress with appropriate shifts in power structure, relationship roles, and rules (adaptability dimension). Both dimensions are descriptive rather than evaluative and require *balancing* of seemingly paradoxical demands. The family must find ways of simultaneously dealing with the necessary coexistence of separateness and togetherness that allow for both autonomy and intimacy (cohesion dimension). It must also find ways of balancing stability with change in order to avoid rigidity or chaos. "Circumplex II" (Olson, Russell & Sprenkle, 1980) reviews the empirical foundations in detail.

The placement of the two major dimensions (family cohesion and family adaptability) into a circumplex model or matrix distinguishes four main quadrants of interaction. These quadrants are further differentiated into extreme and balanced regions, creating a total of 16 possible interaction styles (Figure 1). The labels given to these 16 regions are intended to be descriptive of the relationship system's process, not evaluative. It also is important to remember that the two underlying dimensions of cohesion and adaptability are continuous rather than discrete variables; the markers separating regions are arbitrary.

Family cohesion is "the emotional bonding members have with one another and the degree of individual autonomy persons experience in the family system." Extremes of family cohesion may be described as "enmeshment," which results in limited individual autonomy, and "disengagement," which is characterized by low bonding and results in high individual autonomy. The more "balanced" regions of the family cohesion continuum facilitate intimacy and are described as "connected" and "separate."

Family adaptability is defined as "the ability of a relationship system to change its power structure, role relationships, and relationship rules in response to a situational or developmental stress." Extremes of family adaptability are described as "chaotic" and "rigid," with "structured" and "flexible" styles representing a more balanced approach to simultaneous pushes toward both stability and change.

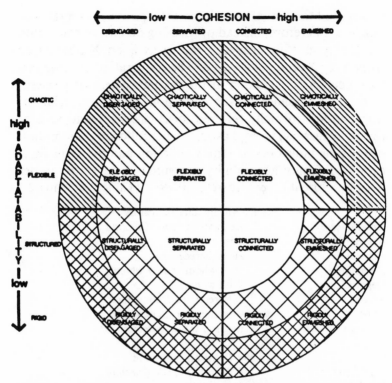

FIGURE I: SIXTEEN POSSIBLE TYPES OF MARITAL AND FAMILY SYSTEMS
DERIVED FROM THE CIRCUMPLEX MODEL

Causal Assumptions

The Circumplex Model was not designed to explain the
etiology of family dysfunction. Its conceptual foundations
are in general systems theory, and, as such, a linear causal
model does not fit comfortably. The etiology of dysfunctional
patterns is not addressed, although hypotheses derived from
the model associate extremes of both family cohesion
(enmeshment or disengagement) and adaptability (chaos or
rigidity) with dysfunction.

Both "cohesion" and "adaptability" are systemic
concepts. That is, the focus is not on one person in the
family, but on each person's relationship with every other

person and the variety of subsystems: spousal, parental, sibling, etc. Therefore, instead of focusing on one person within the family as "disengaged," the focus is on X *disengaged from* Y: or X *enmeshed with* Z. The cooperation of other system members is assumed in the disengagement or enmeshment. This emphasis on shared responsibility for a relationship pattern (formally referred to as circular relatedness or circular causality) is emphasized by the following elaboration of the nine indicators of family cohesion and the seven indicators of family adaptability presented in an earlier paper (Olson, Sprenkle & Russell, 1979). (Tables 1 and 2.)

Family Adaptability Indicators

Sub-Concept	Relevant Systemic Question
Assertiveness	Toward whom?
Control	How shared?
Discipline	Over whom and by whom?
Negotiation	With whom?
Roles	Differentiated from whom?
Rules	Governing which relationship?
System feedback	Between which system parts?

Family Cohesion Indication

Sub-Concept	Relevant Systemic Question
Bonding	Among whom?
Independence	From whom?
Boundaries	Separating whom from whom?
Coalitions	With whom and excluding whom?
Time	Spent with whom and away from whom?
Space	Shared with whom and protected from whom?
Friends	Shared with whom and excluding whom?
Decision making	Shared with whom and excluding whom?
Interests and recreation	Shared with whom and excluding whom?

None of these operations can be performed in isolation: all take the cooperation (accepting, not noticing, openly affirming) of other system parts. Furthermore, who starts the collaborative cycle is unimportant. The existence and maintenance of the cycle is more important than its origin. The question of prior cause is set aside in favor of a circular causal model where A influences B, who influences A in turn. In the circular causal model each element takes turn being cause and effect.

Hypotheses Relative to Optimal Family Functioning

As noted above, the two main dimensions of cohesion and adaptability are descriptive of family process and are not evaluative. Both cohesion and adaptability, however, can be related to outcome variables such as family health or family functioning.

Optimal family functioning is addressed within the family's cultural context, both private and public. The *optimal balance* of togetherness and separateness, stability and change depends upon the family's life cycle category (Olson, Russell, & Sprenkle, 1980) and the family's own expectations about what is desirable and expected. The latter is often mediated by ethnic, religious, and social class membership. The major hypotheses derived from the model are listed below.

Couples/family with balanced cohesion and adaptability (Hypothesis 1). These relationships will generally function more adequately than those at the extreme of these dimensions. Couples/families without serious problems will have more balanced scores on both of these dimensions. Couples/families with serious problems will have more extreme scores on one or both of these dimensions, and Couples/families with normative expectations which suport behaviors extreme on these dimensions will *not* develop problems as long as *all* the members accept these expectations.

Thus, we would expect to find no problems with a rigidly enmeshed family style among a group of Amish families so long as all family members value and accept that style. If the younger generation were to enter the public school system, confront and come to accept a style that acknowledges more personal freedom, we might then expect to see problems.

Couples/families who change their cohesion and adaptability (Hypothesis 2). These people can deal with situational

Table 1: Family Cohesion Dimension: Indicators of Separateness-Connectedness Balance*.

	DISENGAGED (Very Low)	SEPARATED (Low to Moderate)	CONNECTED (Moderate to High)	ENMESHED (Very High)
Emotional Bonding	Very Low	Low to Moderate	Moderate to High	Very High
Independence	High independence of family members.	Moderate independence of family members.	Moderate dependence of family members.	High dependence of family members.
Family Boundaries	Open external boundaries. Closed internal boundaries. Rigid generational boundaries.	Semi-open external and internal boundaries. Clear generational boundaries.	Semi-open external boundaries. Open internal boundaries. Clear generational boundaries.	Closed external boundaries. Blurred generational boundaries.
Coalitions	Weak coalitions, usually a family scapegoat.	Marital coalition clear.	Marital coalition strong.	Parent-child coalitions.
Time	Time apart from family maximized (physically and/or emotionally).	Time alone and together is important.	Time together is important. Time alone permitted for approved reasons.	Time together maximized. Little time alone permitted.
Space	Separate space both physically and emotionally is maximized.	Private space maintained; some family space.	Family space maximized. Private space minimized.	Little or no private space at home.
Friends	Mainly individual friends seen alone. Few family friends.	Some individual friends. Some family friends.	Some individual friends. Scheduled activities with couple and family friends.	Limited individual friends. Mainly couple or family friends seen together.
Decision Making	Primarily individual decisions.	Most decisions are individually based, able to make joint decisions on family issues.	Individual decisions are shared. Most decisions made with family in mind.	All decisions, both personal and relationship must be made by family.
Interests and Recreation	Primarily individual activities done without family. Family not involved.	Some spontaneous family activities. Individual activities supported.	Some scheduled family activities. Family involved in individual interests.	Most or all activities and interests must be shared with family.

*Olson, Sprenkle, and Russell: Circumplex Model of Marital and Family Systems, II, In J. Vincent (Ed.), *Advances in Family Intervention, Assessment and Theory,* JAI Press, 1980.

stress and changes in the family's life cycle. Couples/families without serious problems will change their cohesion and adaptability to an adjacent level (type) to deal with situational or developmental stress. Couples/families with serious problems will either not change their cohesion and adaptability or will flip to an opposite extreme (on one or

Table 2: Family Adaptability Dimensions: Interrelated Concepts.*

	Assertiveness	Control	Discipline	Negotiation	Roles	Rules	System Feedback
CHAOTIC (Very High)	Passive and Aggressive Styles.	No leadership	Laissez-faire Very lenient.	Endless negotiation. Poor problem solving.	Dramatic role shifts.	Dramatic rule shifts. Many implicit rules. Few explicit rules. Arbitrarily enforced rules.	Primarily positive loops; few negative loops.
FLEXIBLE	Generally assertive.	Equalitarian with fluid changes.	Democratic; unpredictable consequences.	Good negotiation; good problem solving.	Role making and sharing. Fluid change of roles.	Some rule changes. More implicit rules. Rules often enforced.	More positive than negative loops.
STRUCTURED	Generally assertive.	Democratic with stable leader.	Democratic; predictable consequences.	Structured negotiations, good problem solving.	Some role sharing.	Few rule changes. More explicit than implicit rules. Rules usually enforced.	More negative than positive loops.
RIGID	Passive or Agressive Styles.	Authoritarian leadership.	Autocratic; overly strict.	Limited negotiations; poor problem solving.	Role rigidity; stereotyped roles.	Rigid rules; many explicit rules. Few implicit rules. Strictly enforced rules.	Primarily negative loop; few positive loops.

*Olson, Russell, & Sprenkle: "Circumplex Model of Marital and Family Systems, II", In J. Vincent (Ed): *Advances in Family Intervention, Assessment and Theory,* JAI Press, 1980.

both dimensions) to deal with situational or developmental stress. These are examples of the system's ability to execute a "step function" in systems terminology.

Positive communication skills will facilitate couples and families to balance cohesion and adaptability (Hypothesis 3). Positive communication skills include: sending clear, congruent messages, appropriate self-disclosure, empathy, and support. Negative communication skills include sending incongruent messages, disqualifications, and double binds.

Review of Empirical Studies

The circumplex model is now in the process of being used in a variety of projects specifically designed to test the major hypotheses described in the previous section. To date, three of these projects have been completed and the results published: Sprenkle and Olson (1978), Druckman (1979), and Russell (1979). Two more are in the data analysis state: Bell (1980) and Portner (1980). Two additional projects are in various stages of data analysis: DeCastro (1980) and Benigas (1980).

Five of these seven studies have controlled for family life cycle category by limiting themselves to families with adolescents: Russell (1979), Druckman (1979), Bell (1980), Portner (1980), and DeCastro (1980). The adolescent stage of the family life cycle provides a particularly strategic point of investigation since it is a period calling for shifts in the sharing of power and decision making in the family (adaptability indicator) at the same time that issues of identity and individual differentiation (cohesion dimension) come to the fore (Tallman & Miller, 1976). There is now a need for investigations into other stages of the family life cycle.

Most investigators have included a clinical population and a non-clinical comparison group. The clinical populations include: couples in marital therapy (Sprenkle & Olson, 1978), families of female status offenders (Druckman, 1979), families with a runaway adolescent (Bell, 1980), families in family therapy (Portner, 1980), and families with an adolescent "repeat offender" (DeCastro, 1980). One study (Benigas, 1980), includes foster parent families who are part of a state-wide training program, while a final study (Russell, 1979) included families who presented themselves in a non-clinical context but who evaluated themselves and were evaluated by others as representing a range of "adequacy of functioning."

Several studies have included multiple methods of measuring cohesion or adaptability and, thus, have allowed for the collection of validity data in addition to their hypothesis testing. Among these are the studies by Russell (1979), Bell (1980), Portner (1980), and DeCastro (1980). Simulated Family Activity Measure (SIMFAM) (Straus & Tallman, 1971), the Inventory of Parent-Adolescent Conflict (Olson, Portner, & Bell, 1979), and the Kvebaek Family Sculpture Test (Kvebaek, 1979) have been used as behavorial measures. The most frequently used self-report instruments are Family Adaptability and Cohesion Evaluation Scale (FACES) and an adaptation of the Bowerman and Bahr Identification Scale. FACES was developed by Olson, Bell, and Portner (1979) using each of the nine sub-indicators of family cohesion and seven sub-indicators of family adaptability presented in Tables 1 and 2 as the conceptual base for the Likert-type items. The adapted Bowerman and Bahr items tap only the first two sub-indicators of family cohesion (bonding and independence).

Three of the seven studies mentioned above have published results and two others are far enough along to report major findings in a preliminary fashion. Not all hypotheses listed in the section above were tested by each study. The extent to which the model received or failed to receive support by each of these four studies will be discussed below.

The Seminal Studies

Using SIMFAM as an arena for the observation of *control* (adaptability indicator) in 25 clinical and 25 non-clinical (NC) couples, Sprenkle and Olson (1978) found that NC couples shift to a more shared leadership pattern during a period of experimentally induced stress, whereas clinical couples were more likely to continue with either an absence of leadership or with an authoritarian pattern. The NC spouses were more responsive to one another's influence attempts and were less likely to display a wife-dominant pattern. Thus, the hypothesis regarding *adaptability* as measured by sharing of leadership or control received support. No statistically significant differences in the sharing of leadership were found, however, between the clinical and non-clinical groups during the non-stressful periods of the SIMFAM game. Therefore, the major hypothesis of *adaptability* as measured by sharing of control failed to receive support.

Using multiple measures for both family cohesion, family adaptability, and family functioning, Russell (1979) reported mixed, but generally supportive findings with regard to the above hypotheses. This study included 31 non-clinical Catholic family triads with a female adolescent. The families were divided into high and low levels of functioning on the basis of self-report (likelihood of adolescent running away from home) and behavorial data (success at solving problems presented by SIMFAM game).

A visual plot of the families using the self-report indicator of family functioning located 11 of the 15 high functioning families in the central area of the model and *all* of the low functioning families in the more extreme regions of the model as predicted in Hypothesis 1. Hypothesis 1 with regard to family cohesion received support when the self-report measure of functioning was used, regardless of how cohesion was measured. The results using the behaviorial measure of functioning, however, were mixed.

All measures of family adaptability in the Russell (1979) study were observed during the SIMFAM game and were related to the following sub-indicators listed in Table 3: control (pattern of sharing leadership); roles (who leads, follows, supports, rejects, ignores); rules (about shifting family decision-making organization during an induced stress); and system feedback (the family's ability to make use of each

Table 3: Transitional Single Parent Family:
Summary of FACES Scores.

	Mom	17-year-old son	15-year-old daughter	12-year-old son
Emotional Bonding	Diseng.	Diseng.	Diseng.	Diseng.
Independence	Diseng.	Diseng.	Diseng.	Diseng.
Family Boundaries	Bal.	Diseng.	Diseng.	Bal.
Coalitions	Bal.	Bal.	Diseng.	Bal.
Time	Diseng.	Diseng.	Bal.	Diseng.
Space	Diseng.	Bal.	Bal.	Bal.
Friends	Bal.	Bal.	Diseng.	Bal.
Decision Making	Bal.	Bal.	Diseng.	Bal.
Interests and Recreation	Bal.	Diseng.	Bal.	Diseng.
Overall Cohesion	Diseng.	Diseng.	Diseng.	Diseng.
Assertiveness	Bal.	Bal.	Bal.	Bal.
Control	Bal.	Bal.	Bal.	Bal.
Discipline	Bal.	Rigid	Bal.	Rigid
Negotiation	Bal.	Bal.	Bal.	Rigid
Roles	Bal.	Bal.	Bal.	Rigid
Rules	Bal.	Bal.	Bal.	Rigid
System Feedback	Bal.	Bal.	Bal.	Bal.
Overall Adaptability	Bal.	Bal.	Bal.	Rigid

other's successful scoring attempts). A sharing of leadership during non-stressful periods and a moderate shift in leadership during stress were clearly related to the self-report measure of family functioning in the predicted direction. A shared leadership pattern, however, was not significantly related to the behavioral indicator of functioning. Thus, Hypotheses 1 and 2 with respect to *family adaptability* received partial support.

The studies by Bell (1980) and Portner (1980) are discussed jointly since they share the same comparison group of 117 families and use the same measures of cohesion and adaptability: (FACES) (Olson, Bell, & Portner, 1979) and the Inventory of Parent-Adolescent Conflict (Olson, Portner, & Bell, 1979). Bell's clinical population included families where an adolescent (primarily 13-16 years of age) had run away from home (N = 31 families). Roughly three-quarters of the runaways were female. Portner's clinical population included families in therapy where the behavior of an adolescent or parent-adolescent conflict was the presenting complaint (N =

53 families). These families had received an average of four therapy sessions at the time of the study. The majority of the identified patients were 13-16 years of age. Two-thirds were male and one-third were female. The comparison group included families in the same stage of the family life cycle who were recruited from schools and churches in the same geographic area as the two clinic populations. The clinical and comparison families were similar on the usual indicators of socioeconomic status.

A preliminary analysis of the self-report data from FACES shows a greater proportion of the non-clinical families falling in the central area of the model than both types of clinical families, which have a greater likelihood of falling outside the central area. This difference approached statistical significance for the therapy versus non-clinical comparison but was not statistically significant for the runaway versus non-clinical comparison.

When the families were compared on the two dimensions of cohesion and adaptability separately, the clinical families were more likely than the non-clinical families to score on the low end of cohesion and the high end of adaptability. These differences were statistically significant for both the runaway versus non-clinical and the therapy versus non-clinical comparisons. Data using behavorial indicators of cohesion and adaptability have not been analyzed.

Although data on family cohesion and adaptability before and after therapy are being collected by the first author on a variety of cases, only one such study has been completed to date (Druckman, 1979). Fourteen families with female juvenile status offenders were assessed on cohesion and adaptability using several items from the Moos Family Environment Scale (1974) before and after family-oriented treatment. Their scores were compared with scores from 15 families who dropped out of the program very early in treatment. None of the control families received any form of total family therapy, although the identified patients did receive such alternative treatment as placement in a group home for juveniles or psychiatric hospitalization. The status offenses included running away, truancy, drinking, smoking, incorrigibility, and promiscuity. Thus, these are "acting out" adolescents (not hard-core delinquents), and the families were motivated enough to participate in total family treatment. The offenders ranged in age from 12 to 17 years with an average age of 15 years. The majority of families (89%) were caucasian. At pre-test, families had moderately low scores on family cohesion and moderately high scores on adaptability.

The treatment program included both didactic and therapeutic components. It consisted of a two-week residential phase followed by six to eight weeks of follow-up family therapy. The goals of family therapy were not intentionally organized around the circumplex model.

Druckman used the cohesion and independence sub-scales on the Moos Family Environment Scale (FES) as a measure of family cohesion and the organization and control sub-scales as a measure of family adaptability.

At post-test, all the scores had changed in the direction of improved family functioning. Improvement among families who completed treatment, however, was *not* statistically more significant than improvement among drop-out families. Furthermore, the adolescents among the completer families had a higher rate of recidivism than the drop-out sample. It is possible that the teenagers in the experimental group were testing changes in the family system by "acting out." A longer follow-up period may have identified a higher recidivism rate among drop-out families, especially since more than one-third of the teenagers in this group were in hospitals or group homes where there was close supervision at the time of follow-up.

In addition to the concerns named above, however, is the issue of instrumentation. According to a study by Russell (1980), the Moos's cohesion sub-scale failed to receive support for convergent validity when compared with two other indicators of cohesion. Thus, the instrument available to Druckman may not be assessing cohesion as defined in the circumplex model. Russell (1980) suggests that the Moos measures something closer to "support." Finally, the Moos measures only two aspects of family adaptability as used in the circumplex model and does so through self-report rather than through observation of behavior. Adaptability may be more adequately assessed through observational procedures. In summary, then, the Druckman data fails to locate the families of female status offenders in extreme regions of the model. Although families did move toward even more balanced regions of the model by follow-up, this change occurred in control families as well as in the families receiving treatment.

Summary of Empirical Evidence

The studies of Sprenkle and Olson (1978) and Russell (1979) made use of *behavioral* indicators of family adaptability and found fairly clear support for Hypotheses 1 and 2 with regard to that dimension of the model. Preliminary findings from Bell (1980), Portner (1980), and Druckman (1979), using self-report indicators of family adaptability and cohesion, support the model with less vigor. Russell (1979) in her work with normal range adolescents found support for Hypothesis 1 with regard to family cohesion using both self-report and behavioral measures of that dimension, but only when the daughter's assessment of the family's functioning was used as the dependent variable. It may be that measurement error is largely responsible for these inconsistent results. It appears that adaptability, being a process variable, is measured better through observation of behavior than by self reports from family members.

Finally, both the Druckman study (1979) and the Bell (1980) and Portner (1980) studies located clinical families on the low end of the cohesion continuum and the high end of the adaptability continuum. Although their findings are consistent with Hypotheses 1 and 2, one must also recognize that only *one* extreme is represented on each dimension. Nonclinical populations are, indeed, located in balanced regions of the model. These three populations of clinical families in the adolescent stage of the family life cycle who are also presenting acting out (as opposed to intrapunitive behavior), are primarily clustered at one end of each continuum rather than showing up at both extremes. This may be due to similarities in presenting complaints and family life cycle category *or* it may be that dysfunctional systems tend to operate in more limited regions of the model than had been hypothesized. In light of the findings by Russell (1979) and Sprenkle and Olson (1978), the former, at this time, is a more likely explanation than the latter.

Treatment Implications

Multi-system and Multi-method Assessments

It is unlikely that an entire family system will fit neatly into one of the 16 types identified in Figure 1. Different subsystems within any given family may be located in different regions of the matrix. Therefore, it is necessary to separately assess the marital dyad (if present), the parental sub-system, the sibling sub-system(s), and possibly the "older kids" as compared with the "young kids" or "his kids" as compared with "her kids" and "their kids" when dealing with reconstituted families. Each relevant sub-system should be located on both the cohesion and adaptability continua.

The nine sub-indicators of family cohesion (emotional bonding, independence, family boundaries, coalitions, time, space, friends, decision making, interests, and recreation) and the seven sub-indicators of family adaptability (assertiveness, control, discipline, negotiation, roles, rules, system feedback) (Tables 1 and 2) can be used to organize a clinical assessment of cohesion and adaptability. This can be done through an initial history-taking (self-report by family members) and through direct observation of the system in operation (behavioral indicators).

The self-report instrument, FACES (Olson, Bell, & Portner, 1979), can also be used to assist in assessment. Each family member completes FACES independently, making possible a comparison of individual perceptions. With those couples or families for whom an educational approach is appropriate, FACES may serve as the framework for presenting self-information and for choosing where to start making changes, for example, by arranging for more private space or for a clearer discussion of mutual expectations about roles. The instrument takes approximately 20 minutes to complete and can be handled by most children eight years or older.

The scale has accumulated preliminary clinical validity and presumably will accumulate more as it becomes more widely used in both clinical and research settings. More information is needed, however, especially regarding predictive validity and test-retest reliability.

As with any assessment procedure, it is important to use multiple indicators and to make assessment an open-ended, ongoing procedure. The model provides a framework for organizing both the clinically-derived and FACES-derived information regarding a couple or family, and, in the process, suggests appropriate treatment goals.

Setting Treatment Goals

Since there are some empirical data to suggest that families who are more successful in handling situational or developmental stress are located in the central regions of the matrix, couples or families coming for treatment should be moved toward an adjacent cell in the mid-region of the model if they start out at one of the extremes. Then, a chaotically disengaged system would be helped toward a more flexibly separate style of operation while a chaotically enmeshed system would be moved toward a flexibly connected style of interacting. Moving the system *one* level on each continuum is respectful of the family's unique culture and also tempers the tendency for a system to "flip flop" to the opposite extreme when trying to respond to positive feedback induced by the therapist.

Therapists disagree as to how explicit a family system assessment should be. Haley (1976) suggests that couples and families already know what their problem is and that a therapist pointing it out only creates defensiveness and further tightens the system. It is possible, however, to present information to a couple or family that complements the basic wisdom of the system (after all, they have been coping up to now) and blames no one for the current distress. Furthermore, the clinical assessment and summary from FACES (Table 3) can help highlight system strengths as well as possible areas for change. Once the therapist has adequately joined the system, it is possible to involve the couple or family in deciding which of the 16 sub-dimensions listed in Tables 2 and 3 it wants to work on changing.

Case Study[1]

As with any paradigm, the model itself over-simplifies reality and, by necessity, allows certain pieces of information to fade and go unnoticed. Some of the complexity emerges, however, when the model is applied to actual case material. There is no substitute for sensitive and creative clinical skill. Interventions, although guided by a conceptual model, are seldom dictated by a model. The exact interventions and therapeutic techniques used in the following case evolved out of an interaction between the family and the therapists' personal styles. The overall therapeutic goals, however, were guided by the Circumplex Model.

A Transistional Single-Parent Family

The primary unit of treatment was a 38-year-old woman, the four children who reside with her (17-year-old male, 15-year-old female, 12-year-old male, and 4-year-old female), and an 8-year-old son whose custody was being contested and who was living initially with the 34-year-old father. The presenting complaints involved the middle two children: conflict between the mother and 15-year-old daughter and the 12-year-old son's immaturity (specifically playing with small toys and string). This was the woman's third marriage, and

---

1. The co-therapist in this case was Raymond B. Atilano.

her husband's second. The three oldest children are by mother's first husband, who was continuing a relationship with the 17-year-old son but not with the 15-year-old or 12-year-old. A child from the mother's brief second marriage had been given up for adoption at birth and was not discussed to any extent. The 8-year-old and 4-year-old are from the current estranged marriage.

FACES was given to the family to fill out prior to the first interview. As can be seen from Table 3, the instrument was not filled out by the 8-year-old son (who was absent from the first four sessions) or the 4-year-old daughter (who was too young to respond). All four older family members see the family as disengaged, especially the 15-year-old daughter who also perceives herself as unfairly criticized by mother and older brother and as more satisfyingly connected with her peer group. On the adaptability dimension, most members saw themselves as balanced, although the 12-year-old identified patient reported a clear pattern of family rigidity, which his older brother perceived only in so far as discipline was concerned (we later learned he was reporting on the discipline *he*, rather than mother, administered).

The clinical assessment of the family was not entirely consistent with the FACES evaluation. Although the two older children were in conflict and the 15-year-old and mother were distanced and in conflict, the 17-year-old son was acutely aware of what was going on in the family and, in fact, became a taciturn, yet sensitive, reporter of family process. The 12-year-old son displayed a clinging dependency toward his mother, and the 4-year-old daughter literally "ran to the side" of whomever in the family was experiencing tension during the interview. The most dramatic inconsistency between the clinical assessment and the self-report instrument, FACES, however, was on the adaptability dimension. Both therapists identified the family as chaotic. Mother had difficulty controlling the children, discussion over rules was protracted and with no clear outcome, and it was unclear whether mother or eldest son was in charge. The initial clinical assessment was "transitional problems associated with marital separation and preparation for a single parent structure."

Later discussion revealed that the 12-year-old's response on the adaptability dimension reflected the severe discipline he had experienced when his father had been living at home rather than his experience in the current transitional structure. Because of the transitional nature of this family group, both in terms of the marital separation and the family life cycle stage, the therapeutic goals became dual-pronged. In a sense, there were two family groups even within this fragment of a larger family. One system had to cope with the developmental issues associated with adolescence and launching. The other system was confronted with the needs of young children (chronologically and/or emotionally) for stability and security during a period of severe family disruption. Separate goals were needed for each of these subsystems.

The goal was to assist the family in moving toward a flexibly separate style for the mother-teenager sub-system and more structured connectedness for the parental-young-child sub-system. The flexibly separate style was one degree removed from the chaotic disengagement mother and adolescents came in with and was respectful of both the family's current culture and its life cycle stage. The structured connectedness goal for the second sub-system was one degree removed from the rigidity experienced when father was a part of the family though two degrees removed from the disengagement all members reported feeling. The clinical judgment was that a temporary "flip flop" on this dimension was appropriate for the young children during this transitional period.

The complexity of the case increased in the fifth session when the 8-year-old son, who had been residing with his father, joined the family in therapy. He was highly stressed and was serving as a bridge between the two households, attempting to solicit recruits to come spend time with dad, whom he correctly perceived as highly dependent and needy. Mom was overwhelmed with this child's anger and hurt and, for awhile, the turmoil created by these feelings permitted the family to make real progress learning how to have one-to-one encounters that require no "envoys" and allowing for direct expression and acceptance of feelings (intimacy). The therapists encouraged the direct expression of feelings and blocked triangulation attempts whenever they appeared in the therapy session. The 8-year-old, who had taken over his father's mission and earlier appeared like a miniature angry 30-year-old, allowed himself to be hurt and weary. He went through a period of getting attention much as his 12-year-old brother had been doing earlier, by withdrawing, not talking, and, in one session, literally curling up into the fetal position. Subsequent to this movement on the cohesion dimension, the therapists were able to focus on the adaptability dimension. Specifically, the therapists shifted responsibility for direction in the sessions to the mother and waited for her to take control, rewarding her steps in that direction and ignoring her requests to be rescued. Mother was able to increase her executive functioning in the sub-system containing the younger children, and by the time the 12-year-old tested the changes with an incidence of shoplifting, mother was able to repond clearly and decisively, though non-punitively (structure).

There were still problems with the 15-year-old daughter who was manipulating her mother by presenting partial truths and threatening to leave the family. She was involved with a sexually active, physically violent group of peers and, although she was afraid of them, she also wanted to be accepted. Mother alternately ignored and complained about her daughter's behavior. At this point, the therapists made the decision to dismiss the rest of the family and see mother and daughter in separate sessions with the goal of strengthening their personal boundaries prior to attempting, once again, to teach them negotiation and problem-solving skills. In individual sessions, it became clear that the lack of attention she was receiving from her biological father, especially in comparison with the time he continued to spend with her older brother, was clearly tied to the 15-year-old's need for acceptance by the peer group, especially males. In the mother's individual sessions, the work was focused on her own family of origin where she was an adopted child. Through an analysis of childhood memories, she came to understand that her fear of abandonment prevented her from taking a firm stand with her children. In attempting to avoid the cold, nagging, over-control she remembered from her mother, she attempted a "super-understanding" style that made her lose the respect of her children and frustrated her with lack of control. After three tries at marriage, it was clear that there was little hope of finding a man to step in to do the job for her; she would have to do it herself.

In subsequent negotiations, mother made the decision to allow the 15-year-old to live elsewhere during the summer months, though she (the mother) reserved the right to decide where (a balance of flexibility and structure). She arranged for the daughter to spend the summer with her biological father and his new family. Neither father nor daughter had been aware of the other's desire to reinitiate contact. The move meant a break with her peer group, which the 15-year-old did not fight. At last contact, she seemed to be coping well with the responsibilities given her on the father's farm, and mother and daughter had had several comfortable, less conflicted talks.

In summary, then, the two teenagers (but especially the 15-year-old) moved from a disengaged to a separated relationship with their mother. For the 17-year-old the separateness from his mother was flexible; for the 15-year-old daughter the separateness was structured. As mother became clearer about her own personal boundaries, the 15-year-old was able to risk more connectedness with her and the 17-year-old was able to relax some of his parental-child functions. Along with these changes came changes in the mother-younger children sub-system. Mother began to take on more of an executive role, and with a sense of rising competency and self-esteem became more "psychologically available" to the children (structured connectedness).

Conclusion

The model presented here continues to be elaborated and revised as empirical tests of its hypotheses become available. It has the advantage of being both empirically and clinically based and has stimulated a variety of testable hypotheses. Yet, work remains to be done. There is need of data indicating where families representing a range of family life cycle categories tend to be located in the model. Also needed are outcome studies of therapy which have been guided by the model on a variety of populations with a variety of presenting complaints.

Finally, measurement issues continue to present problems. The model is one of "optimal balance," yet traditional measurement and statistical analyses tend to average scores rather than balance them. Capturing the clinical richness of a concept remains a difficult task. Nevertheless, the fact that the model has received some initial support despite challenging problems of measurement is encouraging.

REFERENCES

Bell, R. Adolescent runaways and family interaction. Unpublished Doctoral Dissertation, University of Minnesota, 1980.

Benegis, J. Interaction in foster families: An application of the circumplex model of Marital and Family Systems. Master's thesis in progress, Kansas State University, 1980.

DeCastro, F. Circumplex Model of Marital and Family Systems: Empirical test with families of delinquent and non-delinquent adolescent males. Master's thesis in progress, Kansas State University, 1980.

Druckman, J. A family-oriented policy and treatment program for female juvenile status offenders. *Journal of Marriage and the Family.* 1979, *41* (3), 627-636.

Haley, J. *Problem solving therapy.* San Francisco: Jossey-Bass, 1976.

Kvebaek, D. J. *The Kvebaek family sculpture technique.* Vikersund, Norway, 1979.

Moos, R. H., Insel, P. M., & Humphrey, B. *Combined preliminary manual: family work and group environment scales.* Consulting Psychologists Press, 1974.

Olson, D. H., Bell, R., & Portner, J. Family Adaptability and Cohesion Evaluation Scale (FACES). Unpublished Manual, University of Minnesota, 1979.

Olson, D. H., Portner, J., & Bell, R. Inventory of Parent-Adolescent Conflict. Unpublished paper, University of Minnesota, 1979.

Olson, D. H., Russell, C. S., & Sprenkle, D. H. Circumplex model of marital and family systems: II. Empirical studies and clinical intervention. In John F. Vincent (Ed.), *Advances in family intervention assessment and theory.* Greenwich, CT, JAI Press, 1980.

Olson, D. H., Sprenkle, D. H., & Russell, C. S. Circumplex model of marital and family systems: I. Cohesion and adaptability dimensions, family types, and clinical application. *Family Process,* 1979, *18,* 3-28.

Portner, J. Family therapy and parent-adolescent interaction. Unpublished Doctoral Dissertation, University of Minnesota, 1980.

Russell, C. S. A methodological study of family cohesion and adaptability. *Journal of Marital and Family Therapy,* 1980, 6(4), 459-470.

Russell, C. S. Circumplex model of marital and family systems: III. Empirical evaluation with families. Family Process, 1979, 18, 29-45.

Sprenkle, D.H. & Olson, D.H. Circumplex model of marital and family systems: Empirical study of clinic and non clinic couples. *Journal of Marriage and Family Counseling,* 1978, *4,* 59-74.

Straus, M.A. & Tallman, D. SIMFAM: A technique for observational measurement and experimental study of families in J. Aldous, T. Condon, R. Hill, M. Straus & I. Tallman (Eds.) *Family Problem Solving,* Henesdale, Ill. Dryden Press, 1971.

Tallman, I. & Miller, G. Class difference in family problem solving: The impact of hierarchial structure and language skills. Paper presented at the Annual Meeting of the American Sociological Association, 1976.

Watzlawick, R., Beavin, J., & Jackson, D. *Pragmatics of Human Communication.* New York, W.W. Norton, 1977.

Chapter 2

AN OVERVIEW OF RELATIONAL COMMUNICATION AND IMPLICATIONS FOR THERAPY

L. Edna Rogers Ph.D.
Dennis A. Bagarozzi Ph.D.

An emergent theme in family research and therapy has been a focus on the interactional processes and communication patterns among family members. Since Burgess' (1926) innovative definition of the family as a "unit of interacting personalities," there has been a slow but progressive trend toward the study of the internal dynamics of family systems. The attempts to understand the "psychosocial interior" (Hess & Handell, 1959) of the family, its "politics" (Laing, 1972), or "distance regulation" (Kantor & Lehr, 1975), have underscored the necessity of attending to the processes of communication which constitute the ongoing relationships among family members.

The study of communication processes calls for a theoretical approach that moves away from the more traditional linear model of cause and effect based on monadic measures of individual characteristics, toward a more cybernetic model based on measures of system properties and transactional patterns. What has become known as the "pragmatic" perspective of communication, formulated by the Palo Alto Research Group, emphasizes the systematic approach and the study of conjoint, emergent processes. It attends to what goes on among family members, rather than what goes on *within* each member. This perspective focuses on transactional aspects of communication and the accompanying shift away from psychic variables to the relational patterns manifested in interactional sequences unfolding over time.

A principle assumption of the systematic approach is that the system elements don't add up. This assumption asserts that the relationship among family members (the whole), has characteristics which are different from its individual members (parts), and these characteristics emerge from the interactional patterns of its members. Simmel (1950) captured the flavor of the jointly created aspects of relationships:

> ...the common experience of bad marriages between excellent persons and of good marriages between dubious persons, suggests that marriage, however much it depends on each of the spouses, may yet have a character not coinciding with either of them (p. 129).

This character, the conjoint, interactional effect, *is* the relationship. In human systems, it is further assumed that the co-defining nature of relationships emerges from the inherent mutuality of the message exchange. As Duncan so aptly stated, "We do not relate and then talk, but we relate in talk" (1967, p. 294). Explicitly or implicitly, message exchange involves an ongoing reciprocity of ego and alter casting (Weinstein & Deutschberger, 1964). Simultaneously, claims of identity of self and other are made. The claim, "this is how I see me in relation to you," of necessity implies the converse, "this is how I see you in relation to me." Regarding the ongoing process of message exchange, interactants offer one another definitions which invite an appropriate response. The fate of a definition offered, however, awaits the response of other. In this process, no single participant individually defines the relationship; it is a jointly created "product."

The developing area of relational communication falls clearly within the frame that has just been set. In brief, relational communication requires a perspective that differs from the monadic orientation that dominates existing analytic techniques. Relational analyses focus on communication properties that exist only at the dyadic or system level; relational variables do not reside within individual interactors, but rather exist between them. Relational measurements refer to emergent properties of joint communicative behavior and have no counterpart in the properties of individual or single messages. With this perspective, the *transaction*—the exchange of paired sequential messages over time—is the basic unit of analysis.

The epistemological stance of relational communication centers on interactional redundancies, the behavioral "holon" (Koestler, 1968) which characterize social relationships and their interlinking influences on relational processes and consequences. The purpose of this chapter, therefore, is three-fold: (a) to give a conceptual frame and overview of the methodology developed in the study of relational communication; (b) to present the major theoretical hypotheses and evidence of empirical support; and (c) to draw implications for therapy stemming from this research orientation.

Conceptual Origins of Relational Communication

The major premises of relational communication are rooted in the conceptual insights of Bateson (1936, 1951, 1972) and the writings of his colleagues. In particular, the work of Jackson (1959, 1965), Haley (1963), and Watzlawick, Beavin, and Jackson (1967), have played a predominant role in the development of this perspective. Bateson's propositions that relationships "exist" within the exchange of messages, and that there is a hierarchy of message and relational structure, underlie the work in relational communication.

It was Bateson who most notably supported the idea that a major aspect of message exchange is the ongoing *negotiation* of the definition of the interactants' relationship. He argues that the relationship among individuals is immanent within the messages that pass between them. Not only is content information exchanged in this process, but relational information as well. This duality was termed the "report" and "command" aspects of messages by Bateson. The first refers to referential meaning; the second to relational meaning. Both meanings occur simultaneously, with the relational aspect overlaying the content at a *logically higher, meta level*. It is the patterning of message exchange at the relational level that gives form or structure to the relationship. The relational component provides the larger frame, the context within which the content is interpreted. With a relational communication approach, the focus is on the form of the patterns which characterizes social relationships more than on content (Duncan, 1968). In keeping with this perspective, empirical attention is directed toward the redundancies in interaction sequences which index these patterns and, thus, the shape of the relationships.

Bateson's concepts of symmetry and complementarity, formulated in 1935 and reintroduced later within a psychotherapeutic research context by the Palo Alto Group, have led the way in the empirical development of the relational approach (Rogers, 1979). These concepts represent heuristically opposing interaction patterns of relational definitions of control. Relational control refers to the aspects of message exchange by which interactors reciprocally negotiate their positions relative to one another by redefining, constraining, adapting, accepting, and rejecting one another's definitional presentations. Symmetrical interaction is a pattern of differentiation characterized by the "minimization of difference" in message exchange. Complementary interaction is characterized by the "maximization of difference" (Watzlawick, et al., 1967, p. 169). Complementarity is categorized as "one-up" (↑) or "one-down" (↓), depending on the direction of the initial control maneuver. In a complementary transaction, the interactor's behaviors are fully differentiated. The relational control definition offered by one interactor is accepted by the other. In a symmetrical transaction, the interactor's behaviors are the same. There is a similarity of control definition between the interactors. For instance, with competitive symmetry (↑↑) and submissive symmetry (↓↓), the relational control definition offered by one interactor is not accepted by the other.

Symmetry and complementarity have not only served as major constructs for identifying patterns of relationships, but importantly, they have provided a prototype of the paradigmatic shift from single message variables to transactional measures necessary for indexing communication patterns at the relational level. This conceptual and methodological shift has been a difficult one.

> It is only when we attend to *transactions* between individuals as primary data that a qualitative shift in conceptual framework can be achieved. Yet our grasp of such data seems ephemeral; despite our best intentions, clear observations of interaction process fade into the old, individual vocabulary, there to be lost, indistinguishable and heuristically useless. To put the problem another way, we need measures which do not sum up individuals into a family unit; we need to measure the characteristics of the supra-individual family unit, characteristics for which we presently have almost no terminology (Jackson, 1965, p. 4).

A major part of the work in relational communication has been oriented toward developing a transactional level language and an accompanying methodology for indexing patterns at this level of analysis. Within this perspective, relational control is the main dimension that has been operationalized and researched so far, but it is only one of several important, generic relational dimensions in need of investigation in order to give a more complete "picture" of relationships (Note 1). It is to this analysis of the control dimensions and the evolving methodological process that we now turn our attention.

Methodological Developments

A conceptual guide describing and differentiating the form or shape of relational structure is found in the analogy of a musical score. An overriding goal of the relational approach is to move toward indexing conversational dynamics. But to do this, the individual "notes" or "messages" need to be identified. The "pitch" and "tone" of the notes (on the vertical axis), and the "rhythm" and "tempo" (on the horizontal axis), need to be mapped out over time. To explicate the relational measures that have been developed to index patterned "modulations" the beginning steps of identifying control maneuvers and transactional patterns will be described below.

Relational Communication Coding System

The relational communication coding system measures the control dimension of ongoing messages through which interactors reciprocally define their positions relative to one another. It is designed to index the structure or form of conversations more than content. The coding scheme is designed to apply to the verbal and paralinguistic bands of messages.

A message is defined as *each verbal intervention of each member in a conversation.* The coding system procedures move progressively from identifying message code categories to assigning control directions to these message codes, and to defining transactional patterns that result from the sequentially ordered combinations of message control directions (Note 2).

This scheme has strong ties with the conceptual and operational ground work of Sluzki and Beavin (1965) and subsequent elaborations by Mark (1971). Following Sluzki and Beavin's premise that the control definition of a message is rooted in both its grammatical and response form, the scheme was designed to classify and code each of these aspects for each message. The grammatical codes utilized are:

Grammatical codes

1. *assertion*

2. *question*

3. *talk over*

4. *noncomplete*

5. *other*

Response codes

1. *support*

2. *nonsupport*

3. *extension*

4. *answer*

5. *instruction*

6. *order*

7. *disconfirmation*

8. *topic change*

9. *initiation-termination*

10. *other*

Each message is assigned a three digit code. The first digit designates the speaker. For example, the first speaker would be given the identifying numerical code of 1. The second speaker would be designated as speaker number 2. The second digit denotes the grammatical codes 1 through 5, and the third digit represents the response codes 1 through 10. In this manner, any communicative exchange can be represented by a series of sequentially ordered three digit numerical codes which constitute a discrete message unit. To illustrate this point, the three digit code 129 would signify that the first speaker had initiated the interaction by asking a question. In response to this, the reaction of the second party to the interaction might be recorded as 214, signifying an assertion which answers the question.

The three digit codes are then translated into control maneuvers. These assignments are made on the basis of whether a message is (a) an attempt to assert definitional rights, designed one-up (↑), (b) a request or an acceptance of the other's definition of the relationship, designated as a one-down ( ), or (c) a non-demanding, non-accepting, leveling movement, designated as a one-across (→).

The final step in the coding procedure is to combine the control direction of one message with the control direction of a contiguous message, thereby operationalizing the transactional concepts of symmetry, complementarity, and transition. The similarities or differences between the paired message control maneuvers are used to define basic types of control patterns. Nine transactional or relational units result from the combinations of the three basic control maneuvers (Figure 1).

In a complementary transaction (e.g., ↑↓) the control directions are different and directionally opposite; the definition of the relationship offered by one interactor is accepted by the other. A symmetrical transaction (i.e., ↑↑, ↓↓, or →→), where the control directions are the same, involves one interactor behaving toward the other as the other has behaved toward him or her; there is a similarity in the control attempts offered by the two individuals. In a transitional transaction, where the paired directions are different, but not opposite, (e.g., →↓ or ↑→), one of the interactors offers or responds with a leveling control attempt which minimizes the issue of control. Each of the transactional units provides a measure of the interactors' relationship (a pattern of connectedness) and their sequential grouping provides a "musical score" of the control dynamics (a pattern of patterns of connectedness).

With the application of the relational communicational analysis, numerous interactional indices can be obtained at both the monadic, but more importantly, at the systemic level. Among the communication "properties" indexed by this coding system are: (a). the types of transactional control patterns; (b). the fluidity of relational control; and, (c). the meta-patterns of relational control patterns, for example, the larger configurations of patterns of pattern.

Relational Control Measures

Before turning to an explication of the control measures that have been developed on the basis of this coding scheme, the distinction between logical levels must be clear. (The present literature abounds with a confusion of levels, typically "talking" transactionally, but "measuring" monadically.) In the program of research summarized in this chapter, the term *control maneuver* is used to refer to individual message

	ONE-UP ↑	ONE-DOWN ↓	ONE-ACROSS →
ONE-UP ↑	1. ↑↑	4. ↑↓	7. ↑→
ONE-DOWN ↓	2. ↓↑	5. ↓↓	8. ↓→
ONE-ACROSS →	3. →↑	6. →↓	9. →→

**Figure 1:   Possible Transactional Units Resulting
from the Combination of the Three Basic Control Maneuvers**

behavior, while *control patterns* refer to transactional structure based on the combination of individual control maneuvers. The first level of analysis is monadic in nature; the second is dyadic. One level must not be confused with the other (Bateson, 1972).

Domineering and dominance. In the first set of measures to be reviewed, a distinction is made between domineering behavior (a control maneuver) and patterns of dominance (transactional control pattern). Domineeringness is defined as the sending of one-up messages (—)—verbal statements which attempt to claim the right to be dominant. Dominance is defined as the outcome of the acceptance by one interactor of the other's one-up claims. The more one-up definitions of one person are accepted by the other, the more dominant that person is in that interactive system at that time, in that context.

Both domineeringness and dominance can be indexed in a number of ways. Only the basic measures and ratios will be given here (Note 3). Domineering behavior is operationalized by the proportion of one-up maneuvers transmitted by each interactor in an interaction (Domineeringness = ↑/total messages). The research reported deals with marital dyads. Thus, in these studies the domineeringness ratio refers to the proportion of husband one-up messages divided by wife's proportion (Domineeringness ratio = %↑H/%↑W).

Measures of dominance are based on the one-up complementary transacts and refer to the proportion of one-up statements of each interaction that are followed by a one-down response by the other (Dominance = given ↑, %↓). A dyadic ratio of dominance is obtained by dividing the husband's score by the wife's score (Dominance Ratio = given ↑H, %↓W/given ↑W, %↓H).

Submissiveness and submission. Measures of submissiveness and submission are the structural reverse of domineeringness and dominance.The degree of submissiveness is operationalized by the proportion of one-down maneuvers of each interactor, and submission is operationalized by the proportion of one-down complementary control patterns (Submissiveness = —/total and Submission = given —, %—).

Message control intensity. In search of ways to improve our ability at pattern identification, several measures have been developed that go beyond the original coding scheme and allow for finer distinctions of relational control patterns to be tapped. Message control intensity is a recently devised measure which expands the coding scheme's indexing power in depicting greater variation of message movement. In terms of the musical score analogy mentioned earlier, message intensity scores increase the range of message variability on the vertical axis of the interactional graph, just as time measures of message duration increase the variability on the horizontal axis.

The intensity dimension is based on a distancing continuum implicit in the combined grammatical form and response mode of the message codes. For instance, the response mode which implies the least distance between interactants is "support," a type of response that suggests closeness or agreement with the other's definition. In contrast, the response mode that functionally implies the greatest distance from other is disconfirmation. This mode expresses a negation of the other's right to define the relationship. The grammatical form of the message also has intensity implications. Talkovers, for example, imply more distance from other than a question form. With a distancing conceptualization of intensity—two measures of intensity can be defined. *Message intensity* is the score assigned each messge code according to the distance weighting of both its grammatical form and response mode. *Intensity distance* is the absolute difference between the intensity values of two contiguous messages. The mapping of conversations with the original coding system was limited to the three message directions (↑,→,↓). With the inclusion of a message intensity dimension, the vertical axis is greatly expanded and the nuances of message "pitch" and "distance" between consecutive messages adds to the richness of the methodological and theoretical possibilities.

A particular advantage to the inclusion of an intensity dimension is the increased ability for indexing relational patterns at the meta-pattern level, such as the pattern of patterns. Prior to the development of this expansion, pattern identification was limited to the redundancies of the transactional types, but now a redundancy measure, based on a potentially larger range of fluxuation, is possible.

Transactional redundancy. In the research by Millar (1973), a rigidity-flexibility continuum was devised which indexed the degree of alteration in the transactional pattern. In later studies (Courtright, Millar & Rogers, 1979), this concept is referred to as *transactional redundancy* and is operationally defined as the sum of the absolute deviations from random use of the nine transactional types described by the relational communication coding scheme. Thus, the more a couple tends to use one or a small set of transactional patterns, the more rigid their conversation style.

The most recent measure of redundancy was developed to give a global index of the larger relational patterns that characterize interactors' communicative behavior. It is based on the message intensity scores and gives not only the level of the homeostatic "set point" around which a dyad's control movements tend to vary, but a measure of the dyad's overall variance from their particular set point or baseline level of intensity. This measure, the *coefficient of variation,* represents a standardized index of the overall redundancy of the relational control pattern (Note 4).

The measures that have been developed now span a full range of analytic levels and provide key indicies of relational control patterns. Substantive additions to theory are now more possible with the continuing interplay of indexing larger patterns within which to describe the smaller segments of the pattern and vice versa. The pragmatic approach is concerned not only with the identification of different levels of patterns but with their predictive utility as well. The utility of the control measures ultimately lies in the ability to provide increasing insight into family functioning and relational dynamics— particularly diagnostic and therapeutic insight.

Theoretical Model and Supporting Evidence

The main theoretical frame of relational communication research has been the principles and propositions of the theory of open systems and cybernetics. These models stress the interdependence of system members and the adaptive feedback processes by which relationships emerge, stabilize, and change.

In studying family systems, a major theoretical stance has been the functionality of flexible redundance. This proposition holds that viable, close relationships will manifest interaction patterns that contain sufficient confirmation and acceptance of reciprocally offered relational definitions which produce a relatively predictable, stable set of patterns, yet retain the ability to redefine and modify these patterns allowing relational definitions to be kept up to date and fit fluctuating system dynamics and changing contexts. In contrast, it is hypothesized that interpersonal systems with rigid styles of interaction contain less potential for change and accommodation and will be associated with negative rela-

tional aspects and outcomes. The proposition that rigid interaction patterns are related to various individual pathologies
and inadequate family functioning is one of the most widely
espoused views in the clinical literature on family dynamics
(Beels & Ferber, 1969; Haley, 1964; Jackson, 1959; Murrell &
Stachowiak, 1965; Watzlawick, Beavin & Jackson, 1967).

In stating hypotheses about ongoing processes, the
"talk" is linear, but the thinking must remain cybernetic.
Rigidity of pattern is perhaps as much a symptom as a cause.
Emergent aspects of the cybernetic processes must be recognized. Optimal or adequately functioning systems develop
and maintain sufficient patterns of connectedness, but not
over-amounts of interactional redundancy. Yet, there is
always present the potential strain of what Bateson calls the
"tyranny of pattern." Patterns of relationships contain
within themselves the potential seeds of their own demise.
Recurring patterns and cumulative differentiation have
schismogenetic tendencies (Bateson, 1936). Over time, there
is a progressive potential to move toward "more of the
same" (Watzlawick, Weakland & Fisch, 1974) pattern of differentiation, for example, rigidity. In order to maintain
healthy relationships, therefore, the interaction flow must
contain the fluidity of self-correcting processes that counter
the progressive tendency of schismogenesis. This process,
however, may be extremely difficult for family members to
enact.

The work on relational control builds and expands on
the patterns of differentiation, symmetry, and complementarity. Underlying the research reported are two concepts:
over-reliance on symmetrical communicative patterns
resulting in continuing states of unsettled definitional rights
and relational instability, and over-adherence to complementarity and a lack of alteration of one-up and one-down
messages resulting in over-predictiveness, stifling interaction
patterns and producing relational "rigor mortis." The
former is more likely to produce high levels of tension and

system strain, fraught with failure and frustration to negotiate an operable range of homeostatic variability. The latter is more likely to produce avoidance and the empty, trivial, deadening routinization of relational obligation, pseudo-mutuality or the eventual rebellion against the system.

Both types of rigidity are predicted to be inversely related to positive system functioning. More specifically, it is hypothesized that high amounts of symmetrical and complementary transactional redundance are related to relational strain, lower levels of understanding, lower levels of satisfaction and negative relational consequences and outcomes.

Empirical Support

The research done thus far on the relational communication patterns in marital dyads is quite extensive and no attempt to describe all aspects of the findings is undertaken here. The results presented below are those relating to the main theoretical propositions given above that have guided these inquiries. The unfolding of these empirical findings chronologically correlates with the methodological developments described earlier.

The following studies are based on two data sets of randomly selected marital dyads of intact families with at least one child under 12 years of age. During a personal interview in their home, self-report information concerning the marital relationship was obtained from each husband and wife separately and interactional data were obtained by tape recording each couple's discussion of four different family related topics. The first sample consisted of 65 couples and the second, 96; the number of interactional transactions analyzed was more than 12,000 in the first data set and larger in the second.

Communication Control Patterns
and Domineeringness-Dominance

In the first of a series of studies investigating communication control patterns of marital dyads, Rogers (1972) found that couples with differing levels of relational role strain were characterized by different transactional patterns. Role strain refers to perceived dyadic inequity. It is based on a comparison of each member's marital role expectation and perceived role performance, for example, how each spouse perceives who actually "does" a particular task and who "should" do that task (Note 5). Dyads with high role strain were found to have slightly more symmetrical transactions, but noticeably more neutralized symmetry ($\rightarrow\rightarrow$) in their conversations than did low strain couples. The frequent occurrence of neutralized symmetrical transactions suggest an avoidance pattern that periodically erupts into a competitive status struggle (Lederer & Jackson, 1968). This suggestion is supported by findings that these high strain couples manifested (a) fewer husband one-down transition transacts ($\downarrow\rightarrow$, $\rightarrow\downarrow$), a pattern found to be associated with more conversational harmony and smoothness of flow; and (b) more wife one-up control maneuvers than their low strain counterparts. Furthermore, high strain couples expressed fewer support statements and fewer unsuccessful talk-overs.

Self-report comparisons between couples of high and low marital role strain showed the following: high role strain dyads reported: (a) spending less time together; (b) talking less with one another; (c) talking about fewer topics, particularly more personal topics; (d) being less satisfied with their communication relation; and, (e) being less satisfied with their marital relationship than low strain couples.

The initial set of findings were expanded in a study by Rogers-Millar and Millar (1979) which focused on the control differences of domineeringness and dominance (Rogers-

Millar & Millar, 1979). Wife domineeringness was found to be associated with lower levels of marital and communication satisfaction and higher levels of relational role strain; husband dominance was associated with higher levels of satisfaction and lower levels of strain.

To gain information concerning specific styles that were associated with these distinctions, several message behaviors and exchange characteristics were examined. It was found, for instance, that when wives manifested one-up messages, they offered few accompanying supportive statements to husbands; but when husbands exerted one-up maneuvers, they also gave supportive statments to their wives. Perhaps this was one reason for low satisfaction being related to wife domineeringness, but not to husband domineeringness. With husband dominance, there was stronger correlation of wife giving support than husband giving support when the wife was dominant. Again, this may relate to why husband dominance was more strongly related to the satisfaction indices than wife dominance.

An analysis of talk-over behaviors showed that both the total number of talk-overs and the number of successful talk-overs made by husbands and wives were associated with their domineering behavior but not dominance. Interrupting and taking over the speaker position was clearly a characteristic of a domineering style. Research on sex-related language differences show interruptions to be more of a male characteristic (Zimmerman & West, 1975). Perhaps this style is an added irritant of wife domineeringness, but not of husband domineeringness. Husband dominance was related to fewer successful talk-overs by wife, but talk-over behavior was not related to wife dominance.

Of further interest concerning the dynamics of transactional patterning is the negative correlation found between domineeringness, particularly husband domineeringness, and transactional redundancy. The fewer one-up statements made by the husband, the more rigid the couple's transactional patterns. It appears that domineering behavior, especially on the part of the husband, is necessary for flexibility, (for example, the giving of one-up statements that do not result in complementarity). However, if wives are domineering, the benefits of flexibility are offset with negative relational aspects. Thus, this suggests a functionality of husband domineeringness and dysfunctionality of wife domineeringness.

A replication and expansion of the above study, based on the larger sample of husband-wife dyads, was supportive of the previous findings (Courtright, Millar & Rogers, 1979). In addition, an important finding was the negative association between dyadic control and degree of understanding. With high levels of domineeringness or dominance by either spouse, both members of the dyad had lower levels of understanding. Interestingly, the more domineering or dominant member exhibited lower levels of understanding than did the less domineering or dominant member.

A follow-up study using regression analysis techniques dealt specifically with the association between relational control and dyadic understanding (Millar, Rogers-Millar & Courtright, 1979). The inverse relationship between domineeringness and understanding was substantiated, but the dominance ratio was clearly the strongest predictor of the level of understanding. It was found that the less the equivalency of the dominance pattern, the less each spouse understood the other. In other words, the more rigidly a complementary pattern or dominance hierarchy was exhibited, the less each spouse understood the other.

The accumulated findings suggest the following sequence: the more equivalent the dominance pattern (intermixed with husband domineeringness), the more flexibility in the dyad's interaction; the more frequent discussion about who is to do what when, the more conflict potential in the couple's conversations but the more up-to-date the dyad's expectations of one another. In contrast, the more discrepant the dominance structure, the more rigidity in the dyad's transactional pattern; the less frequent discussion about who is to do what when, the more apparent "harmony" in the interaction; but the less accurate and up-to-date the couple's expectations of each other, the greater the "rebellion" potential.

These findings appear to evidence the functionality of the reciprocal complementary pattern (Bateson, 1949) and the mutually enhancing aspects of parallel relationships (Lederer & Jackson, 1968). The proposition concerning the functionality of flexible redundancy seems to be supported.

Message intensity. The results from the most recent set of investigations concerning message intensity (Rogers, Courtright & Millar, 1982), clearly depict the homeostatic nature of conversations and imply the validity of the cybernetic model of interpersonal relationships. The findings strongly indicate the centrality of the one-across ($\rightarrow$) movements in establishing the couple's "set point" on the intensity axis. In general, this study suggests that one-across statements set the intensity "tone" of the interaction, one-down responses to one-up movements attempt to re-establish this "tone," and the couple as a unit periodically move to a higher "pitch" of one-up responses to one-up movements, only to move back toward their set-point intensity level, for example, a homeostatic set point.

Moreover, these findings suggest differential functions of the one-across statements by different interactors. For instance, it appears that domineering individuals use one-across statements in a non-accepting, but submissive-like manner, while submitting individuals use one-across statements in a non-demanding, but domineering-like way. The message intensity measure was developed in an attempt to increase the precision by which control patterns can be described. The results of this exploratory study suggest that one-across maneuvers are multifunctional movements, while by comparison, one-up and one-down message types are more unifunctional. Thus, one-across messages may represent a different logical type, at a higher abstract level than one-up and one-down messages.

In this same study, the degree of redundancy characterizing a couple's control patterns was predicted, and found to be, negatively related to intensity values and distancing movements. The distancing of one-across responses to the preceding messages was found to be primarily responsible for flexible transaction patterns.

This relationship between message control intensity and transactional redundancy was explored further (Courtright, Millar & Rogers, 1980a) by use of a regression model. The findings revealed that five intensity variables predicted 51% of the variance in the couples' redundancy scores. The best single predictor of transactional redundancy was the intensity distance of husbands' one-across response to their wives' preceding messages. This relationship indicated that the less intensity distance created by these responses, the more redundant, fixed, and rigid the conversational pattern. Conversely, the more the husband moved away from the intensity level of the wife's preceding statement, the less redundant and more flexible this pattern.

This same inverse relationship also was found for the intensity distance between the wives' one-across responses and their husbands' preceding messages. Although both the husband and wife variables are significant predictors, the considerably larger regression coefficients for the husband suggests that the amount of distance created by the husbands' responses is relatively more important in determining the degree of transactional redundancy.

In the most recent research effort the coefficient of variance (CV) measure was developed to provide an overall index of the variation of message intensity in dyadic interaction. A regression analysis indicated that the measure accounted for 88% of the information contained in the 12 separate indices of message control intensity. With this level of synthesizing ability the CV measure has promise as an efficient, shorthand, parsimonious index of an entire interactional pattern.

If the potential of the CV measure is realized, the exploration of research questions will be greatly facilitated. Moreover, the ability to examine specific relational dynamics within this larger, more global frame, and vice versa, will allow more guides for pattern interpretation. The CV measure represents a meta level index with the potential to serve valuable exploratory and diagnostic functions in human relations.

The ongoing research program described has been aimed at developing a methodology for exploring relational dynamics and expanding the conceptual base for understanding these processes. An appropriate question, perhaps the ultimate one, is: What are the implications or payoffs of these various efforts for therapy?

Clinical Implications

Control Patterns and Control Maneuvers

In order for intervention to be effective, one must keep in mind that therapeutic efforts can be directed at modifying either the individual control maneuvers or the relationship control patterns themselves. If control maneuvers are the object of the therapist's attention, successful treatment most likely produces first order changes in the system. If, on the other hand, the therapist's goal is to change the structure of patterned interaction, second order changes are required (Watzlawick, Weakland & Fisch, 1974). The diagnostic task is to determine what type of change is appropriate for a particular couple at a given point in their relationship's development. For example, Rogers (1972) found that couples with high role strain and high inequities in their exchange system were less satisfied with their marriage, spent less time together, talked less as a couple, talked about fewer personal topics, and were less satisfied with the quality of marital communication than couples with low levels of role strain. Furthermore, high role strain couples were found to exhibit more symmetrical control patterns than low role strain couples. These findings might lead to intervention attempts to bring about either first order change or second order change, depending on the needs and goals of a given couple. For example, if a couple's goal is to learn more effective ways of negotiating equitable exchanges, the therapist could achieve success by altering the individual control maneuvers of each spouse without changing the overall control patterns. This would be an example of first order change. The outcome of the intervention is the continuance of the homeostatic balance based on the same underlying assumptions concerning the rules which govern the exchange process (Bagarozzi & Wodarski, 1977), but with a realignment of the equity of the exchange pattern. For example, an overall pattern of complementarity may describe a couple's interaction, but with the husband manifesting more dominance in most contexts. A readjustment might involve the wife's moving into a dominant position in an expanded number of contexts. Thus, the overall pattern has not changed, but an equity of exchange has been promoted within the existing pattern. The distinction of first and second order change is a somewhat arbitrary delineation, depending on which level of patterns one is focusing. One might consider the above example to be a movement from complementarity to reciprocal complementarity (Bateson, 1972) and thus, a second order change. Yet, viewing this example within the larger frame of complementarity, the pattern has not been altered or moved out of the overarching pattern, and thus, the result is considered to be a first order type of change.

The effectiveness of intervention is tied to the therapist's ability to distinguish these levels of pattern and to instigate the appropriate type of change. In general, when a couple is helped to devise a different premise, procedural rules, and control patterns which are consistent with this new premise, second order change can be achieved.

These studies lend additional support to the hypothesis that reciprocal complementarity and parallel interaction styles are more functional and satisfying for couples than rigid and inflexible control patterns. The clinical implications that can be drawn from these findings seem clear and supportive of current intervention strategies which attempt to teach couples how to use contingency contracts and to role take in order to increase their mutual understanding (Bagarozzi & Wodarski, 1977; Jacobson & Margolin, 1979; Wodarski & Baragozzi, 1979). The therapist's task is to disrupt the homeostatic patterns of rigid complementarity and/or symmetrical escalation so that the couple can begin to develop more flexible control patterns.

The type of flexibility achieved as a result of successful intervention will vary from couple to couple. For example, a couple who enters therapy with a control pattern characterized predominantly by escalating symmetrical runs, may be helped to decrease the frequency of symmetrical interchanges and to increase the number of alternating complementary exchanges. A couple presenting a problem pattern of rigid complementarity, on the other hand, might be helped to incorporate some degree of symmetrical interaction into their restricted style, as well as to develop some measure of equivalence in their dominance pattern.

If one assumes that dyadic interactions consist of some finite combination of symmetrical and complementary control patterns, alterations in these terms can constitute a first order change since the outcome of any recombination of these patterns remains a member of the same class. Parallel control patterns, which are considered to be the most flexible and functional by some family therapists (Harper, Scoresby & Boyce, 1977), may be more difficult to achieve than alternating complementarity because parallel control patterns have been found to be of a higher logical order than both symmetry and complementarity (Harper et al., 1977).

Although complementary patterns are characterized by the exchange of opposite behaviors and symmetrical patterns are characterized by the exchange of identical behaviors, parallel control patterns involve an exchange of greater variations of different, but not opposite, behaviors. Parallel control patterns contain elements of symmetry and complementarity, yet are separate and different from them. Therefore, the attainment and maintenance of parallel control styles of interaction requires second order change. Harper et al. (1977) found that individuals who exhibited parallel interaction styles had no difficulty accommodating either symmetrical or complementary control patterns, but individuals who habitually exhibited either complementary or symmetrical control styles could not accomodate parallel control patterns. Second order change to parallel modes of interaction, therefore, may be difficult for some individuals to achieve if one considers that logical typing probably is related to cognitive functioning as suggested by Harper et al (1977).

> It seems theoretically probable that individuals engaged in habitual complementary or symmetrical patterns have fewer cognitive categories. Thus, the alternatives for shifting to a more flexible, productive and, abstract exchange of behavior do not exist. Those people continually engaging in the higher logical level of parallel behavior would appear to have more variety of cognitive categorization, creating the possibility for a greater variation of a different (not opposite) behavior (p. 207).

Further empirical work needs to be done to determine the degree to which individual cognitive abilities might limit or hinder the therapist's attempt to bring about the second order changes that are required to achieve parallel control patterns. It is important for future investigators to learn whether persons who have difficulty engaging in parallel forms of exchange actually do possess fewer cognitive categories than persons who can more readily accommodate such modes of interaction. Such a finding would have important implications for assessment and treatment. For example, if it were discovered that individuals who possess few cognitive categories are less able to engage in parallel interactions than persons who possess a broad variety of categories, one might wish to determine to what extent an adult can acquire a sufficiently broad enough range of categories to enable him/her to engage in parallel control patterns. Similarly, one would want to know how long, on the average, it would take to train an individual to achieve such a goal, and what type of training would be required. For instance, would teaching a person to use more one-across ($\rightarrow$) statements be sufficient for developing parallel control maneuvers, or are different skills required?

On the other hand, one might find that no relationship exists between one's ability to engage in parallel interactions and variety of cognitive categories. In such a case, teaching couples to use more one-across ($\rightarrow$) maneuvers is all that may be required to modify control patterns.

These findings will be valuable not only for diagnostic and treatment purposes, but they also will provide further insight into the relationship between individual differences and interpersonal processes.

Communication Processes, Sex Role Behavior,
and Marital Satisfaction

The data in these studies point to a number of sex role differences in communication control maneuvers that are associated with overall marital satisfaction and satisfaction with dyadic communication processes in general. For example, a domineering style on the part of the wife was found to be negatively associated with marital and communication satisfaction. Furthermore, wives' domineeringness was found to be positively related to marital role strain. Husbands' dominance, on the other hand, was found to be positively related to overall satisfaction and negatively related to role strain.

For these samples of subjects, at least, husbands' dominance seems to be an important ingredient for marital satisfaction. These empirical findings offer support for the second author's clinical observations that there seems to be a disproportionate number of couples who enroll in marital enrichment programs and seek marital therapy where it is the female partner who initiates contact with a presenting complaint such as: "My husband does not know how to communicate with me"; "My husband is not as involved with me as I would like"; "My husband pays little attention to me when he is at home"; and "My husband spends too much time away from home." In many of these cases, the husband is placed in a classic double bind by a wife who wants him to be "more spontaneously" involved with her and interested in her and to become more dominant and take more responsibility for the relationship. In all these cases, the wife can easily be cast in the role of the nag, as she attempts to get her husband to become more active and involved by using one-up (↑) control maneuvers, such as becoming more domineering. As a response to this behavior, the husband withdraws even more. His withdrawn behavior, however, serves as a stimulus for more domineering behavior by the wife, and "more of the same" i.e. first order change techniques are utilized when it is second order change that is needed. A reframing, which breaks the pattern and allows a restructuring of the relationship to emerge, is necessary.

It is sexist to assume that what these distraught wives want is a more traditional, male dominant complementary relationship. Perhaps what is desired is a relationship control pattern which is characterized by alternating complementarity or parallel exchanges where the husband exhibits more executive control than he has been exhibiting in the past. Thus, the very maneuvers that made sense from a first order perspective for correcting the situation trap the couple further in that frame. Watzlawick et al. (1974) suggest that it is the attempted "solutions," not the difficulty itself, that hold the key to second order intervention which will lift the couple from their first order entrapment.

The use of relational control codes may bring insight not only to researchers of interactional processes, but to therapists and clients, as well. Mapping out a couple's control pattern either by the therapist, the couple, or together, may bring a meta level awareness of patterns that was previously indiscernable. It may provide a base for change, in terms of new levels of awareness which are essential for increasing behavioral alternatives and for helping couples learn and experience different styles of message exchange, which may facilitate relational flexibility by enlarging the couple's repertoire of transactional patterns.

If one accepts the premise that all human systems, of necessity, must organize according to some type of hierarchical structure (Haley, 1978), then, the findings presented above which demonstrate a positive relationship between husbands' dominance and marital satisfaction and pattern flexibility might be seen as indicative of the type of hierarchical arrangement that is preferred by the couples who choose to participate in these studies. It would be inappropriate, however, to assume that such a pattern would be desirable or functional for all couples.

It is important to keep in mind that even though effective systems' functioning requires some degree of hierarchization and "executive" management, that as power discrepancies between spouses increase, mutual understanding and marital satisfaction tend to decrease. Taking these findings into consideration, the therapist is faced with the critical task of helping a couple develop a management structure which is mutually satisfying and maintains a fairly equivalent dominance pattern.

To view family systems as communication processes and to stress the transactional nature of these processes are basic premises of the relational approach. In linking this approach with therapeutic application, it must be remembered, as Birdwhistell so aptly states:

> An individual does not communicate...he participates in it. Communication as a system, then, is not to be understood on a simple model of action and reaction, however complexly stated. As a system it is to be comprehended on the transactional level (1955, p. 104).

REFERENCES

Bagarozzi, D.A., & Wodarski, J.S. A social exchange typology of conjugal relationships and conflict development. *Journal of Marriage and Family Counseling,* 1977, *39,* 53-60.

Bateson, G. Culture contact and schisomogenesis. *Man,* 1935, *35,* 148-183.

Bateson, G. *Naven.* Cambridge: Cambridge University Press, 1936.

Bateson, G. Bali: The value system of a steady state. In M. Fortes (Ed.), *Social structure: Studies presented to A.R. Radcliff-Brown,* Oxford: Clarendon Press, 1949, 35-53.

Bateson, G. Information and codification: A philosophical approach. In J. Ruesch & G. Bateson, *Communication: The social matrix of psychiatry,* New York: W.W. Norton and Co., 1951, 168-211.

Bateson, G. *Steps to an ecology of the mind.* New York: Ballantine Books, 1972.

Beels, C.C., & Ferber, A. Family therapy: A view, *Family Process, 8,* 1969, 280-318.

Birdwhistell, R.J. Contribution of linguistic-kinesic studies to the understanding of schizophrenia. In A. Auerback (Ed.), *Schizophrenia: An integrated approach.* New York: The Renald Press, 1955, 99-123.

Burgess, E.W. The family as a unity of interacting personalities. *The Family, 7,* 1926, 3-9.

Courtright, J.A., Millar, F.E., & Rogers, L.E. Domineeringness and dominance: Replication and expansion, *Communication Monographs,* 1979, *46,* 179-192.

Courtright, J.A., Millar, F.E., & Rogers, L.E. Message control intensity as a predictor of transactional redundancy. In D. Nimmo (Ed.), *Communication Yearbook III,* New Brunswick, N.J.: Transaction Press, 1980a.

Courtright, J.A., Millar, F.E., & Rogers, L.E. The form of relational communication: A new measure of interactional patterns, Paper presented at the Speech Communication Association, New York, 1980b.

Duncan, H.D. The search for a social theory of communication in American sociology. In F. Dance (Ed.), *Human Communication Theory.* New York: Holt, Rinehart and Winston, 1967, 236-263.

Duncan, H.D. *Symbols in society.* London: Oxford University Press, 1968.

Ericson, P.M., & Rogers. New procedures for analyzing relational communication. *Family Process.* 1973, *12,* 245-267.

Haley, J. Marriage therapy. *Archives of General Psychiatry, 8,* 1963, 213-224.

Haley, J. Research on family patterns: An instrument measurement. *Family Process, 3,* 1964, 41-65.

Haley, J. *Problem solving therapy.* San Francisco: Jossey-Bass, 1978.

Harper, J.M., Scoresby, A.L., & Boyce, W.D. The logical levels of complementary, symmetrical, and parallel interaction classes in family dyads. *Family Process, 16,* 1977, 199-209.

Hess, R., & Handel, G. *Family worlds,* Chicago: University of Chicago Press, 1959.

Jackson, D.D. Family interaction, family homeostasis, and some implications for conjoint family psychotherapy. In J.H. Masserman (Ed.), *Individual and family dynamics.* New York: Grune and Stratton, Inc., 1959, 122-141.

Jackson, D.D. The study of family. *Family Process,* 1965, *4,* 1-20.

Jacobson, N.S., & Margolin, G. *Marital therapy: Strategies based on social learning and behavior exchange principle.* New York: Brunner/Mazel, 1979.

Kantor, D., & Lehr, W. *Inside the family: Toward a theory of family process.* New York: Harper Colophon Books, 1975.

Koestler, A. *Janus: A summing up.* New York: Vintage Books, 1968.

Laing, R.D. *The politics of the family and other essays.* New York: Vintage Books, 1972.

Lederer, W.J., & Jackson, D.D. *The mirages of marriage.* New York: W.W. Norton, 1968.

Mark, R. Coding communication at the relationship level. *Journal of Communication,* 1971, *21,* 221-232.

Millar, R.E. A transactional analysis of marital communication patterns: An exploratory study. Unpublished Ph.D. Dissertation, Michigan

State University, 1973.

Millar, R.E., & Rogers, L.E. A relational approach to interpersonal communication. In G. Miller (Ed.), *Explorations in interpersonal communication.* Beverly Hills, CA: Sage Publications, 1976, 87-103.

Millar, R.E., Rogers-Millar, L.E., & Courtright, J.A. Relational control and dyadic understanding: An exploratory predictive regression model. In D. Nimmo (Ed.), *Communication Yearbook III,* New Brunswick, NJ: Transaction Press, 1979, 213-224.

Murrell, S.A., & Stachowiak, J.G. The family group: Development, structure, and therapy. *Journal of Marriage and Family Living,* 1965, *27,* 13-19.

Rogers, L.E. Dyadic systems and transactional communication in a family context. Unpublished Ph.D. Dissertation, Michigan State University, 1972.

Rogers, L.E. Symmetry and complementarity: Evolution and evaluation of an idea. Paper presented at the ICA/SCA Asilomar Conference, Monterey, CA, 1979.

Rogers, L.E., Courtright, J.A., & Millar, F.E. Message control intensity: Rationale and preliminary findings. *Communication Monographs,* 1982.

Rogers, L.E., & Farace, R. Analysis of relational communication in dyads: New measurement procedures. *Human Communication Research,* 1975, *1,* 222-239.

Rogers-Millar, L.E., & Millar, F.E. Domineeringness and dominance: A transactional view. *Human Communication Research,* 1979, *5,* 238-246.

Simmel, G. *The sociology of Georg Simmel.* New York: Glencoe Free Press. Translated by K. Wolf, 1950.

Sluzki, G.E., & Beavin, J. Simetria y complementaridad: Una definicion operacional y una tipologia de parejas. *Acta Psiquiatricia y Psiquiatrica y Psicologica de America Latina,* 1965, *11,* 321-330.

Watzlawick, P., Beavin, J., & Jackson, D.D. *Pragmatics of human communication.* New York: W.W. Norton, 1967.

Watzlawick, P., Weakland, J.H., & Fisch, R. *Change: Principles of problem formation and problem resolution,* New York: W.W. Norton, 1974.

Weinstein, E.A., & Deutschberger, P. Tasks, bargains, and identities in special interaction, *Social Forces,* 1964, *42,* 451-456.

Wodarski, J.S., & Bagarozzi, D.A. *Behavioral social work.* New York: Human Sciences Press, 1979.

Zimmerman, D.H., & West, C. Sex roles, interruptions, and silence in conversation. In B. Thorne and N. Henley (Eds.), *Language and sex: Difference and dominance.* Rowley, Mass.: Newbury House, 1975.

Reference Notes

1. See Millar and Rogers (1976) and Millar, Rogers, and Villard (1978) for an expanded discussion of other potential dimensions.
2. A brief review of this coding system is given in this chapter, for a more detailed and complete description see Ericson and Rogers (1973), Rogers and Farace (1975), and Rogers (1979).
3. See Rogers-Millar and Millar (1979) for other indices and an expanded discussion of theoretical issues concerning the concepts of power and control.
4. A discussion of this measure is given in full in Courtright, Millar, and Rogers (1980).
5. For a full description of the development and standardization of this instrument see Rogers (1972).

Chapter 3

METHODOLOGICAL DEVELOPMENTS IN MEASURING SOCIAL EXCHANGE PERCEPTIONS IN MARITAL DYADS (SIDCARB)
A New Tool For Clinical Intervention*

Dennis A. Bagarozzi Ph.D.

*The research described in this chapter was funded through Kansas State University, grant No. 2901-8-9900, BGR-SRO 50197. Appreciation is extended to Frank DeCastro, MS, Paula Weber, MS, Paul Rauen, MS, and Ray Atilano, MS, who helped in the data collection process. Special thanks are offered to Ray Atilano, MS, who worked so diligently writing and running the statistical programs used in the data analysis phase of the project, and to Ronald B. Downey, PhD and Kristopher Arheart, PhD, who served as statistical consultants.

Introduction

Principles of equity and social exchange have been used by family therapists to describe the internal dynamics of familial behavior (Bagarozzi & Wodarski, 1977, 1978). According to this viewpoint, perceptions of prolonged exchange inequities motivate dissatisfied spouses to reestablish a previous homeostatic balance of exchanges within the system by using a variety of interpersonal control strategies and maneuvers. The types of maneuvers utilized by a spouse to reinstate an equitable balance, however, can range from positive interpersonal influence attempts (e.g., polite verbal requests and invitations to negotiate differences) to negative behavior control tactics (e.g., verbal abuse and physical coercion). Although one might expect marriages to be terminated by spouses who experience the exchange system as inequitable and dissatisfying for an extended period of time, there are a variety of barriers which may prevent an individual from leaving an unhappy marriage (Levinger, 1976). Such marriages have been termed "nonvoluntary" (Bagarozzi & Wodarski, 1977). While a person's appraisal of the exchange process and perception of relationship barriers are important for understanding how to evaluate a marriage, two additional perceptions play a significant role in determining how to behave toward one's spouse, i.e., the perception of more attractive alternatives and the commitment to one's spouse and the marriage.

If it is assumed that individuals respond to and act upon the world as it is perceived by them rather than the world as it "really is," understanding how one spouse experiences the other's behavior and perceives the marriage will be an essential source of data for explaining particular responses. The importance of gaining the "insider's" (spouse or family member's) perspective for family diagnosis, treatment planning and evaluation of therapeutic outcome has been stressed by a number of clinical researchers (Gurman & Kniskern, 1978; Olson, 1974).

In order to gain a more complete understanding of the "insider's" perception of the conjugal exchange process, an exploratory study was undertaken. The findings of this research are reported below.

Method

Subjects

The names of 500 full time graduate students were randomly selected from a list of all married graduate students who had enrolled at a large midwestern university during the fall semester of 1979. Data were gathered during the spring of 1980. Questionnaires were placed in the prospective respondents' university mail boxes by three research assistants who periodically checked the mail boxes to determine whether questionnaires had been picked up by respondents. All subjects were asked to return the questionnaires via the campus mail regardless of whether they chose to participate or elected not to become involved in the research project. Of the 500 sets of questionnaires sent to student couples, approximately one-third (165) never reached the couples for whom they were intended for a variety of reasons (e.g., students were no longer enrolled at the university during the spring semester, students could not be located because they had dropped out of school, students had graduated, students did not pick up their mail, etc.).

Of the 335 couples who actually did receive questionnaires, 202 couples (60%) elected to participate. Of the remaining 133 couples who received materials, 25 questionnaires were returned completed by participants whose spouse chose not to participate and 12 individuals returned questionnaires who were no longer married.

Of the 202 intact couples who did return the questionnaires, 67 couples had not completed the questionnaires accurately or sufficiently enough to be included in the final data analysis. Finally, 23 couples were excluded from the final analysis because they were foreign students. Therefore, the results reported in this chapter are based upon the data received from 112 intact couples (224 individuals).

The mean age of respondents was 29.1 years. Ages ranged from 20-63. Sixty-six percent of the sample identified itself as Protestant, 17% as Catholic, 16% as other and 1% of the respondents identified themselves as Jewish. Sixty-three percent of the respondents were college graduates and 34% reported having some college education. Approximately half the sample (52%) reported having no children, 23% had one child, 19% had two children and 3% indicated having three and four children respectively. The mean age of children was 2.5 years. Eighty-four percent of these respondents were employed and worked a mean of 32.2 hours each week. The median income was $7,005 per year with a range of $0.00 to $50,000. For 88% of the respondents, this was their first marriage. The mean length of marriage was six years. Thirteen percent of the couples reported having sought marital counseling.

Instruments

A questionnaire was constructed to assess spouses' perceptions of the exchange process. The questionnaire was designed to assess a spouse's perception of the four major components of the exchange process as outlined by Bagarozzi and Wodarski (1977). Participants were asked to respond to seven point Likert-type scale questions for the following areas: (a) satisfaction with the fairness and equity of the conjugal exchange system, (b) alternative sources of satisfaction which are perceived to be available, (c) commitment to the relationship, and (d) perceived barriers to separation and divorce.

In order to help spouses identify those areas of marital exchange where inequities were perceived, respondents were asked to indicate the degree to which they would like to see changes in their mate's behavior in both instrumental and affective realms of the relationship, such as: household tasks, finances, communication and expression of love and affection, in-laws, religion, recreation, sexual relations, friendships and children.

In order to determine the degree to which respondents felt committed to their marriages and their spouses, they were asked to respond to a series of questions dealing with commitment, thoughts of separation and divorce, willingness to divorce and separate from their spouses if equity was not restored and the degree to which they would be willing to change their own behavior for the sake of improving their marriages. Respondents also were asked to rate the extent to which they experienced satisfaction from engaging in activities and personal relationships outside their marriages and apart from their spouses.

The final part of the questionnaire was devoted to having the spouses evaluate the strength of the barriers that they believed would prevent them from terminating their marriages if it were dissatisfying. These barriers included obligations to children, commitment to marriage vows, religious beliefs, friends, neighbors and relatives, job considerations, legal costs and financial concerns.

As a global measure of marital satisfaction and satisfaction with one's spouse, respondents were asked to answer two seven point Likert-type scale questions: "In general, how satisfied are you with your marriage"? and "In general, how satisfied are you with your spouse"? These two questions can be considered valid indicators of satisfaction with one's marriage and spouse based upon statistical analyses performed during the piloting phase of this research when the questionnaire was being developed. One hundred and sixty two respondents were asked to complete the Lock-Wallace Short Marital Adjustment Scale (1959) and the two Likert-type scale questions described above. When the scores of each of these questions were correlated with the Locke-Wallace Short Marital Adjustment Scale (1959), they were found to correlate significantly for both satisfaction with marriage (r = .73, $p < .01$) and satisfaction with spouse (r = .71, $p < .01$). Based upon these findings, it was felt that the two Likert-type scale questions could serve as a brief, but valid, measure of the respondent's overall satisfaction with spouse and marriage.

Results

Responses to all questions were subjected to a factor analysis. The SPSS factor analysis program was used for this purpose. Initial factors were extracted using a principle component solution with iterations. This procedure yields factors which were extracted with the initial estimates of communalities, the R^2 estimates, which were then improved for the same number of factors in the reduced matrix. Initially, seven factors were produced whose eigenvalues were greater than one. Examination of these factors, however, suggested that a four factor solution would be more interpretable. The four factor solution revealed numerous cross loadings on the third and fourth factor. Therefore, a three factor solution was attempted. This three factor solution proved to be clearly interpretable. The rotational method used to obtain terminal factors was the varimax procedure which gives an orthogonal solution. In addition to the orthogonal solution, an oblique solution (Kaiser, 1963) was performed in order to determine the regularity with which these factors appeared. An examination and comparison of both of these derived solutions showed them to be almost identical in structure. This offers additional support for the robustness of the factors extracted.

Items which did not load significantly on any of the factors were discarded, and a final factor analysis and orthogonal rotation were performed. The results of this analysis appear in Table 1. These three terminal factors were found to account for 53% of the variance.

The items with significant loadings on each factor then were summed to form three subscales of the *Spousal Inven-*

Table 1: Varimax Rotated Factor Matrix With Non Significant Items Deleted*

Variables	Factor Loadings**			Communality
	I	II	III	
Household Chores	.38417	.03731	.03304	.31729
Finances	.42043	.06565	.14138	.22697
Communication of love and affection	.51174	.07306	.06534	.42229
Recreation	.50288	.03331	.04500	.38350
Sex	.46405	.06993	.01271	.37653
Friends	.46676	.01711	.00207	.32848
Satisfaction-Marriage	-.92202	.05988	.07720	.87596
Satisfaction-Spouse	-.87436	.05172	.14189	.87125
Commitment	-.60741	.10001	.20738	.60252
Thoughts of Separation	.77560	.13797	.10475	.81717
Thoughts of Divorce	.75284	.15153	.12067	.80685
Willingness to Separate	.13205	-.75847	.13467	.79556
Willingness to Divorce	.05018	-.82833	.16600	.80519
Obligations to Children	.01848	.39593	.15723	.26804
Marriage Vows	.11012	.67422	.10476	.53757
Religious Beliefs	.14035	.62428	.20972	.52433
Friends, Neighbors, Relatives	.17384	.32847	.50379	.42581
Job Concerns	.13010	.00688	.79731	.56915
Legal Costs	.07631	.04719	.79789	.57182
Financial Considerations	.09751	.01455	.71570	.56711

*Three Factor Orthogonal Rotation Solution:Varimax
**Eigenvalues. Factor I = 5.44, Factor II = 3.05, Factor III = 2.12

tory of Desired Changes and Relationship Barriers (SID-CARB). These subscales represent the major dimensions of spousal perceptions: Factor I = *Change, Dissatisfaction and Commitment,* Factor II = *Willingness to Separate/ Divorce and Internal-Psychological Barriers,* and Factor III = *External-Circumstantial Barriers.*

A Cronbach's (1951) to alpha reliability coefficient was computed for each subscale of the SIDCARB. The reliabilities for each of the subscales were found to be .86, .74, and .80 for factors I, II, and III respectively. The first and second factors were negatively correlated, $r = -.19$ ($p < .01$). The first and third factors were positively correlated $r = .24$ ($p < .001$). The correlation between factor II and factor III was $r = .16$ ($p < .01$).

In order to determine whether there were significant differences between husbands' and wives' perceptions on these three subscales, t-tests for related samples were performed. Analysis of these data revealed no significant differences between husbands' and wives' perceptions on any of the three subscales. Factor I: $t = -1.20$, $p = .24$, Factor II: $t = -.26$, $p = .79$. Factor III: $t = -1.64$, $p = .10$. Since no significant differences were found, standard scores were developed for the entire sample using standard T-transformations. An individual receives a score for each of the three subscales. These three scores together provide the clinician with a profile of how a spouse perceives his/her marriage. A score of 50 constitutes the mean for each standardized subscale, with 10 being the standard deviation.

Discussion

The three factors produced in this analysis clearly point to the various dimensions of individual perceptions of marriage. The first factor highlights one's dissatisfaction and the extent to which changes in one's spouse's behavior are desired. It stands to reason that the more changes one would like the mate to make, the less satisfied one would be with the partner in specific and the marriage in general. Similarly, one would expect that the more dissatisfied a spouse becomes, the less committed that spouse would be to continuing in the relationship and the more frequent thoughts of separation and divorce would become.

The second factor demonstrates the strength that Internal-Psychological Barriers exert in marriage. Inspection of this factor shows that Internal-Psychological Barriers are negatively associated with a spouse's willingness to separate or divorce. It is legitimate to say when barriers are of the internal-psychological type, separation and divorce are less likely to be seen as viable options or alternatives.

The final factor consists predominantly of External-Circumstantial Barriers. It is interesting to note that while the Internal-Psychological Barriers that make up factor II are negatively associated with a spouse's willingness to terminate an unhappy marriage, the External-Circumstantial Barriers comprising factor III are not so associated. One may speculate that barriers associated with a person's internalized "values," "conscience," or "superego" serve as much stronger deterrents to relationship termination, because they are more likely to engender psychological stress in the form of shame or guilt than would the External-Circumstantial Barriers associated with factor III. Questions relating to alternate sources of satisfaction outside the marriage did not load significantly on any of the terminal factors.

Administration and Scoring

The 20 Likert-type questions which make up the SIDCARB can be completed by spouses in a period of a few minutes prior to the intial interview. Scoring the SIDCARB can be done easily by the clinician before meeting with the couple by summing the raw scores for each subscale. Once the raw scores have been completed, the therapist uses a simple conversion table to find the standard score and the percentile equivalent for each subscale.

Intervention: Clinical Uses of SIDCARB

Marital conflict as described by Bagarozzi and Wodarski (1977, 1978) develops when continued perception of exchange inequities cause both spouses to become dissatisfied. Dissatisfaction drives both spouses to reduce the inequity and to restore an equitable exchange system by employing a variety of interpersonal behavior change strategies. When the strategies employed are predominantly coercive in nature, a negatively escalating cycle of mutual coercion results which is extremely difficult to extinguish. As a result of the coercion, communication breaks down, constructive problem solving decreases and successful conflict management becomes less likely.

Unfortunately, both spouses are forced into using "more of the same" coercive tactics, because these tactics have been successful to some degree, in the past. This periodic reinforcement of coercive interpersonal strategies only insures that the cycle will be repeated from time to time.

Based upon the paradigm presented above, the therapist can be said to have two major goals in mind when working with distressed couples: To help them develop an exchange system which both spouses perceive and experience as fair and equitable, and to reduce the use of punitive, coercive, and dysfunctional behavior change maneuvers and replace them with problem solving techniques and conflict negotiation strategies which are more functional, flexible, and satisfying.

The treatment procedures outlined below are based on the premise that behaviors exchanged between spouses have both real and symbolic value and meaning for the parties involved, and that spouses respond to each other according to how they perceive and interpret the behaviors and intentions of their mates. Therefore, the therapist must address the behavioral acts themselves as well as their symbolic meaning in order to be effective.

Initial Phases of Treatment:
The Context of Change

As in all forms of psychotherapy, the therapist's first task is to establish a trusting relationship with the couple. Both spouses should feel that the therapist's goal is to help them improve their relationship without favoring one spouse over the other or siding with one spouse against the other. In addition to communicating neutrality, the therapist has the added task of helping spouses perceive their relationship as one of mutual collaboration and cooperation rather than as a competitive struggle. This change may be difficult to accomplish, however, when couples have a history of mutual coercion, punishment and hostile interaction. In such instances, it may be necessary for the therapist to provide the couple with specific ground rules for communicating and behaving in the sessions before such perceptual changes can be brought about.

If spouses are locked in a deadly struggle, the therapist might attempt to negotiate a temporary "truce" or "cease fire" for an agreed number of sessions. During this "truce" period, the couple can be taught to use conflict negotiation strategies to resolve differences and problems of lesser importance which are not as emotionally charged as those for which they originally sought treatment. If they are successful in resolving these lesser problems, they will be more likely to use their newly acquired skills to tackle more serious differences.

When one spouse is presented as the "identified patient" with "the problem," the therapist can help the spouses change their perception of the problem by indicating that the problem affects their relationship, and that in order for their relationship to improve, both spouses will have to work together to resolve the problem. It does not matter whether the "well" spouse acknowledges any responsibility for maintaining the problem behavior. What does matter, however, is whether the spouse can be motivated to make behavioral changes in order to improve the relationship.

The therapist's goal in the initial sessions, therefore, is to change the couple's perception of their relationship from one where spouses see themselves as adversaries who are trying to change each other's behavior to one where both spouses see themselves as collaborators who are trying to overcome a problem which is threatening their relationship. Solving the presenting problem then becomes a superordinate goal that can be acheived only through the concerted effort of both spouses. If the therapist is successful in having the couple perceive the problem in this manner, some of the emotional reactions associated with the problem can be defused.

Frequently, however, one spouse expresses doubt as to whether therapy can help the relationship. This spouse usually is reluctant to participate in treatment and blames the other spouse for the sorry state of affairs. In such cases, the therapist must concentrate on involving the less willing spouse in the treatment process. The degree to which the therapist is successful in doing this will depend upon the reluctant spouse's commitment to the relationship, the strength of the barriers, and the reward potential of the mate. If one assumes that the reluctant spouse is less dependent on the relationship, the therapist might concentrate on having the more committed spouse increase inputs into the marriage by providing more rewards for the less committed spouse. This will have several effects. It will: make the giving spouse more appealing, make the interactions more pleasurable, and require the less committed, less involved spouse to become more involved in the relationship in accordance with the norms of reciprocity. If this goal can be accomplished, the spouses may experience a renewed commitment to the relationship, because they can anticipate that a more equitable and rewarding exchange system is possible in the future.

It is important to realize that the initial stages of treatment are crucial to its outcome. The therapist's task in these early sessions, therefore, is to bring about an atmosphere where change can take place. This requires the reduction of mutual punishments and hostile behavioral exchanges between spouses, the development of a collaborative set, and the creation of an expectation that more rewarding and equitable exchanges can be negotiated.

Assessment Process

The SIDCARB has proven to be a valuable assessment tool and treatment aid. The Change-Dissatisfaction-Commitment subscale provides the therapist with valuable information about those areas of the marriage where inequities are perceived and where spouses would like to see changes brought about. It also gives a good indication of how dissatisfied each spouse is with the current exchange system in general. By checking the percentile rank for each spouse, the therapist can assess the severity of inequities experienced by each spouse. In addition, the clinician can get some idea about each spouse's verbal commitment to making the marriage work. Later on, as treatment progresses, the therapist can observe and evaluate the extent to which each spouses's behavior is consistent with his/her verbal statments about commitment.

When the Change-Dissatisfaction-Commitment subscale is used in conjunction with subscales II and III (Internal-Psychological Barriers and External-Circumstantial Barriers) the therapist is provided with an insider's perception of barriers to separation and divorce even though the marriage is perceived as inequitable and dissatisfying. Insights about the extent to which the marriage is perceived as a non-voluntary association by each spouse can be gained by comparing the barrier scores of both spouses. This also allows one to speculate about which spouse has more power in the marriage by being less interested and invested in maintaining the relationship (Waller & Hill, 1951).

During this assessment phase, it is important for the spouses to become aware of the valued resources they possess which can be used later as exchange commodities. I have found it helpful to have spouses list the personal qualities each possesses and believes to be valued by the mate. Similarly, each spouse is asked to identify specific behaviors and qualities in his/her spouse that are rewarding and pleasing. To aid the couple in this process, spouses are asked to list their own resources and those of their mate according to five categories. These include: physical attributes, intellectual abilities, emotional characteristics, material resources and services performed.

By comparing the responses of both spouses, the clinician can determine whether the resources a spouse perceives himself/herself to possess actually are valued as exchange commodities by the mate. Making this distinction between what one spouse perceives to be rewarding to his/her partner and how that partner actually feels about, perceives, evaluates, and interprets that same behavior is an important piece of information for the therapist to obtain, because spouses may disagree about the value of their own inputs and those of their mate's as well as the worth of the resources exchanged between them. This often results in spouses differentially perceiving the fairness of various "exchanges" (Bagarozzi & Wodarski, 1977). This is true especially when couples are embroiled in conflict (Gottman, Notarius, Markham, Bank, Yoppi & Rubin, 1976).

The problem identification process should help both partners focus on specific behaviors that are to be the target of treatment. For example, if a spouse identifies the area of "friends" as a major concern, it is essential for the therapist to help that spouse pin-point what specific behaviors he/she would like to see changed in his/her mate concerning that spouse's interactions with friends. The therapist's job is to help the spouse identify, for example, whether it is the amount of time the partner spends with friends, the friends themselves, the activities engaged in, who the friends are, etc. The more specifically the problem is stated, the more able the therapist will be to have the couple focus on and begin to negotiate a more satisfying way of resolving this issue.

The therapist then gathers data about how the couple has tried to resolve this difficulty in the past. The object of this information gathering process is to determine what types of coercive techniques have been utilized by both spouses and how they have been reinforced.

In the process of making these inquiries, the therapist attempts to help both partners become more empathic by having them discuss together their interpretations, perceptions and feelings about each other whenever one spouse exhibits a problem behavior. In addition, the therapist can have each spouse discuss the intentions attributed to the mate whenever a particular problem behavior is exhibited. The therapist can then help both spouses see that they frequently misinterpret the intentions of their partners. Here, the therapist can help the couple disrupt the negative response chain which often follows whenever malevolent intentions are attributed to a spouse. The couple can be taught to "short circuit" this process and to institute another response chain which is more functional. For example, spouses can be taught to "check out" the intentions of their mates before retaliating with a counter coercive strategy.

In some instances, the therapist might relabel the meanings of some behaviors or reframe the intentions of a spouse in order to produce a more positive atmosphere and to change the context of the interaction.

Another goal of the assessment phase is to help both spouses take some responsibility for their part in maintaining the problem behaviors. This is important, because each spouse will be required to make changes in the characteristic mode of responding if interaction patterns are to be changed. This may be difficult to do when one spouse has been singled out as the "identified patient." Frequently, attempts to have the "well" spouse acknowledge any responsibility for maintaining the problem are met with resistance. A number of techniques can be employed to overcome this obstacle. For example, the SIDCARB can be used to locate areas of concern where both spouses desire change. By focusing on mutually shared concerns, the therapist can get both spouses to look at their own behavioral contributions to maintaining the problem. If no areas of mutual concern can be identified, the therapist can show how one spouse's concerns are linked to the concerns of the other. Finally, if the therapist cannot demonstrate a logical link between problems, a problem area identified by each spouse can be selected as the area to be the focus of treatment. Such a procedure will set the stage for trade-offs which will take place later on in therapy when contingency contracts are introduced. Taking responsibility for one's own behavior is an essential prerequisite to changing the spouse's views about how relationships operate and how to go about gaining more satisfying and equitable exchanges.

Treatment: The Working Phase

The procedures outlined thus far and the ones to follow may seem strange and unorthodox to behaviorally oriented clinicians. However, they have been developed to treat distressed couples who present themselves for therapy rather than to participate in marital enrichment programs, educational experiences, experimental studies, etc. Frequently, these couples may be put off by structured assessment procedures and step by step treatment processes which they perceive as alien, mechanistic, rigid, and impersonal. In many instances, couples come in for treatment in a highly emotional state or in the throes of a crisis which has to be dealt with immediately. Finally, some couples may be resistant to the use of formalized assessment procedures, questionnaires such as the SIDCARB, and the collection of baseline data. When this happens, it is essential for the therapist to be flexible, to meet the couple on its own ground and to talk the couple's language. Under such circumstances, the SIDCARB can be introduced later on in therapy, once a trusting relationship has been established.

Keeping in mind the goals of eliminating negative behavior change strategies and establishing a more equitable exchange system, the therapist proceeds to move the couple in the direction of negotiating differences. Depending upon the couple, the therapist might use a direct approach by introducing contingency contracts which are stated explicitly and negotiated openly, or have the spouses contract and negotiate their differences in an informal, low keyed and almost off handed manner by giving the couple directives that will help them informally institute more equitable exchanges.

Having spouses formally negotiate more rewarding exchanges has been the major focus of some behaviorally oriented clinicians for some time (Azrin, Naster & Jones, 1973; Patterson, Hops & Weiss, 1976; Stuart, 1976). While this approach has been shown to be effective with minimally distressed couples, its appropriateness for healing severely distressed relationships has yet to be demonstrated (Gurman & Kniskern, 1978). Although no empirical data have been presented to indicate that contingency contracts produce negative treatment outcomes, some clinicians have cautioned against their use (Jacobson & Margolin, 1979). In this author's opinion, contingency contracts constitute one possible treatment procedure to be used in the treatment of disturbed relationships. Like any other treatment strategy, the therapist's decision to use a particular technique should be based upon its appropriateness for a given couple.

In order to establish a more equitable exchange system, a number of techniques can be used. Some of these will be discussed briefly in the next section.

Case Study

The Philips Family

Mr. Philips (age 25) and Mrs. Philips (age 27) presented themselves for treatment. At the time of their request, they had a 3-year-old daughter. Mr. Philips had a personal history of child neglect, abuse, abandonment and loss of significant parental figures throughout his life. He had a history of drug and alcohol abuse and periodic psychiatric hospitalizations during his adolescence. At the time of treatment, he had been drug free for six months.

Mrs. Philips had experienced a somewhat more stable home life than her husband. She had lived with her mother until her mother's death. Her mother had had a series of marriages and relationships with men who moved in and out of the home. Although her home life was chaotic, her mother did provide some degree of stability and support. Mrs. Philips had sought individual therapy on a number of occasions but had never been hospitalized. Before meeting Mr. Philips, she had had a series of dissatisfying relationships with men with whom she had lived. These relationships were punctuated by bouts of mutual verbal abuse and physical violence. This pattern continued, to a lesser degree, in her relationship with Mr. Philips.

This couple entered treatment in a highly distressed state. Mrs. Philips was extremely anxious and Mr. Philips was depressed. The frequency of their arguments had been increasing, and Mrs. Philips had become assaultive. Mr. Philips had retaliated by leaving home on a number of occasions. Their initial interview was characterized by mutual blaming and accusations. In order to stabilize the relationship, it was necessary to set specific ground rules for their conduct in the sessions as well as for how they were to behave at home. A temporary truce was negotiated between the spouses, and they were given specific guidelines for how to "communicate" in the therapy sessions. Modeling, role playing and shaping were used to accomplish this goal. These practices helped to restructure their interactions and allowed the spouses to discuss their feelings about the relationship. When their interactions had become less volatile, the couple was asked to complete the SIDCARB. An analysis of both Mr. and Mrs. Philips' responses to the SIDCARB revealed the following:

Mrs. Philips had extremely high scores on the Change-Dissatisfaction-Commitment subscale of the SIDCARB. However, she had extremely high scores on both Willingness to Separate/Divorce and Internal-Psychological Barriers and External-Circumstantial Barriers subscales.

Mr. Philips, on the other hand, scored at the mid point on the first subscale and had extremely low scores on both the Willingness to Separate/Divorce and Internal-Psychological

Barriers and External-Circumstantial Barriers subscales.

As can be seen from the above profile, Mr. Philips was less committed to maintaining the relationship than Mrs. Philips (i.e. he had more power). Her attempts to coerce Mr. Philips to put more effort into the relationship, however, only resulted in Mr. Philips reducing his inputs by emotional and physical withdrawal. Mrs. Philips responded with more coercion which culminated in her physical attack on Mr. Philips. When they presented themselves for therapy, Mrs. Philips expressed the fear that Mr. Philips would leave her and their child.

Although Mr. Philips was the "identified" patient, both spouses were willing to work on the relationship. The SID-CARB was used to help this couple identify areas where changes were desired. It was not difficult to have them locate an area of mutual concern, however, because Mrs. Philips had indicated that *all* areas of the marriage were problematic!

The broad area of change identified by both spouses was "communication of love and affection." Mrs. Philips listed a number of behaviors that she would like Mr. Philips to modify. He, in turn, listed a variety of behavioral changes that he felt would make the relationship more satisfying. When both were asked to rank these behaviors in order of their importance, Mrs. Philips said she wanted her husband to "be more honest." Mr. Philips said he wanted his wife to "nag less and be more encouraging." When asked to be more specific, Mrs. Philips said she wanted Mr. Philips "to come home on time and to tell me when you are going out with your friends and when you will be home late at night." Mr. Philips explained his request as meaning that he did not want his wife to tell him things repeatedly such as "feed the baby" and only ask him to "do something one time" and to "tell me I've done O.K. when I finish feeding her."

After each spouse had pin-pointed specific behaviors to be modified, how frequently they were to be exhibited, in which situations they were to be performed, etc., the stage was set for helping them negotiate a more satisfying exchange system. An informal contractual approach was used with this couple. This procedure is described below. It entails a number of steps, each of which has a specific goal or purpose.

Increasing empathy through role taking. Spouses are asked to discuss how they feel, what they say to themselves about their mate and what is believed to be the mate's intentions whenever that spouse exhibits a behavior or fails to perform a given response. Spouses are cautioned, however, to speak from their own vantage point but not to accuse, attack, etc., their mates. The other spouse is asked to listen attentively and to summarize both the content and feelings expressed by his/her mate. By doing this, a number of goals are achieved: (a) each spouse has the opportunity for self expression, (b) the frequency of personal attacks is reduced, (c) by hearing one's spouse summarize what was said, the other knows he/she has been heard and understood, (d) a more positive atmosphere is created, and (e) empathy for one's spouse is developed.

> During this process, Mrs. Philips described, in detail, her fears, apprehensions and the sense of dread she experienced whenever Mr. Philips was out at night and she did not know his whereabouts. She vividly talked about her concerns that he had been in an accident, gotten into trouble with the law, returned to drugs or alcohol, or abandoned her and her child. Sometimes these fears caused her to "go into a panic".

After each spouse has had the opportunity to discuss the issue under consideration, the next step is introduced.

Correcting perceptions, relabeling behaviors and reframing intentions. At this juncture, the offended spouse is asked to discuss his/her perceptions of the mate's intentions. Frequently, malevolent intent is attributed to the spouse. The spouse who has been accused then is asked to discuss his/her "true" intentions. Three responses are possible: (a) the spouse offers a logical non-malicious explanation, (b) the spouse denies any hostile intent, or (c) the spouse admits that the actions were intended to hurt, punish, or coerce the mate. If the spouse offers a logical explanation that is accepted by the partner, the therapist can help the couple discuss how to treat this situation in a more satisfying manner the next time it arises. If, on the other hand, the offended spouse does not accept the explanation, the therapist can indicate acceptance of that spouse's explanation, but will teach the couple some new procedures which may help them avoid such "misunderstandings" in the future. The therapist also might agree with the offended spouse and not accept the explanation offered, but instead of attributing a negative intent to the behavior, reframe the behavior as being well intentioned. Finally, if the offending spouse admits malicious intent, the therapist can relabel the behavior as a problem solving strategy that failed because both spouses are still unhappy. The therapist then can proceed to teach the spouses a new way to "resolve their differences."

> When Mrs. Philips was asked to discuss her perceptions and attributions concerning Mr. Philips' intentions when he was away from home for extended periods of time, she indicated that this meant he did not love her and their child. Mr. Philips' reply to this accusation was that he was "just out with friends, having a good time," and that "I always come home to you, because I love you." Mrs. Philips agreed that he always came home, but that she was "afraid to be alone when he was gone." Her response to his behavior frequently was coercive. She would refuse to engage in sexual relations, verbally berate him, etc., and a cycle of mutual coercion would ensue.
>
> Since Mrs. Philips agreed that her husband did eventually come home and that he had not gone back on drugs or used alcohol for a substantial period of time, the therapist used this oportunity to "teach" them how to resolve this problem in a more satisfying manner (indicating that Mr. Philips' behvior was well intentioned). An informal contract was negotiated in which Mr. Philips agreed that he would only go out on specified evenings and that he would telephone his wife if he planned to come home after midnight. At that time, he would tell her where he was and when to expect him home. If he came home at the agreed upon time, she was to tell him that he had "done O.K.," and she "loved" him when he was "honest." During the time she was at home alone, Mrs. Philips was instructed to "think differently." She was to say to herself that

Mr. Philips had "proved his honesty" by telephoning her, and that he was going to show her "how much he loved her by coming home on time." Mr. Philips was instructed to write these comments on 3 × 5 index cards so that she would remember them accurately and to read these statements to herself whenever she began to "worry."

The remainder of the session was spent going through a similar procedure with Mr. Philips concerning his spouse's "nagging" and her lack of "encouragement."

This informal process allows the distressed couple to engage in trade-offs which are not stated explicitly in rigid contractual terms, and it deals with problem behaviors as well as the spouses' cognitions, perceptions, and interpretations, which frequently serve as antecedent cues in a response chain which results in the use of coercive behavior change maneuvers. By focusing on the cognitive processes, the therapist attempts to short circuit this response chain and replace it with a different one which leads to the enactment of positive behavior change strategies.

After helping the couple resolve inequities in one area of the relationship, the therapist moves to the next area of concern. For the Philips family, this was "friendships."

Closer examination revealed that Mrs. Philips did not approve of her husband's friends and feared that they might influence him to return to drugs. She also wanted Mr. Philips to spend more time at home with her and their child. Mr. Philips indicated that he did not mind spending time at home with Mrs. Philips, but he did need some time at home where he could be "left alone" and "watch television without interruption." In exploring these requests in more detail, the therapist discovered a relationship or "link" between both spouses' requests. Because Mrs. Philips worked during the day, she wanted to spend time with her husband during the evening "talking or doing things as a family." Mr. Philips' job as a construction worker, however, left him quite tired in the evening, and he enjoyed relaxing after meals by watching television. Mrs. Philips' response to his watching television was to use coercion and punishment. She would stand in front of the television, play the radio, turn off the television etc. Mr.

Philips' response was counter-coercive (e.g., leave the house, shout obscenities, or shut off the radio and again switch on the television.)

An interesting turn of events took place as the therapist was working with this couple to establish an informal contract. Mrs. Philips asked if their agreements could be written down because they had a hard time remembering. At this juncture, more formal contracts were instituted. The couple went to work in the areas of child rearing and financial management. In order to work on the latter concern, a referral to a financial counselor was made (Bagarozzi & Bagarozzi, 1980). The couple continued in therapy while working with the financial counselor who helped them deal with the realities of their financial situation. Treatment was terminated after 12 sessions. Post treatment evaluations using the SIDCARB showed a reduction in the Change-Dissatisfaction-Commitment subscale scores for both Mr. and Mrs. Philips. Barriers' subscale scores, however, remained about the same for both spouses.

The Broader Context of Therapy: Symbols and Meanings

The Philips family is a good example of how contracting and exchange procedures can be introduced in a manner which is acceptable to the couple. Contracting, stimulus control, and cognitive restructuring techniques were particularly helpful with this couple because they enabled both spouses to bring a much needed order into their lives and predictability to their relationships.

The point is missed, however, if the goal of treatment is seen only as the establishment of contractual agreements which couples can use to govern their relationship in specified areas of interaction and exchange. The meaning of the behaviors exhibited by each spouse is something which the therapist must keep in mind in order to understand the significant role they play in the relationship, the genesis of conflict, and its resolution. For example, having Mr. Philips call his wife was more than a modification in his usual behavioral pattern. It was a symbolic message to Mrs. Philips that she was cared about and would not be abandoned. Similarly, when Mrs. Philips reinforced Mr. Philips for coming home on time, her praise was interpreted as a validation of his self-worth and his importance to Mrs. Philips.

In the broader context, one can understand this couple's mutually coercive strategies as attempts to gain control of the relationship, to establish certain rules for interaction and exchange, and as each spouse's struggle to regulate the degree of separateness and connectedness that is personally acceptable and tolerable. The therapist need not address these issues directly, but understanding their significance in the relationship will enable him/her to deal with them indirectly in working with the couple to establish more satisfying and equitable exchanges. In this sense, exchange contracts are seen as a means to effect structural changes in overall relationship patterns rather than as ends in themselves.

Summary

In this chapter, history of the SIDCARB has been traced from its philosophical and theoretical origins, through its methodological developments, to its clinical uses as an assessment tool and therapeutic aid. A case example was provided to illustrate how the SIDCARB was used to tap each spouse's subjective perception of the relationship, the areas where changes were desired, and the barriers which were perceived to stand in the way of relationship termination even though the exchange system was experienced as dissatisfying and inequitable. A number of intervention strategies were discussed which can be used to address both the individual, cognitive components which play a significant role in the genesis and maintenance of disordered relationship patterns and the behavioral, interactional processes themselves. Techniques which have been developed for working with severely distressed couples and resistant spouses were discussed. Specific attention was given to the use of informal contractual procedures and cognitive intervention strategies which have been found to work well with disorganized couples because they provide structure and predictability for both spouses. Although contingency contracting is discussed as one of the possible treatment tools that can be used to bring about more satisfying and equitable exchanges between spouses, it is considered only as one means to bring about structural changes in the overall relationship patterns and interaction processes and not as the primary goal of treatment.

REFERENCES

Azrin, N.H., Naster, B.J., & Jones, R. Reciprocity counseling: A rapid learning based procedure for marital counseling. *Behavior, Research and Therapy,* 1973, *11,* 365-382.

Bagarozzi, D.A., & Wodarski, J.S. A social exchange typology of conjugal relationships and conflict development. *Journal of Marriage and Family Counseling,* 1977, *3,* 53-60.

Bagarozzi, D.A., & Wodarski, J.S. Behavioral treatment of marital discord. *Clinical Social Work Journal,* 1978, *6,* 135-154.

Bagarozzi, J.I., & Bagarozzi, D.A. Financial counseling: A self control model for the family. *Family Relations,* 1980, *29,* 396-403.

Cronbach, L.J. Coefficient alpha and the internal structure of tests. *Psychometrika,* 1951, *16,* 297-334.

Gottman, L., Notarius, C., Markham, R., Bank, S., Yoppi, B., & Rubin, N.E. Behavior exchange theory and marital decision making. *Journal of Personality and Social Psychology,* 1976, *34,* 14-23.

Gurman, A.S., & Kniskern, D.P. Research on marital and family therapy: Progress, perspective and prospect. In S.L. Garfield & A.E. Bergin (Ed.), *Handbook of psychotherapy and behavior change: An empirical analysis (Vol. 2),* New York: John Wiley & Sons, 1978.

Jacobson, N.S. & Margolin, G. *Marital therapy: Strategies based on social learning and behavior exchange principles,* New York: Brunner/Mazel, 1979.

Kaiser, H.F. Image analysis. In C.W. Harris (Ed.), *Problems in measuring change*. Madison: The University of Wisconsin Press, 1963.

Levinger, G. A social psychological perspective on marital dissolution. *Journal of Social Issues,* 1976, *32*, 21-47.

Locke, H.J., & Wallace, K.M. Short marital adjustment and prediction tests: Their reliability a validity. *Marriage and Family Living* 1959, *21*, 251-255.

Olson, D.H. Insiders and outsiders view of relationships: Research strategies. Paper presented at the symposium on Close Relationships. University of Massachusetts, 1974.

Patterson, G.R., Hops, H., & Weiss, R.L. A social learning approach to reducing rates of marital conflict, in R. Stuart, R. Liberman, & S. Wilder (Ed.), *Advances in behavior therapy,* New York: Academic Press, 1976.

Stuart, R. An operant interpersonal program for couples, in D.H. Olson (Ed.) *Treating relationships*. Lake Mills: Graphic Publishing, 1976.

Waller, W., & Hill, R. *The family: A dynamic interpretation*. New York: The Dryden Press, 1951.

THERAPY WITH FAMILIES IN CRISIS AND UNDER STRESS

Chapter 4

PARENTAL COPING AND FAMILY ENVIRONMENT:
Critical Factors in the Home Management and Health Status of Children with Cystic Fibrosis*

Hamilton I. McCubbin, Ph.D.
Joan Patterson
Marilyn A. McCubbin, R.N.
Lance R. Wilson, Ph.D.

*Paper presented at the annual meeting of the American Public Health Association, New York, November 1979. This project was funded by the Agriculture Experiment Station, University of Minnesota, St. Paul. The authors would like to acknowledge the families who participated and who gave so much to advance our understanding of their personal situation. We would like to thank Dr. Warren Warwick, Director of the University of Minnesota Cystic Fibrosis Center whose commitment to the CF children and their families made this project possible. We would like to thank Drs. William Hueg, Keith Huston, Signe Betsinger, and Keith McFarland of the Institute of Agriculture, Forestry and Home Economics who supported the research project. We would also like to note the significant contributions of Karen Reigstad, R.N., Marsha Zuckerman, MSW, Joan Comeau, MS, Michael Morris, Elizabeth Cauble, MSW, as well as our patient and supportive secretary, Diane Felicetta, all of whom worked with, and guided this research effort, in a personal way.

Introduction

Cystic fibrosis, one of the most common chronic diseases of childhood, is now considered the most serious lung complication in children (Travis, 1976). Genetically transmitted through a recessive gene from both parents, it is found predominantly in Caucasians and is estimated to occur in a ratio of 1:1,000 to 1:1,500 live births. The exact defect causing the disease is not known. Despite advances in therapy in recent years increasing longevity into adulthood, the disease is still eventually fatal.

Physiologically, the disease affects the exocrine glands with a variability in the amount of involvement in each organ system. Mucus obstruction of the pancreatic ducts causes digestive disturbances with an inability to digest fats and protein resulting in inadequate weight gain in the growing child. Lung involvement is characterized by thickened bronchial mucus which interferes with the normal functioning of the respiratory system by obstructing airways and interfering with the normal cleansing action of the lungs. The sweat glands contain an abnormally high concentration of salt. Intestinal obstruction also can occur due to increased mucus in the intestinal glands. Treatment of cystic fibrosis involves a complex time-consuming regimen of daily therapy carried out in the home environment. The family is called on to make long-term intra-familial, social and psychological adaptations to this form of chronic stress. Children with cystic fibrosis are now surviving through adolescence into young adulthood so that more stages of the family life cycle are affected.

The long term treatment of a child with cystic fibrosis involves a complementary relationship between the health care team, as well as the family and its willingness and ability to follow through with the treatment program in the home. In an effort to enhance medical-family relationships and strengthen the family's capability to respond to the demands of cystic fibrosis, several important questions need to be answered.

- Why is it that some families respond well to the demands of this chronic illness, while other families struggle and are not able to provide the family environment called for by the situation?
- Are there coping strategies parents employ which facilitate family adjustment and play a part in improving the child's health?
- What aspects of the family environment are associated with improvements in the CF child's health?

This study examines these questions with the expectation that health professionals may improve the child's physical health and psychological well-being by emphasizing parental coping strategies and family environment dimensions.

The majority of research studies on the psychosocial effects of cystic fibrosis focus on the deleterious impact of the disease process on the afflicted child and its crippling effect on family life. The emphasis has been on the maladaptation and the dysfunctional aspects of family coping and adjustment to the chronic illness. For example, Lawler, Nakielny, and Wright (1966) found problems of anxiety, depression, and preoccupation with death in all 11 children they studied. Marked psychopathology and marital discord were also present in a majority of the parents of these children. Spock and Stedman (1966) found children with cystic fibrosis to be highly anxious and in need of strength and support. Parental anxiety and sympathy for the child resulted in the provision of a more permissive, overprotective environment in the home. In a study of 20 children, Tropauer, Franz, and Dilgard (1970) revealed both anxiety and depression in the children and their mothers. Despite emotional conflicts and maternal responses ranging from overprotectiveness to rejection, this study concluded most mothers were still able to perform effectively. Severe emotional reactions of parents including anxiety, depression, denial, hostility, and immobilization, both to the initial diagnosis and long-term care of the child have been recorded by several investigations (Meyerowitz & Kaplan, 1967; McCollum & Gibson, 1970).

The first major effort to emphasize the need for a total family environment perspective in the treatment of cystic fibrosis (Turk, 1964), concluded that, financial stresses did not deprive the family of essentials (food, clothing, shelter), but the emotional and social stresses did result in deprivation in family relationships and activities. Communication breakdowns among family members and among the family and relatives and neighbors were especially noted; parents had inadequate time for leisure activites with the family and by themselves and less energy for the marital relationship. Meyerowitz and Kaplan (1967) noted that the presence of a child with cystic fibrosis played a part in precipitating a chain of events leading to a major adjustment in family role definitions and interactions. The expected course of family development was altered due to the stress of long-term illness. Decreased geographical and occupational mobility affected the family's social and economic resources. Reduced time for familial participation in the life of the community and the perceived negative attitudes of extended family and neighbors brought about feelings of social isolation.

Few investigators have turned their attention to the identification of coping behaviors and family characteristics which promote the family's and child's optimal long-term adaptation to cystic fibrosis. Venter's (1982) most recent interviews with 100 cystic fibrosis families involving 129 afflicted children revealed two major functional coping strategies. Positive family functioning involved coping by sharing the burdens of the illness among family members and with persons outside the family, as well as, coping by endowing the child's illness with meaning. The latter coping strategy of searching and finding some broad philosophical or religious framework to make the event of their child's illness comprehensible to them has also been cited by Chodoff, Friedman, and Hamburg (1964) as a normal coping response by families of children with malignant disease.

In an effort to continue this line of scientific inquiry on family coping and family environment as viable targets for strengthening family adaptability, this study will: (a) examine the range of coping strategies families use and find helpful; (b) examine the family environment; and, (c) determine if there are any relationships between family coping strategies, family environment and the child's physical health.

Methodology

Sample

Subjects were 100 families who have one or more children with cystic fibrosis (CF) and who were seen at periodic intervals in the Cystic Fibrosis Center, Pediatric Outpatient Clinic at the University of Minnesota Hospitals, Minneapolis, MN. The Cystic Fibrosis Center is a regional program attracting and treating patients from a five-state area. All families seen at the center who had at least one dependent CF child living at home were notified and asked to participate. Of the 224 families listed, we were unable to determine the status of 48 families. Of the resulting 176 we were able to contact, 31 families (18%) refused to participate and 145 families (82%) agreed to complete the questionnaires. The intial cut-off for receipt of questionnaires (seven months after initial letters) resulted in 100 families of which 90 were two-parent families and ten which were single-parent families (all headed by mothers). Of the two-parent families, 85 were in their initial marriage. The median length of marriage was 12.6 years with a range of one to 40 years. The number of children per family ranged from one to 11, with a median of two children. The family income was between $20,000-$25,000 per year. The parent and family characteristics are presented in Table 1.

Table 1:   Characteristics of Parents in the Sample

	Mothers	Fathers
Median Age	35.0 years	37.0 years
Education		
Median	12.5 years	12.5 years
High School Diploma	89.0%	90.0%
Bachelors	20.0%	25.0%
Masters	3.0%	4.4%
Doctorate	1.0%	2.2%
Occupation		
Professional	13.0%	22.0%
Managerial	5.0%	13.2%
Sales Worker	6.0%	7.7%
Clerical	17.0%	3.3%
Laborer	4.0%	42.9%
Farm Manager	—	6.6%
Service Worker	6.0%	1.1%
Homemaker (and retired)	49.0%	3.3%
Employment Status		
Not Employed	49.0%	3.3%
Employed, Part-Time	27.0%	1.1%
Employed, Full-Time	22.0%	79.1%
Employed, Full-Time Plus	2.0%	16.5%
Religion		
No Religion	3.0%	7.7%
Protestant	51.0%	49.5%
Catholic	43.0%	39.6%
Other	3.0%	3.3%
Race		
Caucasian	93.0%	92.3%
Native American	6.0%	5.5%
Black	—	1.1%
Latino	—	1.1%
Other	1.0%	—

Of the 100 families in the sample, 93 families have one child member at home with cystic fibrosis, and seven families have two chidren with cystic fibrosis living at home. Of the total 107 CF children, 63 (59%) are females and 44 (41%) are males. The median age is nine years with a range of three months to 28 years.

Procedures

Following the investigators' receipt of the family's letter of consent, each family was sent questionnaires designed to record parental coping strategies in the management of cystic fibrosis. Each parent was asked to complete the coping inventory, and the parents' perceptions of the family's psychosocial environment (parents were asked to complete the questionnaire *together* and single parents completed the inventory alone, preferably without the consultation of children or significant others). Concomitantly, the research team cooperated with the medical team within the Cystic Fibrosis Center to obtain the necessary criterion indices of the child's health as measured in terms of changes in the child's height, weight, and pulmonary functioning. These child measures were recorded at two points in time (during the same time period in which family measures were recorded).

Instruments

Parental coping with cystic fibrosis. *CHIP—Coping Health Inventory for Parents, Form A* (McCubbin, McCubbin, & Cauble, 1979) is an 80-item questionnaire checklist developed to provide information about how parents individually perceive their overall response to the management of the CF member in the family. The coping behaviors, such as "Believing that my child(ren) will get better" or "Talking with the medical staff (nurses, social worker, etc.) when we visit the medical center," are listed and parent(s) are asked to record how "helpful" (0-3) the coping items were to them in managing the home-illness situation.

The psychometric details of the development of CHIP are presented elsewhere (McCubbin, McCubbin, Patterson, Cauble, Wilson & Warwick, 1982). Briefly, three coping patterns derived from factor analysis representation 71% of the variance of the original correlation matrix. Cronbach's alphas, computed for the items on each coping pattern indicating respectable reliabilities of .79, .79, and .71 for the respective coping patterns described as follows.

The first coping pattern is composed of 19 behaviors which center on family and the parents' outlook on life and the illness. The first coping pattern is labeled *Maintaining Family Integration, Cooperation, and an Optimistic Definition of the Situation.*

Coping pattern II consists of 18 behavior items and focuses on the parents' efforts to maintain a sense of well-being through social support, maintaining self-esteem, and managing the psychological tensions and strains. This coping pattern is therefore labeled *Maintaining Social Support, Self-Esteem, and Psychological Stability.*

Coping pattern III involves eight coping behaviors and focuses on the interface between the parent, the medical staff and its program, as well as parental effort to understand and master the medical information needed to cope with this chronic illness. This coping pattern is labeled *Understanding the Medical Situation Through Communication With Other Parents and Consultation with the Medical Staff.*

Coping scale scores were computed for each of the three patterns by means of an unweighted summing of a parent's helpfulness ratings (0-3) across behavior items within each pattern. The three parental coping scores were correlated with the criterion indices of changes in the child's health.

Family environment in the care of the CF child. Parent(s) were asked to fill out the Family Environment Scale (FES) (Moos, 1974) composed of 90 true-false items that evaluate the social climate of all types of families. The FES is composed of ten subscales which measure the interpersonal relationships among family members, the directions of personal growth emphasized in the family, and the basic organizational structure of the family. The psychometric details of the development of the FES are discussed elsewhere (Moos & Moos, 1976). Briefly, the FES was validated from data from more than 1,000 individuals and a representative sample of 285 families. The ten subscales have moderate to high internal consistencies (ranging from .64 to .79 using the Kuder-Richardson Formula 20), and acceptable test-retest reliabilities (ranging from .68 to .86). The average subscale intercorrelation is approximately .20, indicating that the subscales measure distinct though somewhat related aspects of family social environments. The seven subscales, which focus on family functioning, and have received emphasis in prior studies and were utilized in the present study were:

Family Interpersonal Relationship Dimensions. Cohesion or the extent to which family members are concerned, helpful, and supportive of each other; expressiveness or the extent to which family members are allowed and encouraged to act openly and to express their feelings directly; and, conflict or the extent to which the open expression of anger and aggression or generally conflictual interactions are characteristic of the family.

Family Personal-Growth Dimensions. Independence or the extent to which family members are encouraged to be assertive, self-sufficient, to make their own decisions, and to think things out for themselves; and, active-recreational, the extent to which the family participates actively in various recreational and sporting activities.

System Maintenance Dimensions. Organization, the extent to which order and organization are important in the family in terms of structuring of family activities, financial planning, and the explicitness and clarity of rules and responsiblities; and, control, the extent to which the family is organized in a hierarchical manner, the rigidity of rules and procedures, and the extent to which family members order each other around.

These seven indices were also correlated with the criterion indices of changes in the child's health.

Criterion Indices

Child's health status. Two indices of child's health operationally defined by the medical director of the CF Clinic, were selected for this investigation. The first index was the statistical average of two independent measures of percent of predicted capacity of the child's height, and percent of predicted capacity of the child's weight. Predicted score is based on sex and height norms arrived at from a sample of 300-400 normal school children. The second major index was the statistical average of four independent measures of the child's pulmonary functioning. First, percent of predicted capacity of the child's small airway, the earliest index of disease measured by the percent of the expected average of the total volume of air expired divided by total time for the forced expiratory maneuver; midexpiratory flow x .50 vital capacity; and, midexpiratory flow x .75 vital capacity. Second, percent of predicted capacity of the child's mixed airway, an index of the obstruction of the larger airways as measured by the percent of the expected average amount of forced expiratory flow in .75 second and 1 second. Third, percent of predicted capacity of the child's vital capacity, the percent of the expected amount of air expired in a forced expiratory maneuver, and fourth, percent of predicted capacity of the child's peak flow, the percent of the expected maximum flow of air expired in a forced air maneuver. For the sake of simplicity in presentation and discussion, the two major criterion indices were named Height/Weight Index and Pulmonary Functioning Index, respectively.

These two indices were recorded at two different periods which were approximately two to three months apart and occurred during the same period in which family data (coping and environment) were recorded. Changes in the child's health (as measured by the Height/Weight Index and Pulmonary Functioning Index at two times) were calculated and the difference scores were used in subsequent analyses as the criterion measures.

Statistical Analysis

The statistical analyses focused on the relationship between the independent variables of:

- parental, family, and CF child characteristics (age, education, number of children, income, child's age, and sex);
- mother's coping strategies;
- father's coping strategies;
- the family's environment,

and *each* of the dependent measures of changes in child's Height/Weight Index and changes in child's Index of Pulmonary Functioning.

The resulting significant ($p < .05$) independent variables were entered into multiple regression analyses equations in order to determine the amount of variance in the criterion variables that was explained by each set of independent variables.

Results

Sociodemographic Variables and CF Child's Health

A range of sociodemographic factors have been examined previously in association with CF children's health, but the findings are inconsistent. In our efforts to identify the best combination of independent explanatory variables for changes in child's health, two-parent, two-family, and three child variables were examined. Inspection of the sociodemographic data (Table 2) reveals that improvement in the child's Height/Weight Index was *not* associated with any of the independent variables. Positive change in the child's Index of Pulmonary Functioning, however, was *inversely* related to father's *age* (r = *.24* p < .05).

Parental Coping and CF Child's Health

The data presented in Table 3 substantiate the hypothesis that parental coping patterns are associated with both indices of child's health. Specifically, *mother's effort to maintain family integration, cooperation and an optimistic definition of the situation* (Coping I) plays a significant (*r* = .20, *p* < .05) part in positive gains in the child's growth as reflected in the Height/Weight Index. Additionally, improvements in the child's overall Index of Pulmonary Functioning was associated with mother's coping pattern II of *maintaining social support, self-esteem, and psychological stability* (*r* = .23, *p* < .05).

Father's coping patterns are of equal importance. Specifically, father's effort to *maintain social support, self-esteem and psychological stability* (Coping II) is associated with improvements in the CF child's health as reflected in both the Height/Weight Index (*r* = .22 *p* < .05) and the Pulmonary Functioning Index (*r* = .31 *p* < .01).

Family Environment and CF Child's Health

The final data set of independent variables to be considered are the seven indices of the CF child's family environment. The composite profile of all 100 families on the Moos Family Environment Scale (*FES*) is presented in Figure 1. The standard scores computed from the Sample Mean Score indicate that the CF families fall well within the normal range of standard scores set for the Family Environment Scale.

The zero-order correlations between the seven scales and the indices of changes in child's health are presented in Table 4. The correlational data do not offer support for the

Table 2:   Correlations of Parent, Family, and Child Characteristics with Indices of Changes in Child's Health.

Indices of Child Health Status	Height/Weight Index			Pulmonary Functioning Index				
	% Height	% Weight	AVE % HT/WT	% Small Airway	% Mixed Airway	% Vital Capacity	% Peak Flow	Average % Overall Pulmonary
Parent, Family and Child Characteristics								
PARENTS:								
Mother's Age	-.14	.03	-.03	-.11	-.09	-.20 *	.03	-.12
Mother's Education	.03	-.05	-.02	.06	.02	-.01	.03	.03
Father's Age	-.11	.08	.03	-.16	-.16	-.22 *	-.16	-.24 *
Father's Education	.02	.04	.04	-.02	-.05	-.04	-.14	-.08
FAMILY:								
Number of Children	.02	-.13	-.09	.10	.15	.06	.16	.15
Income	.15	.01	.06	-.13	-.04	-.04	-.25 *	-.16
CHILD (CF):								
Sex:[1] Male	.11	.02	.06	-.12	.05	.08	.04	.00
Female	-.11	.02	-.06	.12	-.05	-.08	-.04	.00
Age	.05	.16	.12	-.20 *	-.09	-.14	-.03	-.16
Birth Order	-.06	.03	.01	.00	.08	-.05	.10	.03

[1]Coded as Dummy Variable for analysis

*p<.05

Table 3:   Correlations between Parental Coping Patterns and Indices of Children's Health.

Child Health Indices	Height/Weight Index			Pulmonary Functioning Index				
	% Height	% Weight	AVE % HT/WT	% Small Airway	% Mixed Airway	% Vital Capacity	% Peak Flow	Average % Pulmonary
Parental Coping:								
Mother I-Integration Cooperation, Optimism	.06	.19*	.20*	−.03	.07	.04	.01	.12
Mother II-Support, Esteem, Stability	.11	.07	.12	.25*	.22*	.13	.10	.23*
Mother III-Medical Communication and Consultation	.12	−.09	−.03	.21*	.13	.02	.09	.15
Father I-Integration Cooperation, Optimism	.17	.05	.10	.15	.06	.09	−.08	.08
Father II-Support, Esteem, Stability	.22*	.14	.22*	.32**	.31**	.16	.12	.31**
Father III-Medical Communication and Consultation.....	.18	.03	.09	.03	.08	.01	.00	.04

*p ≤ .05
**p ≤ .01

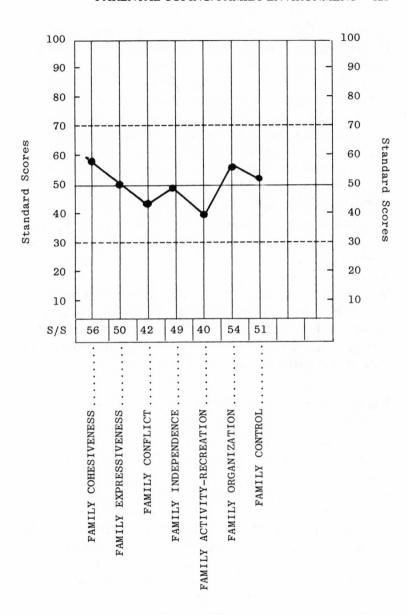

**Figure 1:   CF family profile
on the Family Environment Scales (Moos, 1974).**

hypothesis of an association between improvement in child's Height/Weight Index and the seven dimensions of family environment. Improvements in the child's Pulmonary Functioning Index, however, were associated with two dimensions of family environment, that is, an *active recreational orientation(r = .23p   .05) and family control* (r = .20p   .05). In other words, the extent to which the family participates actively in various recreational and sporting activities *and* the extent to which the family is organized in a hierarchical manner with rules and procedures have a positive association with improvements in the child's pulmonary functioning.

In summary, the zero order correlational analyses reveals that of the 20 sociodemographic, parental coping, and family environmental measures, six show significant association with the criterion measures of changes in the child's health. Figure 2 presents the significant independent variables in a graphic scheme relative to the dependent measures of changes in Height/Weight and changes in pulmonary functioning. The above process of variable selection retained five independent variables for multiple regression analysis.

Regression I: Changes in Child's Height/Weight Index

The two significant predictors for the criterion of Height/Weight Index were Mother's Coping I: *Maintaining Family Integration, Cooperation and an Optimistic Definition of the Situation* ($r = .20$, $p < .05$) and Father's Coping II: *Maintaining Social Support, Self-Esteem and Psychological Stability* ($r = .22$, $p < .05$). The regression analysis summarized in Table 5 indicates that the two predictors considered together were important in explaining the variability in changes in this index of the child's health status. The significant multiple R ($F = 3.4728$, $p < .05$) with the two independent predictors (mothers and fathers coping) explained 8% of the variance in this criterion.

Table 4: Correlations between Family Environment and Family Compliance and Indices of Child Health.

Family Index of Compliance and Child Health Status	Family Compliance Index	Height/Weight Index			Pulmonary Functioning Index				
		% Height	% Weight	AVE % HT/WT	% Small Airway	% Mixed Airway	% Vital Capacity	% Peak Flow	Average % Overall Pulmonary
FAMILY ENVIRONMENT:									
Cohesiveness	.26**	.05	-.13	-.07	.32**	.07	-.01	-.04	.13
Expressiveness	.15	.15	.08	.10	.07	-.07	-.05	-.14	-.04
Conflict	-.22**	.14	.03	.06	.05	.02	.05	-.14	.00
Independence	.05	.04	.00	.00	.24*	.13	-.16	.10	.13
Active-recreation Orientation	.13	.08	-.02	.02	.15	.27**	.25*	.06	.23*
Organization	.17*	-.10	-.14	-.15	.17	.02	-.02	.10	.10
Control	.04	-.10	-.08	-.07	.30**	.16	.07	.02	.20*

*p ≤ .05
**p ≤ .01

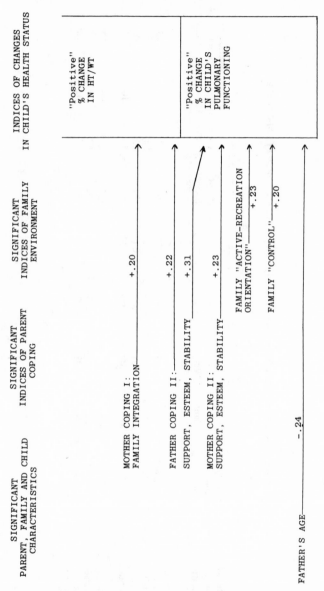

Figure 2:   Graphic presentation of the relationship between significant 1. parent, family, and child characteristics; 2. indices of parent coping; and, 3. indices of family environment with the criterion indices of changes in child's health status (CF).

Table 5: Regression Analysis of Child Health Status Height/Weight Index on Mother's Coping I and Father's Coping II.

Multiple Regression	beta	F	Multiple R	R^2	Adjusted R^2
Predictors					
Mother's Coping I: Maintain Family Integration, Cooperation and Optimism	.1954	2.8675	.2416	.058	.046
Father's Coping II: Maintain Social Support, Self Esteem and Psycho-logical Stability	.1719	2.2190	.2929*	.085	.061

*$F = (2,74) = 3.4728$, $p < .036$

Regression II: Predictors of CF Child's Pulmonary Functioning Index

At the time of this analysis, data on changes in CF Child's pulmonary functioning were only available on 55 chidren. (Pulmonary functioning tests are unreliable for children under approximately two years of age). Using the SPSS listwise deletion procedure for multiple regression analysis, the study reveals that five independent variables—(a) father's Coping II—*Maintaining Social Support, Self-Esteem, and Psychological Stability*; (b) *family "Control"*; (c) family *"Active Recreational Orientation"*; (d) Mother's Coping II—*Maintaining Social Support, Self-Esteem*, and *Psychological Stability*; and, (e) *father's age*—may be considered together in explaining the variability in the children's pulmonary functioning.

In examining the statistical results of the multiple regression analysis with listwise deletion presented in Table 6, only four independent variables would be considered in the final prediction equation. The summary in Table 6 indicates that father's coping II, *Maintaining Social Support, Self-Esteem, and Psychological Stability*, an *Active Recreational Orienta-*

tion, family Control, and *father's Age* explain 18% (12% adjusted) of the variability in the CF child's Index of Pulmonary Functioning. Together, they have a multiple correlation of .42 (f(4,55) = 2.9482 p = .028). The remaining independent variable, mother's coping II, Maintaining Social Support, Self-Esteem, and Psychological Stability, improves our understanding of the total range of factors which inflence children's pulmonary functioning, but does not add in an appreciable way to the total amount of variance explained. This remaining variable had a partial correlation of .01099 with a non-significant (p = .936) test of .6520.

In summarizing the regression analyses, changes in the Height/Weight Index may be partially explained by two parental coping patterns, that is, father's coping effort to enhance his self-esteem with social support and maintaining psychological stability, and mother's coping through maintaining family integration, cooperation, and an optimistic definition of the situation. The most parsimonious set of family variables associated with changes in the Pulmonary Functioning Index are: father's coping efforts to enhance his self-esteem with social support and maintining psychological stability; family efforts to be active and involved in recrea-

Table 6:   Regression Analysis with Listwise Deletion
for Children's Pulmonary Functioning.

Regression Statistics	betas	F	Multiple Regression*	R^2	Adjusted R^2
Family Predictors					
Father Coping II: Social Support, Esteem and Psychological Stability	.2536	3.9257	.3082	.0950	.0794
Family Active Recreational Orientation	.1650	1.5962	.3721	.1385	.1082
Family Control	.1514	1.4509	.3940	.1552	.1099
Father's Age	−.1513	1.4249	.4202	.1765	.1167

*F = (5,55) = 2.9482 p < .02

tional activities; family efforts to maintain rules and regulations through control; and, father's age where the younger the father, the greater the improvement in the CF child's pulmonary functioning.

Discussion

The findings of this study add in an appreciable way to the identification of parental coping strategies and aspects of family life which facilitate family adaptation to managing a child with cystic fibrosis. The study clarifies specific coping patterns and dimensions of family behavior which also contribute to improvements in the CF child's health.

Improvements in the CF child's height and weight were associated with two of the 20 independent variables examined. A relatively small percentage of the variance is explained by the two coping strategies; one advanced by mother, *Maintaining Family Integration, Cooperation, and an Optimistic Definition of the Situation*, and the other by father, *Maintaining Social Support, Self-Esteem, and Psychological Stability*. In other words, mother's effort to maintain and suport family togetherness, to promote cooperation among members to get the family tasks done, which include meal preparation and monitoring the CF child's nutritional intake, taking good care of all medical equipment, having the CF child seen at the clinic/hospital on a regular basis, and maintaining a positive outlook on the stressful situation contribute to the CF child's physical growth and development.

Of equal importance, father's coping strategy is directed at maintaining his psychological stability and emotional well-being. This coping pattern includes efforts to establish relationships and friendships, entertaining friends at home, as well as going out with his spouse. It would appear that father's social and emotional well-being plays a contributory role in creating a family atmosphere which also promotes the CF child's physical development.

The family process through which parental coping strategies have an effect on the child's physical development is only speculative at this time. It is reasonable to argue that the tasks associated with managing the CF child in the home, which have been documented in the psycho-social research conducted to date (McCollum & Gibson, 1970; Meyerowitz & Kaplan, 1967; Turk, 1964; Travis, 1976), place coniderable strain on the family unit and particularly, the parents. A major source of strain is the day-to-day routine of providing medical care directed at keeping the lungs clear of obstructing secretions to prevent or reduce infection and damage to the bronchial walls and a special diet. The process of promoting physical growth and development involves, in some cases, the family commitment to frequent feedings, possible dietary restrictions, or at least planning for meals and monitoring the child's intake. This is supplemented by medical procedures involving aerosol administration of drugs, postural drainage with percussion and vibration of the chest, exercises, and physical activity. The burden of responsiblity lies with the family. Because effective treament is a matter first of medical competence and second of parental ability to exert a lifetime of daily effort in the child's behalf, the crux of the prognosis is social—the family's ability to secure competent medical care early and the ability to carry out the medical recommendations (Travis, 1976). Parents appear to cope with this demanding medical regimen by creating a family atmosphere characterized by cohesiveness, cooperation, and optimism. In addition, they must take care of their own emotional and social support needs. The importance of family cooperation, sharing responsiblities and maintaining optimism has been noted previously (Venters, 1982).

Improvements in the CF child's pulmonary functioning are associated with a combination of parental coping patterns, family environment variables, and a background factor. Specifically, the efforts of both parents to maintain social support, self-esteem, and psychological stability are important. In order for parents to respond to the demands of family life, perform the complex and demanding tasks of medical treatment in the home environment, as well as promote the social and emotional development of its members, parents individually need *to care for themselves,* through social support, relationships with friends and each other, and through tension management devices such as ventilating anger and involvement in hobbies and work.

There are two dimensions of the family environment that also are associated with improvements in pulmonary functioning. Families develop an *active recreational orientation* and employ family *control* in an effort to manage the child in the home. Considering the complex medical treatment regimen with an emphasis on physical activities to promote the child's pulmonary functioning, it is not surprising that these two family dimensions should emerge as being of paramount importance. First, families are encouraged to develop a family environment in which the family members are called on to participate actively in various recreational and sporting activities. This family orientation, complemented by actual family activities which involve the CF child, play a positive role in promoting the child's pulmonary functioning.

Second, in response to the demand that the family unit perform medically technical and physically demanding procedures and at the same time maintain a stable family organization, the CF families see themselves as functioning in a hierarchical manner with rigid rules and procedures. Although Moos (1974) intended the Control subscale of the Family Environment Scale to be a negative dimension of family life, that control may be an appropriate and valued characteristic in a family with a CF member. This is not to say that control in general is beneficial to any family unit, but rather to underscore the observation that control appears to be a vitally important family dimension in promoting the CF child's pulmonary functioning.

The final predictor, the father's age, is inversely related to changes in the CF child's pulmonary functioning. The younger the father, the greater the improvment in the child's overall test of pulmonary functioning. In light of studies which point to the physical and psychological hardships of maintaining a quality medical care program in the home setting, it was predictable that father's age would be associated with the child's health. If we take into consideration the total medical program and its emphasis on physical activity as a vital part of the medical regimen, younger parents, particularly fathers, are an asset to families managing CF children in the home.

This investigation and its findings, which emphasize what parents *do* to cope and what dimensions of the family environment are important, can be contrasted with prior research which accentuate the hardships families face and the deleterious effects of having a CF child. The findings suggest possible targets for health education programs as well as family therapy. Such programs should focus on helping parents develop social support systems, maintain their self-esteem, and devise functional family rules and hierarchical family structures. The value of the family's active recreational orientation also should be considered when planning a comprehensive intervention program. Of equal, if not greater importance, the study offers empirical evidence in support of a health care philosophy which includes the family as an integral part of the total treatment package. A serious commitment to the care of the CF child would legitimately involve the family.

The findings support the efforts of physicians, nurses, social workers, and other members of the health team to involve family members, and fathers in particular, in the health education and counseling process. This study is supportive of social work efforts to bring different families of CF children together to share their personal experiences and promote social support. The research findings and the emergence of parental coping and family environment measures also would support present efforts to develop home monitoring programs (Warwick, 1978). This would involve the use of daily diaries and other home recording measures on children, family coping, and functioning. Through such measures, to be shared with the medical staff at Reginal CF Centers, it is expected that we can provide medical care and family support in a more timely manner. This type of computer-assisted program also is expected to decrease the severity of medical complications, promote parental adjustment and compliance, and demonstrate that remote computer monitoring of the patient and family will reduce cost and increase the efficiency of the medical team.

Prevention Intervention for Families: The Case of Chronic Illness

This study suggested that parental coping and family functioning are viable targets for prevention-oriented intervention. Prevention as a public health framework is viewed as a continuum of activities directed at protecting the health of family members and the well-being of the family unit. These activities include: (a) health education and promotion; (b) early diagnosis and treatment; (c) limiting the impact of dysfunction or disability; and, (d) rehabilitation.

Family health education and promotion are classified as efforts directed at *primary* prevention or intervention before a family problem is manifest. Early diagnosis and treatment of family dysfunction are considered to be *secondary* prevention while limiting the impact of family dysfunction, and efforts directed at rehabilitation are classified as *tertiary* prevention. Public health activities are directed at families with chronically ill children with the expectation of reducing or eliminating the factors which curtail parental coping and adaptation, and enhance parental coping and family functioning in order to maximize the family's ability to handle present and future strains.

Prevention Strategies: The Commitment to Health

In accepting prevention as a part of our clinical work with families under stress, we are called on to view family crises as an opportunity to promote family well-being. Not only can we make use of the community and its programs and services in support of families under stress, but also, perhaps more importantly, we can use the family situation as an opportunity to improve its problem-solving, coping, and interpersonal relationships.

In the case of chronic illness, family patterns of managing life's situations are likely to be disturbed and family members are likely to face difficulties and changes for which they have no ready-made solutions. The father, for example, may be angry with the mother's commitment to providing care to the CF child, and he, therefore, struggles with the dilemma of accepting the situation or attempting to change things to gain more attention for himself. So extensive may be the disruption of family routines and way of life that the family unit may not know where to begin rebuilding. To the extent that the parents' sense of competence has been challenged, they may be uncertain about whether they are capable of improving the situation.

Therefore, *current,* rather than retrospective emphasis, in family history-taking and the use of *problem-solving concepts* in treating families under stress are important aspects of prevention-oriented intervention (Compton & Gallaway, 1975; Golan, 1978; Hoff, 1978; Parad, 1966). To rely on the traditional therapeutic strategies of sorting out the family's "past," health professionals may ultimately sacrifice a vitally important opportunity to relate to the family's immediate and presenting problems and felt need. The parents' need to understand the medical situation, manage the disturbing changes in family relationships, and develop a range of coping strategies need to be given priority.

Problem-solving strategies can include sharing information with families which order and explain the family's experiences and responses. Other types of information include reports of experiences of others in a similar situation and descriptions of coping methods others may have used and found helpful.

One of the most useful forms of problem-solving appears to be the provision of social support (Cobb, 1976) to families who find themselves in such situations which leave them unsure whether their personal, material, or interpersonal resources are adequate to the demands being made on them. One form of support is offered by the "helper" (who may or may not be a professional) who is accepted as an ally by the members of the distressed family. Guided by the premise that the family unit is capable of helping itself, the helper offers encouragement and understanding as well as specific information which helps them feel understood and appreciated (emotional support) capable of managing life's hardships (esteem support) and, a sense of belonging to a larger group of persons/families from the same socioeconomic strata (network support).

In summary, the fundamental strategies for prevention-oriented intervention (Golan, 1978; Rapaport, 1966a, 1966b), which are pertinent to the situation of working with families coping with a chronically ill child include: (a) keeping an explicit focus on the present family crisis; (b) helping families to gain a conscious grasp of the crisis in order to enhance purposeful problem-solving; (c) helping parents to deal with and overcome doubts of adequacy and self-confidence; (d) helping with interpersonal communication and assisting families in achieving a balance in individual growth and meeting family needs; (e) offering basic information and education regarding the medical aspect of the problem; (f) helping to develop social support; (g) helping to master the medical procedures involved in home care of the chronically ill; and, (h) creating a bridge to community resources and opening the pathways of referral.

Summary and Conclusions

Of the family research conducted to date in cystic fibrosis, a disproportionate amount has been devoted to understanding the hardships families face. In contrast, the present investigation attempted to identify parental coping strategies and specific dimensions of family life and their relationship to improvements in the child's health in terms of changes in child's height, weight, and pulmonary functioning. Although subject to the constraints of a single sample of families, without the benefit of cross validation, the findings offer evidence to support this line of scientific inquiry.

Given the heavy demands of caring for a chronically ill child at home and the natural tendency for parents to invest a significant proportion of their personal self and energy in the care of the child, this study calls attention to the need for parents to balance this concentrated care with personal investments in themselves, in the marital relationship, and in the family as a whole.

A basic challenge to our findings concerns the direction of causation. The statistical relationships might represent the influence of child's health status on parental coping strategies and the family environment. Because independent and dependent measures were collected during the same period, it was not possible to formulate a conclusive statement of the direction of influence. It is reasonable to believe, however, and to have some confidence in the argument that parental coping strategies and the family's environment evolve over time and in response to a range of pressures from other family members, values, parental needs, and the demands of the total medical regimen. Therefore, they are not likely to be caused by small incremental changes in the child's health alone.

The present data would suggst that health education programs and professional interventions which focus on adaptive coping behaviors and a physically active, organized family environment would ultimately signify meaningful payoffs for the families, as well as for the child with cystic fibrosis. The findings of this line of research should renew our interest in prevention oriented programs, our sensitivity to family health practice (Pratt, 1976) and particularly the impact of the family on the child's health. The study underscores our need to work with families as a "total unit" where and when possible, particularly if interventions are designed to shape and support parental coping and family functioning, thereby promoting the health of children with cystic fibrosis.

REFERENCES

Chodoff, P., Friedman, S.B., & Hamburg, D.A. Stress, defenses, and coping behaviors: Observations in parents of children with malignant disease. *American Journal of Psychiatry,* 1964, *120,* 743-749.

Cobb, S. Social support as a moderator of life stress. *Psychosomatic medicine,* 1976, *38,* 300-314.

Compton, B., & Galaway, B. Social Work Processes, Homewood, IL: Dorsey Press, 1975.

Golan, N. *Treatment in crisis situations.* New York: The Free Press, 1978.

Hoff, L. *People in crisis: Understanding and helping.* Reading, Mass: Addison-Wesley, 1978.

Lawler, R.H., Nakielny, W., & Wright, N.A. Psychological implications of cystic fibrosis. *Canadian Medical Association Journal,* 1966, *94,* 1043-1046.

McCollum, A.T., & Gibson, L.E. Family adaptation to the child with cystic fibrosis. *The Journal of Pediatrics,* 1970, *77,* 571-578.

McCubbin, H.I., McCubbin, M.A., & Cauble, E. *CHIP: Coping health inventory for parents,* Form A, 1979. Available from Family Social Science, University of Minnesota, St. Paul, MN 55108.

McCubbin, H.I., McCubbin, M.A., Patterson, J., Cauble, E., Wilson, L., & Warwick, W. *CHIP: Coping health inventory for Parents: An assessment of parental coping patterns in the care of the chronically ill child.* In H. McCubbin, (Ed.), *Family stress, coping and social support.* New York: Springer Publishing, 1982.

Meyerowitz, J.W., & Kaplan, H.B. Familial responses to stress: The case of cystic fibrosis. *Social Science and Medicine,* 1967, *1*, 249-266.

Moos, R. *Family environment scale and preliminary manual,* 1974. Available from Consulting Psychologists Press, 577 College Avenue, Palo Alto, CA 94305.

Moos, R.H., & Moos, B.S. A typology of family social environments. *Family Process,* 1976, *15*, 357-370.

Parad, H. *Crisis intervention: Selected readings,* New York: Family Service Association of America, 1966.

Pratt, L. *Family structure and effective health behavior: The energized family.* Boston: Houghton Mifflin Co., 1976.

Rapaport, L. The state of crisis: Some theoretical considerations. In H. Parad (Ed.), *Crisis intervention: Selected readings.* new York: Family Service Association of America, 1966(a).

Rapaport, L. Working with families in crisis: An exploration in preventative intervention. In H. Parad (Ed.), *Crisis intervention: Selected readings.* Family Service Association of America, New York: 1966(b).

Spock, A., & Stedman, D. Psychological characteristics of children with cystic fibrosis. *North Carolina Medical Journal,* 1966, *27*, 426-428.

Travis, G. *Chronic illness in children: Its impact on child and family.* Stanford: Stanford University Press, 1976.

Tropauer, A., Franz, M.N., & Dilgard, V.W. Psychological aspects of the care of children with cystic fibrosis. *American Journal of Diseases of Children,* 1970, *199*, 424-432.

Turk, J. Impact of cystic fibrosis on family functioning. *Pediatrics,* 1964, *34*, 67-71.

Venters, M. Familial coping with chronic and severe illness: The case of cystic fibrosis. In H. McCubbin (Ed.), *Family stress, coping, and social support.* New York: Springer Publishing, 1982.

Warwick, W.J. *Computer monitoring of long-term care for cystic fibrosis. Washington, D.C.: Smithsonian Science Information Exchange, 1978.*

Chapter 5

FAMILY THERAPY WITH DEVELOPMENTALLY DELAYED CHILDREN

An Ecosystemic Approach

Ramon G. Corrales, Ph.D.
Janice Kostoryz, M.A.
Laurence Ro-Trock, Ph.D.
Barbara Smith, O.T.R.

Introduction

The dynamics of families with developmentally delayed children have not been adequately examined from the unique perspective of family systems theory. Professionals have commented on the traits or characteristics of the parents (Gath, 1977; Torrie, 1973), but previous work has not focused on the *entire* family as a unit of study. Tremendous effort has been expended to provide quality services to the handicapped child through educational, medical, and social services, but these interventions have not addressed the needs of all family members. Our belief is that the developmentally delayed (DD) child is a member of and plays specific roles in a variety of social systems. Our theoretical viewpoint suggests that there are no clear-cut divisions among these different systems, thus, it is fruitless to discuss where one influence ends and another begins.

Since 1978, a four-member team consisting of two family therapists, an occupational therapist, and a social worker has conducted an exploratory study directed toward an increased understanding of the characteristics of families with a handicapped child. This chapter offers a descriptive report of preliminary observations of 24 families who agreed to participate in the pilot phase of this research. The research phase of the project explored how family interactional patterns influence the child's functioning and how family reorganization affects the child. In this regard, there seems to be a parallel between families of developmentally delayed children and families with psychosomatically ill children. In their discussion of psychosomatic illness in children, Minuchin et al. (1975) state that the psychosomatically ill child feels both protected and scapegoated by his/her parents. If this process is allowed to continue for a substantial period of time, the child may be rendered incompetent in many areas of life functioning. Consequently, dependency increases.

One may assume that having a handicapped child is a traumatic experience for families. Many parents seem to follow a predictable sequence of shock, denial, and grief after learning of their child's handicap (Gath, 1977). They, then, begin the difficult process of raising the child. Family systems theory has not previously been applied in understanding the unique context of families with a DD child. Literature integrating the major descriptors of families with handicapped members and family systems theory is practically nonexistent, although there is considerable literature of an anecdotal nature recognizing that the handicapped child affects, and is effected by, the family in a rather profound way (Torrie, 1973).

In addition to being sparse, the current literature addressing the characteristics of families with handicapped children is limited in scope. At the time of this research, the authors were aware of only two studies that even superficially utilized systemic principles (Gath, 1977; Holt, 1957).

Methodology

The general prupose of this project was to explore, from the unique perspective of family systems theory, the characteristics of families who had a profoundly handicapped child. Most of the handicapped children in our sample were organically or functionally deaf and blind.

A sample of 30 families with DD children was recruited from a group of 70 families identified in the western portion of Missouri. At the time of this writing, the findings include data from 24 of these families with DD children between the ages of one to eight years of age. All family members currently residing in the home, including the DD child, participated in a three-hour, semi-structured interview. Each family was interviewed by a male and female member of the four-pers on team. The other two members acted as observers, took extensive notes, and recorded each component of the interview from behind a one-way mirror. These notes later were content analyzed to assist in a more complete description of family characteristics. The social worker/parent-teacher from the child's education program also observed the interview. Immediately prior to the interview, the family was introduced to the entire team. The three-hour session was videotaped with the family's knowledge and permission.

The family assessment interview followed a semi-structured format that included a three-generational family developmental history beginning with the courtship of the couple through the birth of the children. The involvement and reaction of the extended family members to the marriage and the grandchildren were explored, as well as the current nuclear family's relationship to the extended family. In addition, each family was required to perform three family "tasks" while the interviewers were out of the room. Families were asked to: (a) define a family problem; (b) discuss how they would like their lives to be 5-10 years from now; and (c) complete a Family Bond Inventory (FBI). Of primary importance was how the family discussed these stimulus issues (process) rather than what they said about them (content).

In order to assess the dynamics of interpersonal processes, the Beavers-Timberlawn Family Evaluation Scales (Lewis, Beavers, Gossett & Phillips, 1976) were used. These scales were developed to measure family interaction in a number of critical areas of family process such as: structure, mythology, goal-directed negotiation, autonomy, and affect. A global health-pathology measure also was utilized (Lewis, Beavers, Gossett & Phillips, 1976) as a gross measure of overall family health. The Family Bond Inventory (Fullmer, 1972), an instrument developed to help practitioners identify family alliances and coalitions, was used to assess structural characteristics of the families interviewed in this study. Although data concerning this instrument's reliability and validity have not been reported, the research team found the FBI to be a valuable clinical tool. The Genogram (Bowen, 1966, 1972), a structural diagram of a family's three-generational relationship system designed to uncover toxic issues in the family, also was employed in this investigation. Some of these issues might include: sex, parenting, child rearing, etc., which often are problematic for many families. Finally, a telephone interview was conducted to help the investigators identify additional problem areas and concerns of family members.

In order to achieve the goal of better understanding the characteristics of families with DD children, the following questions were posed:

1. What are the structural characteristics of families with a DD child? These include: overt power, parental coalitions, and closeness.

2. How congruent are the mythologies of such families? Mythology refers to an ongoing group perception of the qualities and capabilities of the individual family members. When the group appraisal of itself is congruent with that observed by outsiders, it is defined as high in congruency. The more congruent a family's image of itself is with that of the observer's, the healthier a family is thought to be.
3. How effective are these families in solving family tasks? Task resolution involves two aspects; the efficiency of the family in arriving at decisions and the degree to which the family encourages negotiations among all members.
4. How much autonomy is permitted for individual family members? Autonomy refers to the extent to which separation and uniqueness are tolerated and encouraged.
5. What is the predominant affect of families with DD children? Affect is separated into four categories according to Lewis et al. (1976): range of feelings, mood and tone of the family group, degree of unresolvable conflict, and the amount of empathy present.
6. What are the toxic issues in families with a DD child?
7. To what extent do parents with a DD child report marital tensions as a primary concern? The initial telephone contact was used to locate possible areas of marital tension.

Relationships Among Variables

1. *What is the relationship between each of the Beavers-Timberlawn Evaluation Scales and the Global Health-Pathology Scale?*
2. *Is there any relationship between a congruent mythology and effectiveness at solving family tasks?*
3. *Is there any relationship between autonomy and a strong parental bond?*
4. *Is there any relationship between marital tension and a parental alliance with the DD child?*

Because of the relatively small group of families in this investigation and reliance on observational measures, two highly qualified experts in family therapy, one male and one female, were chosen to assess the 24 families. Both therapists were chosen because of their considerable experience and training in family process and family therapy. The two raters had extensive training and experience in the use of all instruments in this study. The results of the ratings on the Beavers-Timberlawn Evaluation Scales are detailed and summarized in the frequency tables in this chapter.

For reporting purposes, the scores of the two experts were combined to give an average mean rating for each family. Only four scores of the raters had a spread of more than one scale point, indicating high consistency between the raters. Two of these ratings were on "invasiveness," one on "permeability," and one on "clarity of expression."

Structural Characteristics: Power, Parental Coalition, and Separateness-Connectedness

Ten of the 24 families fell at the chaotic extreme of the overt power scale (Table 1). Families at the chaotic extreme were most disturbed. In such families, communication is obscure and indirect. Power is neither clearly claimed nor shared. Toward the positive end of the scale, families clearly are "led" or "egalitarian." Seven families were rated within the positive domain.

The majority of families (19) were rated as having either a "weak parental coalition" or a "parent-child coalition" (Table 2). Five families were rated at the desirable end of the continuum on this variable. Beavers (1977) suggests that the effectiveness of the family is closely tied to the quality of the parental coalition. The most dysfunctional situation is a parent-child alliance where a child displaces one of the spouses. By contrast, a strong parental coalition refers to the parents ability to work effectively together as a team (Beavers, 1977).

Table 1:   Frequency Distribution of Scores by Expert Raters on the Beavers-Timberlawn Evaluation Scale for Overt Power.

Description	Scale Points	Frequency	Percentages
Chaos	1	4	16.7
	1.5	6	25.0
Marked	2	1	4.2
dominance	2.5	3	12.5
Moderate	3	3	12.5
dominance	3.5	4	16.7
Led	4	2	8.3
	4.5	1	4.1
Egalitarian	5	---	---

Table 2:   Frequency Distribution of Scores by Expert Raters on the Beavers-Timberlawn Evaluation Scale for Parental Coalitions.

Description	Scale Points	Frequency	Percentages
Parent-child	1	3	12.5
coalition	1.5	6	25.0
	2	2	8.3
	2.5	3	12.5
Weak parental	3	5	20.8
coalition	3.5	4	16.7
	4	1	4.2
	4.5	---	---
Strong parental	5	---	---
coalition			

Families were found to be evenly disbursed along the closeness continuum (Table 3). The concept of closeness is complex because two separate qualities are involved—clarity of boundaries and sharing and intimacy. In previous work, Beavers (1977) noted that in severely disturbed families, individual boundaries were replaced by fusion and suffocating closeness. In the healthiest of families, closeness and individuality were seen as complementary (Beavers, 1977).

Table 3:   Frequency Distribution of Scores by Expert Raters on the Beavers-Timberlawn Evaluation Scale for Closeness.

Description	Scale Points	Frequency	Percentages
Amorphous, vague, and	1	2	8.3
indistinct boundaries	1.5	2	8.3
among members	2	4	16.7
	2.5	3	12.5
Isolation, distancing	3	8	33.3
	3.5	3	12.5
	4	1	4.2
Closeness, with distinct	4.5	1	4.2
boundaries among	5	---	---
members			

To elaborate on the family structure scores presented in Tables 1, 2, and 3, families rated at least functional in overt power seemed confused and misdirected. These difficulties took many forms. For example, some parents would go through the entire interview without speaking to each other, even when the interviewers left the room. In other situations, communication between the parents was often sidetracked through one of the children. In still other instances, children could not be controlled by their parents. They turned over plants, pulled books from shelves, emptied desk drawers, and pushed over the camera. Interestingly, we observed that the parents of these children became uncomfortable if the children left the room, even for a minute, to get a toy or a drink.

Interactions among family members who scored at the midpoint on the parental coalition scale were often oppositional rather than cooperative. One parent tended to be most verbal and controlled the interaction. In extreme cases, this parent appeared to be the final authority on all topics, the other spouse and children deferring to his/her leadership. Other members in this type of family tended to complement the dominant member by being quiet, passive, or receding. In contrast, in families where there was a solid parental coalition, leadership and power were respectfully shared. Moreover, there was a relaxed, easy quality to familial interaction with even the youngest member contributing.

Mythology

The majority of families in the sample were seen as incongruent by the raters. Only four of the 24 families were viewed as "mostly congruent" while 14 were rated "somewhat" to "very incongruent," with six falling midway between "mostly" and "somewhat incongruent."

In these families, raters reported considerable reality distortion in the parents' perceptions of the handicapped child. For example, one father clung desperately to the belief that his physically and mentally retarded son eventually would play basketball and help manage the family farm. Although one could infer from the mother's tears that she was having a different internal reaction, the myth was not challenged by her or the older siblings. At the congruent end of the continuum, there were families who, despite some difficulty, were able to describe the realistic capabilities of their children and talk of their hopes and fears for the future.

Table 4:   Frequency Distribution of Scores by Expert Raters on the Beavers-Timberlawn Evaluation Scale for Family Mythology.

Description	Scale Points	Frequency	Percentages
Very congruent	1	---	---
	1.5	---	---
Mostly congruent	2	3	12.5
	2.5	1	4.2
	3	4	16.7
	3.5	2	8.3
Somewhat incongruent	4	4	16.7
	4.5	8	33.3
Very incongruent	5	2	8.3

Goal Directed Negotiation Processes

Since all families have problems to solve, two aspects determining the health or pathology of a family system are efficiency and the negotiation process. In order to assess these two dimensions, each family was given a series of three, five-minute tasks to perform. They were asked to do the following: "plan something together as a family"; "discuss some simple circle drawings" which each member had made of the physical location of his family members; and "discuss a family problem, either large or small." After giving the instructions for each task, the interviewers left the room and returned five minutes later. The interactions were rated from behind a one-way mirror.

Task Efficiency and Encouragement of Negotiations.

Table 5 shows that 12 of the 24 families were rated as "poor" to "extremely inefficient" on task efficiency. Five were seen as approaching "good." The remaining seven fell between "good" and "poor." Fifteen of the 24 families were rated as providing "low" to "no encouragement" during the negotiation process. Four were seen as offering "high" encouragement and five were rated as providing "moderate" encouragement (Table 6).

Families who demonstrated no encouragement often sat awkwardly for most of the five-minute segments, one member occasionally making a futile attempt to start a conversation. In other instances, one parent quickly would decide "the answer" to the task without eliciting others' viewpoints. In still other examples, parents would rely on one of the children to provide most of the input. In some situations, a family member would noticeably be left outside the family interactions; his comments either would be ignored or never solicited. By comparison, families seen as most encouraging

Table 5: Frequency Distribution of Scores by Expert Raters on the Beavers-Timberlawn Evaluation Scale for Task Efficiency.

Description	Scale Points	Frequency	Percentages
Extremely efficient	1	---	---
	1.5	---	---
Good	2	3	12.5
	2.5	2	8.3
	3	5	20.8
	3.5	2	8.3
Poor	4	1	4.2
	4.5	7	29.2
Extremely inefficient	5	4	16.7

Table 6: Frequency Distribution of Scores by Expert Raters on the Beavers-Timberlawn Evaluation Scale for Encouragement of Negotiation Processes.

Description	Scale Points	Frequency	Percentages
High encouragement	1	---	---
for all members	1.5	1	4.2
	2	3	12.5
	2.5	2	8.3
Moderate encouragement	3	2	8.3
	3.5	1	4.2
Low encouragement	4	7	29.2
	4.5	6	25.0
No encouragement	5	2	8.3
of negotiation			

would solve tasks efficiently and solicit input from all family members. This was done in a spirit of negotiation and compromise.

Autonomy: Clarity of Expression, Personal Responsibility, Invasiveness, and Boundary Permeability

Autonomy consists of four elements: clarity of expression, the assumption of personal responsibility, the amount of invasiveness found in the system, and the permeability of the boundaries among family members. The essence of autonomy as a general concept is individuation; thus, one way of assessing the autonomy of a family system is to determine its tolerance for individuation as reflected by these four concepts. Tables 7 through 10 indicate how the sample families were rated on each of these four dimensions.

More than half the families were rated as being "somewhat vague" to "hardly anyone is ever clear," on the clarity of expression scale (Table 7). Families judged to be "most clear" in their communication encouraged input and directness from all members. This type of communication style promotes task efficiency and effective functioning. In family systems that were judged to be less effective, communication patterns were vague and misleading. We observed that less effective families punished members who openly expressed their thoughts and feelings.

Responsibility refers to the extent to which family members accept the burden of their own feelings, thoughts, and actions. In families rated most positively on this dimension, there was more frequent use of "I" statements, and less scapegoating than in those families whose members assumed less responsibility for their own actions.

Families who participated in this study were evenly distributed along the invasiveness continuum (Table 9). At the positive extreme, all family members were allowed uniqueness, seemed to have a strong sense of self, and, most importantly, did not attempt to disqualify or interpret another's view of reality.

As an example of the least healthy extreme, a mother reported concern, because in her words, "I'm not sure I'm putting the right words in my daughter's mouth." Interestingly,

Table 7:   Frequency Distribution of Scores by Expert Raters
on the Beavers-Timberlawn Evaluation Scale for Clarity of Expression.

Description	Scale Points	Frequency	Percentages
Very clear	1	---	---
	1.5	1	4.2
	2	1	4.2
Somewhat vague	2.5	4	16.7
and hidden	3	3	12.3
	3.5	4	16.7
	4	4	16.7
Hardly anyone	4.5	6	25.0
is ever clear	5	1	4.2

Table 8:   Frequency Distribution of Scores by Expert Raters
on the Beavers-Timberlawn Evaluation Scale for Responsibility.

Description	Scale Points	Frequency	Percentages
Members are regularly	1	---	---
able to voice respon-	1.5	1	4.2
sibility for individual	2	2	8.3
actions			
Members sometimes voice	2.5	6	25.0
responsibility for indiv-	3	3	12.5
idual actions, but tactics	3.5	3	12.5
also include sometimes	4	4	16.7
blaming others, speaking			
in 3rd person or plural			
Members rarely, if ever,	4.5	5	20.8
voice responsibility for	5	---	---
individual actions			

this same family did not remain in the waiting room to be
called by the interviewers, which was the usual procedure, but
rather, opened two doors and went unannounced into the in-
terviewing room. This action can be viewed as indicative of
the lack of physical boundaries which can be seen as symbolic
of the invasive interactional patterns in this family system.

Scores on the permeability dimension were rated heavier toward the end of the continuum which reports members as "unreceptive" (Table 10). Beavers (1977) suggests that receptivity to another's communications (permeability), including even the youngest children, is a powerful way for a system to assert that its members are important. By contrast, in dysfunctional family systems, there is a "practiced obliviousness" to another's comments.

Table 9:   Frequency Distribution of Scores by Expert Raters on the Beavers-Timberlawn Evaluation Scale for Invasiveness.

Description	Scale Points	Frequency	Percentages
Many invasions	1	2	8.3
	1.5	1	4.2
	2	3	12.5
	2.5	3	12.5
Occasional invasions	3	4	16.7
	3.5	3	12.5
	4	5	20.8
	4.5	3	12.5
No evidence of invasions	5	---	---

Table 10:   Frequency Distribution of Scores by Expert Raters on the Beavers-Timberlawn Evaluation Scale for Permeability.

Description	Scale Points	Frequency	Percentages
Very open	1	---	---
	1.5	1	4.2
Moderately open	2	2	8.3
	2.5	5	20.8
	3	4	16.7
	3.5	4	16.7
Members frequently unreceptive	4	8	33.3
	4.5	---	---
Members unreceptive	5	---	---

Affect: Range of Feelings, Mood and Tone, Unresolvable Conflict and Empathy

Family affect refers to four dimensions: range of feelings (expressiveness), mood and tone, unresolvable conflict, and empathy. Tables 11 through 14 provide a summary of the scores on these variables. Although there were a few exceptions, the vast majority of family scores fell toward the unhealthy end of the continuum in the areas of range of feelings and mood and tone. Scale scores for unresolvable conflict and empathy were more evenly distributed.

Eighteen of the 24 families exhibited marked restrictions in their ability to express a range of feelings (Table 11). In terms of mood and tone, the most frequent affective rating was depression or hopelessness. Table 12 indicates that 10 of the 24 families fell in this category.

Since conflict is ubiquitous in all families, the ratings in Table 13 referred to unresolvable conflict. Ratings were determined by looking for recognition of the conflict, use of avoidance or denial, and evidence of recurring conflict and impairment of group functioning. Approximately half of the families were seen as having some unresolvable conflict but without impairment or only slight impairment of group functioning. Slightly less than half were rated as having definite conflict with moderate to severe impairment of group functioning.

Empathy refers to the capacity to experience another's feelings, volitions, or ideas. Table 14 shows that the 24 families were somewhat evenly distributed between consistent empathic responsiveness and grossly inappropriate responses to feelings, with most of the scores clustered from 2.0 to 4.0.

Toxic issues

The nuclear family can be thought of as a subsystem that is linked with other subsystems. One of these subsystems is the extended family. Many problems or concerns of the nuclear family may not be confined to that unit and may include the extended family network. As stated earlier, the Genogram was used to uncover toxic issues (Guerin & Pendagast, 1976).

Table 11:   Frequency Distribution of Scores by Expert Raters on the Beavers-Timberlawn Evaluation Scale for Range of Feelings.

Description	Scale Points	Frequency	Percentages
Direct expression of	1	---	---
a wide range of feelings	1.5	---	---
Direct expression of	2	3	12.5
many feelings despite	2.5	3	12.5
some difficulty			
Obvious restriction in	3	2	8.3
the expression of	3.5	5	20.8
some feelings			
Although some feelings	4	3	12.5
are expressed, there is	4.5	7	29.2
masking of most feelings			
Little or no expression	5	1	4.2
of feelings			

Table 12:   Frequency Distribution of Scores by Expert Raters on the Beavers-Timberlawn Evaluation Scale for Mood and Tone.

Description	Scale Points	Frequency	Percentages
Usually warm, affec-	1	---	---
tionate, humorous, and	1.5	1	4.1
optimistic			
Polite, without impres-	2	4	16.7
sive warmth or affection;	2.5	4	16.7
or frequently hostile			
with times of pleasure			
Overtly hostile	3	1	4.1
	3.5	4	16.7
Depressed	4	3	12.5
	4.5	3	12.5
Cynical, hopeless,	5	4	16.7
and pessimistic			

**Table 13:   Frequency Distribution of Scores by Expert Raters
on the Beavers-Timberlawn Evaluation Scale for Unresolvable Conflict.**

Description	Scale Points	Frequency	Percentages
Severe conflict with	1	2	8.3
severe impairment of	1.5	4	16.7
group functioning			
Definite conflict, with	2	2	8.3
moderate impairment of	2.5	1	4.2
group functioning			
Definite conflict, with	3	4	16.7
slight impairment of			
group functioning			
Some evidence of unre-	3.5	5	20.8
solvable conflict, without	4	5	20.8
impairment of group	4.5	1	4.2
functioning			
Little or no	5	---	---
unresolvable conflict			

**Table 14:   Frequency Distribution of Scores by Expert Raters
on the Beavers-Timberlawn Evaluation Scale for Empathy.**

Description	Scale Points	Frequency	Percentages
Consistent empathic	1	---	---
responsiveness	1.5	2	8.3
For the most part, an	2	3	12.5
empathic responsiveness	2.5	3	12.5
with one another, despite			
obvious resistance			
Attempted empathic	3	5	20.8
involvement, but failed	3.5	4	16.7
to maintain it			
Absence of any	4	2	8.3
empathic responsiveness	4.5	4	16.7
Grossly inappropriate	5	1	4.2
responses to feelings			

We have found the Genogram to be a very useful tool for tracking information and providing input about intergenerational dynamics. This instrument has not been standardized, however, so information gathered through the use of this technique should be seen as suggestive and interpretive.

The interviews, during which the Genograms were administered, were videotaped and relevant comments recorded by the raters. A content analysis of the Genogram, both the recorded comments of the observers and the videotaped segment, was undertaken to determine those issues that were problematic. A compilation of the results is reported in Table 15. It should be noted that this categorization does not assess the severity of the issues. They are "more or less" unresolved as seen by family members. Also, these categories are not mutually exclusive since a reported difficulty with money or sex would likely appear as a marital concern.

In a quarter of the families interviewed, there was some discussion or hint of marital separation with an additional nine families alluding to marital conflict. Twelve families reported difficulties with in-laws. There was a wide range of difficulties reported, such as: acceptance of the child by the in-laws, alcoholism, or belated grieving over the death of a parent. Many issues surfaced concerning the birth and acceptance of the handicapped child. These included sadness or depression on the part of all family members at not having a normal child, and feelings of resentment or anger at the medical community because of the way they (the parents) were told their child was handicapped. Frequently, the oldest non-handicapped female child was shouldered with the responsibilities of caring for the handicapped sibling.

Marital Tension

Information from the telephone interview revealed that 15 of the 24 families reported marital stress as a concern during the initial contact.

Relationships Among Variables

Mythology, permeability, range of feelings, overt power, task efficiency, and mood and tone all were found to be significantly related to the overall health of the family, as demonstrated in Table 16, showing the relationship between each of the 14 Beavers-Timberlawn Evaluation Scales and the Global Health Pathology Scale (Lewis, et al. 1976).

It was surprising to find no relationship between the strength of the parental coalition and the global measure of family health, because family systems lore considers this dimension to be of critical importance for healthy family functioning. Similarly, only one of the four components of autonomy—permeability—was found to relate significantly to a strong parental coalition, $r = .50$, $p < .05$.

A significant relationship was found between a congruent family mythology and task resolution effectiveness, $r = .78$, $p < .01$.

Fifteen of the 24 families reported marital stress or tension during the initial telephone interview. Of these 15 families, 13 were rated as families where one parent had formed a coalition with the handicapped child.

Virtually all families interviewed reported extraordinary demands on their time and energy as the result of caring for a handicapped child. This demand often was directly associated with the severity of the handicapped condition. As a result of the physical and emotional demands of the handicapped child, it is almost inevitable that an alliance of some magnitude will develop between the child and the one responsible for his/her care. Assuming it is one of the spouses who is shouldered with this extra burden, it is very reasonable to see how this situation would produce strain in the marital subsystem and weaken the parental bond.

Discussion

This investigation has provided considerable data describing some of the major characteristics of families who

Table 15:   Toxic Issues as Determined by the Genogram Interview.

Toxic Issues

Family	Money	Sex	Parenting	Children	Marital	In-laws	Alcohol	Death	Religion	Educational Level	Work	Handicapped Child
1								x				x
2	x	x			x	x						x
3			x	x	x	x					x	x
4					x*	x					x	
5												
6					x						x	
7			x		x	x						
8	x				x*						x	x
9	x		x		x		x					

10	11	12	13	14	15	16	17	18	19	20	21	22	23	24
					×	×	×				×	×	×	×
		×			×				×		×			
								×						
			×											
									×					
					×	×								
	×	×	×	×	×	×	×						×	
		×	×	×	×*		×	×*		×*	×*			
			×				×			×	×			
				×				×		×				
					×					×				
					×					×				

Table 16:   Zero-Order Correlation Coefficients Between Beavers-Timberlawn Evaluation Scales and the Global Health-Pathology Scale.

Beavers-Timberlawn Evaluation Scales	r
Overt Power	.4944*
Parental coalitions	.0791
Closeness	.1156
Mythology	.5545**
Task efficiency	.5003*
Encouragement of the negotiation process	.3502
Clarity of expression	.3252
Responsibility	.3722
Invasiveness	.1616
Permeability	.5186**
Range of feelings	.5691**
Mood and tone	.4845*
Unresolvable conflict	.3596
Empathy	.3733

*r. < .05.
**r. < .01.

have severely handicapped children. This description has been presented in the form of a discussion about variables considered central to family systems theory. The results of this study may be interpreted as supporting the concept that many families with a severely handicapped child display interactional characteristics that are dysfunctional. Approximately 75% of the families in this study were seen as having either a weak parental coalition or a parent-child coalition. Consistent with this observation, more than half of the families reported marital stress, and many are continuing in family therapy. More than 75% of the 24 families with DD children exhibited varying degrees of reality distortion (mythology). This was true especially in terms of their attitudes about the handicapped child. In terms of family mythology, investigators have found that families who are most dysfunctional tend to have extremely incongruent mythologies

(Ferreira, 1963). In some cases, even very bizarre behavior on the part of the identified patient is considered to be normal by other family members (Beavers, 1977). We found that more than half the families in this study seemed to have difficulty expressing feelings. More than half were rated as depressed or pessimistic in their mood and tone, and almost half were seen as having unresolvable conflicts with some impairment of group functioning. Finally, 50% were seen as lacking empathic responsiveness.

From this investigation, it was determined that the magnitude and number of difficulties among families who have DD children is large. Although it seems reasonable to assume that the presence of a severely handicapped child will increase the likelihood of a system becoming dysfunctional, it remains for future investigations to determine whether these difficulties are greater than would be found in a comparable sample of families with nonhandicapped offspring. Moreover, this investigation did not address the question of why a small percentage of families are functioning very well in spite of the presence of a handicapped member. Heuristic and practical considerations suggest a need for research replication and methodological refinement, further research to discover the characteristics of healthy families with developmentally delayed children, improved instrumentation consistent with the assumptions of family systems theory, and the availability of family therapy for families with developmentally delayed children. The significance of the study lies in the exploratory and descriptive nature of its findings. Evidence from this investigation suggests that programs designed to serve this population should have a strong family focus that recognizes the umbilical nature of the relationship between the handicapped child and other family members, and how the presence of a severely handicapped child might disrupt normal functioning and development in a number of critical areas of family life.

*Features of Theory and Therapy of Families
with Developmentally Delayed Children*

After two years experience with families of DD children, observations and generalizations are tentative with respect to theories and therapies. The patterns we described reflect a summary of our work with these families. They are clear enough, however, to convince us that they are valid to a large degree.

The decision to embark on a research project with handicapped children and their families was based on a number of assumptions and observations. Fundamentally, it is assumed that the birth of a handicapped child changes the structure and interactional characteristics of a family in a way that is different from the impact of a non-handicapped child. The birth of a handicapped child can be conceptualized as precipitating a family crisis. Unfortunately, such a crisis never seems to pass. Typically, parents experience shock, denial, and grief after learning their child is abnormal. The grieving for the loss of the "normal" child has no closure, in a manner that occurs when a loved one dies. Thus, it is assumed that the grieving is more prolonged and potentially more profound among family members with a DD child. Also, it is assumed that in families with non-handicapped offspring, the child's development proceeds at a fairly predictable rate until the child leaves home. The developmental process with children who are severely handicapped, however, may involve a lifetime of "perpetual parenthood," accompanied by involvements with many agencies (DeMeyer, 1979). Therefore, the predictable passage of children through the normal developmental stages of weaning and individuation from preschool through adolescence are not present in the same form for families with DD children. Parents of DD children repeatedly make reference to their 5-year-old "baby" and the fact that "he'll never leave us." At the same time, the life expectancy of the DD child is often uncertain. This poses a continuous threat to the family's current and future structure. When asked to discuss their family in five-to-ten years, conversation regarding the future of the DD child often is avoided. A kind of existential "limbo" appears to exist. Parents are faced, at a much earlier time, with their own eventual death and the implications their death might have for the life-long care of the DD child. Issues of institutionalization are paramount. Although recognizing the practical necessity of this possibility, families struggle painfully with their own feelings of inadequacy and often equate institutionalizing the child with no longer loving him/her. Not only is a family decision required, but judgments and pressure from the extended family and community come into play. At the height of frustration, one mother cried that not only was she trying to consider what was best for the child, but also felt herself faced with the impossible task of "pleasing everyone."

It is no wonder that the majority of families with DD children, which we observed, create patterns of functioning reflecting a type of rigid homeostatic balance that they believe is necessary for their survival. When stressed by such future uncertainties and pressures from a variety of external systems, families typically attempt to cope by narrowing, rather than expanding, their alternative choices and find themselves unwittingly caught in a cycle of doing "more of the same" to solve their problems (Watzlawick, Weakland & Fisch, 1974). Although their coping patterns are not working, they are at least familiar. This often appears to be a safer alternative than risking a change when the stakes seem so high.

For the reasons mentioned above, therapy with families of DD children requires skill and sensitivity. Based on our clinical experience, the following therapeutic implications are offered:

Issues of joining and rapport building are exceedingly important with these families. A great deal of skill is required in reading and respecting the analogical rules of the system.

We believe that the extent to which therapists are required to "enter the family's model of the world" and to "positively connote" the homeostasis is greater in working with these families than in working with non-DD families.

It is believed that these families are less apt to seek therapy on their own. Therefore, issues of therapy initiative need to be very carefully addressed. We have used paradoxical techniques to get stronger responses from families in the direction of their wanting therapy more than we want it for them. This issue was often unclear among families who stopped therapy before we had any solid indicators of systemic change. The initiative issue continues through the middle phase of therapy, because these families perceive their range of alternative choices as more limited than non-DD families. Divorce, for example, as a solution for parents of DD children is seen as a much bleaker alternative than it is in the general population.

Because developmental phases and tasks are different for these families, the goals and indicators of change are different. For example, in a non-DD family where the identified patient is a shy, school-phobic, 7-year-old boy, the therapist might set three indicators of change: (a) the boy succeeds in going to school every day (averaging perhaps one absence a month); (b) the husband and wife go out, recreationally, as a couple approximately four times a month; and (c) the boy initiates some type of play activity with a friend at least twice a week. For a family with a severely handicapped child, however, going to school and initiating friendships are less consciously chosen activities. Furthermore, parents have more than the average obstacles in securing babysitters. These parents report that willing babysitters are hard to come by, let alone securing sitters whom the parents can trust to handle medical emergencies. For these families, we have to set indicators of change that are tailored to their specific family and social context.

We encounter ecologically related issues more often than in our therapy with non-DD families. All of the families we work with have a social worker/parent-teacher assigned to them through the school program or Department of Mental Health, and it is essential to work closely with the special educators in the school system. Extended family relationships play a more significant role than we have observed in non-DD families. Grandparents and relatives have a very strong response to the handicapping condition and often serve as the only acceptable babysitters. Therefore, it becomes all the more important to define clearly our position as therapist in relation not just to the family unit, but also vis-a-vis other professional and social contexts in which the family is a subsystem. The ecosystemic approach, therefore, seems to be well suited for working with these families.

REFERENCES

Beavers, W. R. *Psychotherapy and growth*, New York: Brunner/Mazel, 1977.

Bowen, M. The use of family theory in clinical practice. *Comprehensive Psychiatry*, 1966, *7*, 345-374.

Bowen, M. Principles and techniques of multiple family therapy. In J. Bradt & C. Moynihan (Eds.), *Systems therapy*. Washington, DC: Groome Child Guidance Center, 1972.

DeMeyer, M. K. *Parents and children in autism*, V. H. Winston & Sons, Washington, DC, 1979.

Ferreira, A. J. Decision-making in normal and pathologic families. *Archives of General Psychiatry*, 1963, *8*, 68-73.

Fullmer, D. W. Family group consultation. *Elementary School Guidance and Counseling*, 1972, *7*, 130-136.

Gath, A. The impact of an abnormal child upon the parents. *American Journal of Psychiatry*, 1977, *130*, 405-410.

Guerin, P. & Pendagast, E. Evaluation of family system and genogram. In P. Guerin, (Ed.), *Family therapy: Theory and practice*. Gardner Press, Inc., New York: 1976, 450-464.

Holt, K. S. The impact of mentally retarded children on their families, M.S. Thesis, University of Manchester, 1957.

Lewis, J.M., Beavers, W.R., Gossett, J.T., & Phillips, V.A. *No single thread: Psychological health in family systems.* New York: Brunner/Mazel, 1976.

Watzlawick, P., Weakland, J., & Fisch, R. *Change: Principles of problem formation and problem resolution.* New York: W.W. Norton and organization and family therapy. *Archives of General Psychiatry,* 1975, 32, 1031-1038.

Torrie, C. Unpublished paper: A preliminary report on parent observations and needs as they relate to programs for deaf-blind children in the south central region, 1973.

Watzlawick, P., Weakland, J., & Fisch, R. *Change: Principles of problem formation and problem resolution.* New York: W.W. Norton and Co., Inc., 1974.

Chapter 6

VULNERABILITY AND INVULNERABILITY TO THE CULTS
An Assessment of Family Dynamics, Functioning, and Values[*]

Florence W. Kaslow, Ph.D.
Lita Linzer Schwartz, Ph.D.

[*]This research was supported by the Faculty Scholarship Support Fund, Phase III, of the Pennsylvania State University during 1979. Appreciation is expressed to our research assistants, Nadine Joy Kaslow and Richard Tanenbaum, both graduate students in psychology, at the University of Houston and Virginia Commonwealth University respectively, for their assistance in questionnaire construction, compiling a list of subjects, and data collection. Acknowledgement is also made to Tom Warms, at Ogontz Campus of Pennsylvania State University, for his contribution in computer analysis of the data.

Introduction

No unidimensional mural can adequately convey what constitutes healthy family functioning. What is needed is a complex, multi-hued tapestry which encapsulates numerous

165

dimensions characteristic of healthy families regardless of their socioeconomic status, ethnicity or race, level of educational attainment, size of family, or the occupations of their members. We prefer "healthy" to "normal" as the descriptive term for individuals and families that usually function at an optimal level. Normal tends to denote average, and that conveys mediocrity, some rigidity and conservatism, and an absence of creativity. The model utilized here is mainly a synthesis and expansion of the work of Beavers (1977); Kaslow (1980); Lewis, Beavers, Gossett and Phillips (1976); Maslow (1962).

The chapter begins with a summation of the eight variables according to which (Beavers, 1977) all families, whether healthy or optimal, average or mid-range, dysfunctional or pathological, can be evaluated. This is followed by a brief overview of the contemporary cult phenomenon. Next, the data derived from a comparative study of ex-cult and non-cult members and their parents will be presented and discussed in light of the typology and characteristics of healthy, mid-range, and dysfunctional families. Some observations of therapeutic issues which surface and strategies being utilized in treating cult members or their families are described. Finally, some hypotheses regarding vulnerability and invulnerability to the cults are formulated and suggestions made for future empirical research.

Systems Orientation

Optimally functioning families reflect a *systems orientation*; the family has a sense of itself as a unit in which all members feel that they have a special and meaningful relationship with each other. There is an inherent knowledge that the whole is more than the sum of the parts as it embodies the individuals, their interactions and transactions. They are certain who is a member of the family and who is not. Others may be included in activities and welcome in their home, but there is no acting as if they are truly family members. Sometimes, the family elects to participate together as a unit; at other times, some members prefer to be with or undertake projects with non-family members (Whitaker & Wynne, 1974). These non-family involvements are perceived positively as they provide exposure to a broader world view and prevent the stifling of individuality. The system is *open* and responsive to outside input and challenges, yet stable enough to offer security and continuity (Kaslow, 1980).

Rigidity, rather than openness, typifies the mid-range family (Beavers, 1977). New acquaintances do not gain entry to the system easily; they are scrutinized to assess their acceptability. Predictability is preferable to novelty. In dysfunctional families, one of two patterns is apt to be present. In the first, there are virtually no boundaries between the family as a group and the outside world. Non-members move in and out in a haphazard way; who really belongs is hazy, as when children each have a different father. The second group of multiproblem families operates quite differently; they isolate themselves, living without contact with extended family or communal support systems.

The healthy family has a definite, yet flexible, structure. There is a recognition of the ever-changing nature of the process of living. The mid-range family is more static and closed, preferring to conserve traditional values and ways; the dysfunctional family is frightened by harbingers of growth and change because these disrupt what little certainty they have in a tumultuous world.

Boundaries

In the healthy family, there are clearly demonstrated *intrafamilial boundaries* among the generations (Minuchin, 1974). The parents, as the architects and executives, function effectively in their spouse and parent roles. Children are not parentified and can concentrate on the concerns of childhood such as play and school. Grandparents have their own unique, respected status, and are realistically regarded as being part of a third, separate, but equally valued, generation.

In mid-range families, it is not uncommon to hear a mother say "My daughter and I are great friends. We do everything together!" Such possessiveness and lack of differentiation places everyone at a disadvantage, since children can have many friends, but they only have one set of parents. If that position is abdicated, a deficit is created. Another aspect of "boundary issues" is the recognition of the need for privacy of each individual and among generations. In healthy families, the ideal is not total togetherness; rather, there is time and space for children to play and work without their parents. There is ample time for adults to be alone together, at home and away, and to pursue their own interests apart from their spouse or parent roles. There is intimacy but not intrusiveness; privacy, but not distance. Each one can have his/her own friends and hobbies without the others feeling shut out when the preference is for a non-family activity.

In mid-range families, youngsters are apt to be told not to close their bedroom door or whisper on the phone because they should not have secrets from their parents, who foster a public image of family solidarity. They become quite annoyed when the adolescents prefer to spend Sunday with friends rather than visiting Grandma. In pathological families, lack of space is often a serious problem. It is hard to feel whole and separate when one shares a bedroom with siblings, when others listen in on phone conversations, or open mail —all not uncommon infringements on personal boundaries.

In healthy families, adult sexual needs are satisfied within the marital relationship. Neither parent would cross generational boundaries to become seductively involved with the child or grandparent generation. Yet, such transgressions often occur in multiproblem, disturbed families. In mid-range families, sexual topics are often not discussed, and there are many prohibitions on sexual behavior. Children's ease with their sexuality seems to be directly correlated to the frequency of parental sexual gratification. Across generations, affection, caring, and nurturing love may flow, but a child should not be triangulated to fulfill his/her parents' emotional or sexual needs.

Context

Contextual issues concerning communication constitute the third characteristic. Healthy families utilize few double bind messages, and verbal and nonverbal messages are congruent; who is being addressed is easy to discern (Epstein, Bishop, & Levin, 1978).

When statements are clear and requests for clarification encouraged, a good interchange can occur leading to completion of a feedback loop. One can say, "I disagree because" and move on to the next transaction until misunderstanding or disagreement is worked through. There is no build-up over time of unresolved issues like those that plague pathological and mid-range families, resurfacing periodically amidst "here we go again" disillusionment. Rather than trying to use solutions or orders repeatedly found to be unworkable, hoping vainly that someone will finally react in a new way, as dysfunctional families tend to do, healthy families engage in creative problem solving.

In the mid-range family, members are apt to look, act, and sound alike, parroting the expected views and answers. Since there is less differentiating and more emphasis on unanimity, it may not be safe to disagree with one's parents. More denial and repression of disapproved thoughts and feelings occur. In pathological families, long silences, screaming matches, or double bind messages may be the primary mode of communication.

Power

In the modern healthy family, the relationship of the marital pair is generally an egalitarian and mutually supportive one (Sprenkle & Olson, 1978), and parents share power and authority. Under these circumstances, power is not abdicated to the children. The latter are encouraged to participate in the decision-making at their level of development, and this increases as they get older. They are given age-appropriate responsibilities, and the parents intuitively model claiming one's own thoughts, feelings, and behavior.

In an egalitarian relationship, respect for each other's individuality and happiness are higher values than being "right." The children, recognizing the strong parental alliance, rarely try to "divide and conquer." "The children's awareness of parental cohesiveness and rational use of power contributes to their growing feeling of trust in their parents, in themselves, and in each other. And they identify with, and ultimately internalize, a sense of potency and competency into their own self image" (Kaslow, 1980).

A different scenario emerges when the father is an authority figure or master and the mother an acquiescent martyr-slave, as is the case in some rigid, traditional, mid-range families. Here, male and female roles are specific and stereotypic. More severely pathological families may be headed by a domineering, boisterous, or manipulating wife-mother and a passive, though hostile or absent husband-father. In other cases, one or several children may tyrannically boss their parents around. The need for control of one's anger and hurt, plus the strong urge to make others act in certain ways, keep power and control battles in the foreground in these tempestuous families.

Autonomy and Initiative

Healthy parents realize that the youngsters will grow up and move out and the nuclear family, per se, will cease to exist if they have successfully fostered competence and independence. They also know that their adult children, although they will live elsewhere, will still be affectionately invested in the family. Their relocating is anticipated as a normal developmental emancipation despite some sense of loss. The capacity to create an environment in which one's offspring can get the love and guidance they need while still gradually fostering independence evolves from the parents' valuing of their own individuality and a fulfilling marital relationship. In the healthy family when the children depart, the parents are still very much in the world; active and productive, and often delighted to concentrate again on themselves and each other. They still care about their children, but do not long for earlier phases of the family life cycle.

By contrast, loneliness and sadness are more typically expressed in mid-range families who have been possessively invested in, and apt to live vicariously through their youngsters. Parents may convey the message, "After all we have done for you, how can you take off and desert us? Where is your loyalty?"

In schizophrenic families, the projected relocation of a family member who has been part of the "undifferentiated family ego mass" is likely to set in motion a series of crises since the tenuous equilibrium is threatened (Bowen, 1974). In borderline families, the leaving of young adult members may be perceived as desertion or abandonment.

Affect

The sixth constellation encompasses *affective issues*. The healthy family experiences and expresses a broad repertoire of emotions (Epstein, et al., 1978). Hurts and losses are discussed and grieving is permissible. Since they do not fear displays of strong feelings, anger and disappointment, fury and sorrow, can be shown. Consequently, they can also express the positive emotions of happiness, joy, playfulness, and triumph. They can listen, empathize, and sympathize with each other, and optimism and humor are dearly valued commodities.

In contrast, mid-range families do not permit experiencing or sharing their fury, hurt, confusion, exhilaration, and affection with each other. Since feelings are the emotional currency of intimate living, much of this is lacking and the apparent closeness is more pseudomutual than real (Wynne, Ryckoff, Day & Hirsch, 1958). It is necessary to repress strong feelings since they are perceived as dangerous to the calm order of life.

Napier and Whitaker (1978) posit that all families have "family wars." Yet these differ in the three kinds of families. In dysfunctional units, the battling is hostile, destructive, repetitious, and often futile. In the mid-range family, a smoothly functioning facade may be sought, even if it covers much dissension. In the healthy family, disagreements are brought out into the open in the service of understanding everyone's feelings and thoughts, and with the goal of finding an equitable solution. To feel is to risk being hurt and to risk knowing the marvelous sensation of peak experiences. This cannot occur if feelings are denigrated or if one is told not to trust his/her intuitions and observations.

Conflict Negotiation and Task Performance

The seventh aspect is *negotiation and task performance* (Beavers, 1977). Negotiation entails hearing what everyone has to say and trying to reach a solution by incorporating part of everybody's input rather than at a level of compromise which is lower than where everyone began. Healthy families find this process stimulating, challenging, and fun.

By contrast, in mid-range families that are authoritarian, tasks are assigned by the reigning power(s). Their execution may be reinforced by rewards; failure to do chores may result in loss of privileges or allowance or other punishment. Children are expected to conform to parental decrees as to what should be done and when; they have little choice of duties, and tasks are rarely rotated.

Chaos prevails in the dysfunctional family in which everyone expects someone else to do what needs doing, or roles are so rigidly enforced that if one person is ill or away, no one can substitute. Attempts to get things accomplished may ignite the family ritual war dance.

Transcendental Values

The healthy families identified in various studies (Beavers, 1977; Sprenkle & Olson, 1978), and those observed by the first author have a definite belief system that is applicable in the family and extends to include a sense of connectedness in "time and space with their past and future family history, and with the larger world. They are not in conflict with their external environs but feel a kinship to the rhythm of the cosmic universe" (Kaslow, 1980).

The data do not show convincingly whether the transcendental value system has to be a religious one. Yet, almost invariably, families rated as "healthy" by clinicians and researchers have viewed their religious observances as a binding force and a source of comfort. They have a belief in some kind of a supreme being or force in nature and a well-defined ethical system of values. Whitaker and Wynne (1974) mention continuity of the values that are transmitted through time across generations in optimal families.

Mid-range families are likely to be involved in organized religion on a more automatic, unquestioning basis—going to church or synagogue because "it is the thing to do" rather than because in this way they find a personal connectedness from which is derived a framework for meaning and value. Attendance may be mandatory and may be an area of contention since repetitive services and rigid structure are not conducive to evolving one's own set of transcendental values.

Pathological families are usually religiously unaffiliated since the structure of church is too demanding and confining. They cannot tolerate being involved in the community or to find a haven in fundamentalist sects. The value system may be predominantly a survival ethic or an extension of the law of talion (i.e. an eye for an eye, a tooth for a tooth).

Healthy families harbor an optimistic outlook about life and their ability to live a satisfying and productive existence. This ingredient, invaluable for bolstering coping capacities in times of stress, is lacking in dysfunctional and mid-range families. The latter two are prone to pessimism, to waiting for the next streak of bad luck to befall them since life is a series of hard knocks. In the mid-range family, it may be a more balanced view—a combination of optimism and pessimism and an expectation of some good times.

The Contemporary Cult Phenomenon

In times of economic instability, family disorganization, and political uncertainty, some people turn for comfort, security, easy answers, and direction to groups under the aegis of an authoritarian, powerful, charismatic leader. Often, because personal and social upheaval contain existential elements related to the lack of a sense of purpose and meaning in life, such as those alluded to previously in some mid-range and dysfunctional families, the search for affiliation and direction leads one to a fundamentalist, proselytizing, religious-type organization. Such forces have contributed to the rise and spread of the cult phenomenon in the past 15 years, a period in which young Americans, estimated to number in the millions, have joined such cults as the Divine Light Mission, Church of Scientology, Unification Church (the "Moonies"), International Society for Krishna Consciousness (Hare Krishna), and Children of God. These five are the most prominent of the estimated 2,500-3,000 current cults in the United States.

According to the literature, young adults who have succumbed to the ploys of cult recruiters have tended to be upper-middle-class students who are lonely, depressed, uncertain, outerdirected, and searching for *the* answer to society's problems and their own, who have been yearning for acceptance, and for a "cause" to which to be committed. The interaction of this constellation and the perfect timing of cult recruiters enhances susceptibility. Recruiters seek converts at critical times in the person's life—the first weeks on a new campus, during exams, near graduation, when they are apt to be most forlorn. Recruiting and conversion techniques are similar in the aforementioned cults. Recruiters are alerted to the characteristics of "prospects" and taught how to approach them (Lofland, 1977; Stoner & Parke, 1977).

The initial overture occurs on campus or near a transportation terminal. The recruiter begins a casual conversation with the prospect and eventually extends an invitation to "come home for dinner with my friends and me so that we can discuss our work for peace (or orphans, or the aged) some more." During the interchange, the potential recruit has begun to reveal something of his/her ideas, concerns, yearnings, and preferences. This information is frequently used later in the conversion process.

The second phase takes place in a house or apartment where cult members live. The prospect is greeted warmly, complimented on some facet(s) of his/her appearance, repeatedly told how great he/she is, and how happy the group is that he/she came to visit. This strongly positive approach is called "love-bombing" (Lofland, 1977). It flatters the prospect's weak ego to a point that is difficult to resist. Conversation revolves around the uplifting work of the group and their deep investment in their mission, usually without any mention of a church affiliation. Later, an invitation is extended to spend a low-cost or free weekend with them and more of their friends at a lodge, camp, or ranch.

During phase three, transportation is provided to the retreat. During the ride there, inspirational songs are sung by recruiters and prospects, esprit de corps is stimulated, and there is more talk of the group's projects and the prospect's personal assets. On arrival at the destination, usually late at night, each prospect is assigned a personal companion. This escort does not leave the prospect's side, answers (or sidesteps) his/her questions, and seeks to keep the recruit completely involved in the business of the weekend. Lectures, group singing, organized games, directed discussion, and meals fill the hours; there is little time for sleep and none for privacy. The constant activity and companionship leave the prospect with little energy or time to review and digest what is happening (Landes, 1976). Such a controlled environment is crucial to the success of indoctrination techniques. Once recruited, the young adult "is subjected to repetitive lectures, chants, and rituals that have a hypnotic effect; is kept in an encapsulating environment that allows for no contradictions or outside information; and is manipulated by highly effective conditioning techniques and psychological pressures. Probing questions and negative comments are met with resistance designed to make the individual feel guilty for such behavior" (Schwartz & Kaslow, 1981). Those who succumb to the indoctrination process experience marked changes in personality as they assume a new identity within the cult (Conway & Siegelmann, 1978).

The characteristics that cults share in common are: (a) active recruiting techniques; (b) a charismatic leader, almost invariably male; (c) demand for total submission to authority; (d) restriction of communications to and from the outside world; (e) isolation from family; (f) practices of physiologic deprivation (of sufficient food, balanced diet, and sleep); (g) propagation of fear and hatred of outsiders, claiming they are "of Satan"; and (h) a requirement to earn money and turn over all assets to the cult.

Parents of those who convert and withdraw into their new way of life are baffled at the sudden disappearance of the youth. If they manage to see their child, they are shocked by the transformations in personality and physical appearance and grief-stricken at being totally deserted and replaced by the new cult "family."

At this stage, parents bring their distress to clergy, therapists, attorneys, and public media—anyone who will listen—pleading for help. Their reports have spearheaded investigations by journalists (Stoner & Parke, 1977), research and treatment endeavors by therapists (Singer, 1979a), and projects such as this one. They have also led to law suits in which parents have sought conservatorship powers to regain custody of their offspring (Katz v. Superior Court, 73 Cal App. 3rd 952, 141 Cal Rptr. 243, 1977) or, rarely, an ex-cult member sues the group on the grounds of fraud (Titchebourne v. Church of Scientology, Oregon, 1979).

Kaslow-Schwartz Study

Mindful of the conflicting and often hortatory articles that have appeared in the professional literature and the lay press, we sought to determine: (a) whether there were real personality differences in the pre-cult or early college years between young adults who had and had not been in cults; (b) whether there were differences in the dynamics and structure of the nuclear family between the two groups; and (c) the young adults' perceptions of cult groups and their own vulnerability to their appeals.

Methodology

The original intent was to obtain a sample of 62 non-cult members and their parent(s) and 62 ex-cult members and their parent(s). Young adults were to be matched on the following variables: age, education, and race. These three variables were selected because the literature (Schwartz, 1979; Stoner & Parke, 1977) indicates that the majority of young people who have joined such cults as the "Moonies," Hare Krishna, and the Church of Scientology are well-educated, white young people who are in their late teens and early twenties.

Obtaining a non-cult sample was relatively easy. A total of 62 sets of questionnaires (62 to young adults and 107 to parents) were sent to the non-cult group. The response yielded a non-random sample of 51 young adults (21 males and 30 females) and 75 individual parents, representing 35 complete family units. The goal of having a sample of equal size of ex-cult members and their parents, however, was not realized. The resistance we met in seeking an ex-cult population was puzzling at first. Conversations with and letters from the parent segment provided four clues to the resistance: (a) continuing fear of harassment by the cults; (b) defensiveness about the family situation which we were raising as a possible contributor to one's vulnerability to the cults and the resentment this segment of the questionnaire engendered; (c) a strong desire not to revive the traumatic experience in their children, to try to protect them from reliving the pain and not to risk reactivating their interest in the cult; and (d) a need to have this troublesome phase of their lives remain closed. We have no explanation for the lack of response from the many professionals we contacted whom we knew were working with ex-cult members. We sent out 17 questionnaires to ex-cult members and 26 to their respective parents. In the end, nine ex-cult members (7 male and 2 female) and 15 parents of ex-cult members, representing five complete family units, constituted the ex-cult sample. The small size of this sample precluded meaningful statistical analysis, so that the findings reported here are preliminary and suggestive.

A consent form, explanation of the study, Adjective Check List, and Young Adult or Parent Questionnaires were mailed to all prospects, along with a stamped, pre-addressed envelope to increase the probability of response. Confidentiality and anonymity were guaranteed.

Demographic Data

A total young adult sample of respondents, comprised of 51 non-members and 9 ex-cult members, exhibited some shared characteristics. They fell predominantly in the 20-24 year age range; were heterosexual in sex preference (43/51, 9/9); had never been married (43/51, 6/9), were well-educated (28/51 and 6/9 were college graduates and 18/51 were enrolled in college); were employed full- or part-time; were of above average or superior intelligence with cumulative averages at college of 2.5 or higher (out of a possible 4.0), and were from upper-middle and upper-income suburban families (36/51, 8/9).

In terms of religion, respondents were 73% Jewish, 20% Catholic or non-fundamentalist Protestant, and 7% "other." These clearly disproportionate percentages reflect the "snowball" effect since the authors and research assistants are Jewish and drew many of the non-cult respondents from among their friends, students, and others known to them in university settings with a high proportion of Jewish students. Only four young adults reported that they came from very religious homes, while most subjects attended religious services a few times a year or not at all. These data were confirmed in the parents' responses.

Interestingly, 7/9 ex-cult members had been moderately or very active in high school extracurricular activities, as had 47/51 non-cult members. Both sets of figures dropped drastically, however, when the subjects attended college, with none of the ex-cult members rating themselves as very active and 5/9 indicating that they rarely participated in extracurricular activities. Of those who never joined a cult, 30/51 were either moderately or very active in college, and 20/51 rarely participated.

Of the subjects who had had psychotherapy, four ex-cult members entered therapy between the ages 21 and 25 (possibly post-cult) and 10/18 non-cult members entered treatment between ages 16 and 20. Most had been in therapy one year or less, although one ex-cult member and 7/18 non-cult young adults were in therapy for more than a year. None of the ex-cult sample reported having had any family member hospitalized for mental illness. A total of seven non-cult members, however, had a close relative who had been so hospitalized. Parents of non-cult members reported mental illness in their own families of origin or families of procreation with much greater frequency (33/75) than did ex-cult parents (1/15). All of the young adults had at least one sibling, although there was a tendency for ex-cult members to be the youngest child (5/9) and non-cult members to be the oldest (24/51).

Our data indicate that all nine ex-cult members had tried drugs, with 55.6% of this sample having used drugs minimally. By comparison, 81% of the non-cult group had used drugs minimally or not at all. A total of 60% of the non-cult group had tried drugs. Of the parents, one ex-cult parent and one non-cult parent used drugs moderately often. The young adults in both samples used alcohol minimally or not at all.

Tentative Profile of Cult Members and Their Families

Despite the difficulty of securing a larger sample of ex-cult members, an important element in the data collected was the corroboration of ex-cult members' perceptions by their parents, and the differences in trends that seem to emerge in the two groups. Inspection of responses to the Adjective Check List showed that the ex-cult members rated themselves and were rated by their parents as more pessimistic, more unloved, more insecure, and less successful in interpersonal relations than did the non-cult members. In addition, the ex-cult members saw themselves as sadder and less confident in their pre-cult period than their non-cult peers did as freshmen. Parents of ex-cult members also saw their children as tending more to underachievement in that period than did parents of non-cult subjects.

In examining relationships within the nuclear family, young adults and their parents agreed, in ex-cult families, that the parents tended to spend less leisure time with their spouses than was the case in non-cult families. Ex-cult parents also reported more conflict in the marriage, less mutual understanding and consideration for each other, and more involvement in decision-making for their children than did non-cult parents. On the young adults' matching questions, ex-cult members found their parents more protective of them. They also perceived themselves as more alienated from their families and more distant from their siblings than did non-cult young adults. Although the data support the common view of somewhat more stressful relationships in families where there has been a cult member, they do not support the strongly pathological family portraits painted by *in*-cult subjects in the previously cited studies. It is interesting to note, also, that non-cult subjects cited close and satisfying family relationships as one reason that they felt and feel invulnerable to cult recruiting.

Two additional factors stand out in differentiating ex-cult and non-cult young adults. The ex-cult members reported less sense of meaningfulness and purpose in life and less of a sense of their own identity than their non-cult peers in the pre-cult/early college period. Again, the strong sense of identity was cited by the non-cult sample as contributing to their invulnerability.

Queried directly about the cult experience, the ex-cult members reported, in retrospect, that they had been "brainwashed" when they became involved. Only two indicated that they had left the cult voluntarily. Most had been attracted by the feelings of belonging they experienced in the cult and reported that the cult has provided not only a sense of acceptance, but also a sense of purpose and feelings of achievement and fulfillment. They indicated that young people become involved with cults because they feel lonely and alienated, feel a need for structure and rules in their lives, and because of a sense of "inner weakness." Since leaving the cult, they perceived themselves as more responsible individuals, more tolerant of their parents, and more successful in interpersonal relations. These responses differ markedly from the uncertainty expressed by several ex-cult members interviewed by Beckford (1978). This variation may be due to the deprogramming and psychotherapy undergone by many of our American sample, experiences apparently not undergone by the British sample.

The data support our earlier hypotheses (Schwartz & Kaslow, 1979) that those who are most vulnerable to the cult mystique: (a) lack a sense of inner direction; and (b) have a weak relationship with their father. On the non-paired questions of the Young Adult and Parent Questionnaires concerning family relationships, ex-cult members did not perceive the parents' marriage or parent-child relationships in the same way that their fathers did, although the youths' responses tended to agree moderately well with their mothers' responses on these items. This statement comes from a comparison of data derived only when everyone in the family unit had responded and the data could be cross-tabulated. Non-cult young adults' responses agreed moderately well with those of both parents.

One other factor appeared with sufficient frequency to merit noting. A much higher percentage (by 2:1 ratio or more) of non-cult parents reported equality in their relationship in the family constellation in terms of authority and power. Despite the fact that the five complete ex-cult family units that responded in our study constitute five more than anyone else has reported, this number is too small for meaningful statistical analyses or generalizations to be made.

Interpretation of Data

Those who are vulnerable to cults appear to come from mid-range and dysfunctional families. Lacking a sense of an open system that specifies clearly who is a member and who is not, and longing for a strong sense of affiliation and belonging, they can exchange their family of origin for the cult family—hoping to find in the new what was lacking in the old. Lacking a sense of the solidity and need-gratifying potential of the family unit, they are vulnerable to promises that the new group will take care of them and make life easier. Healthier young adults go home and try to rework conflict areas; they do not escape by severing all ties and replacing them in such a totalistic way.

Frequently, in joining a cult, one gives up all privacy. There is an oceanic "we-ness" that engulfs members as concerns for individual personhood and goals are subjugated to the primacy of the cult's dictates and objectives. For those needing symbiotic attachment, the assignment of another member as a constant companion seemingly fills the loneliness void. It appears from our limited sample of ex-cult members that they were not joiners in college; evidently, they saw themselves as unacceptable isolates and were pleased at the overtures made by and compliments received from recruiters. A healthy, young adult who treasures separateness as well as valuing friendships would find the cult milieu stifling and intolerable.

As described earlier, healthy families communicate specifically and clearly; open dialogue is encouraged. Conversely, in the cults, as in many mid-range and disturbed families, one does not question rules, doctrines, or the order of things. Everything is what the leader says it is, even if there are gross inconsistencies. Messages often are presented in a vocabulary specific to the cult, usually garbled or vague, so that "outsiders" cannot understand and the distance between cult member and family is broadened as they no longer speak the same language.

Young people who are lured into the cults want someone to tell them what to do and when. The cult leader has absolute power and the member is to submit completely. It appears from our findings that those who had a weak relationship with their father and who also perceived him as weak, find comfort and strength from the autocratic, omnipotent leader. They finally get answers as to what is expected and some safe structure that helps them control the desire for drugs or sex. For those who come from authoritarian, father-dominated, mid-range families and then are thrust into the permissive atmosphere of college, the chance to revert to a more familiar and predictable world, while still rebelling against the disliked parental authority, has much appeal. This is not to say that becoming involved with a cult is necessarily an informed, conscious, or deliberate decision.

So, too, with autonomy and initiative. In the dysfunctional family, although one may be goaded to "fend for yourself," it is likely that they have not had sufficient nurturance to have an internal reservoir of strength and coping strategies to do that. The young person from the "average" family may have been so overprotected or enmeshed, with the parents doing so much for him/her that the freedom of college life with its concomitant responsibilities may be experienced as overwhelming. The cult demands the dependence to which they wish to retreat.

For those from emotionally volatile dysfunctional families, the calm, loving cult community appears to be a welcome pacifier; an antidote to the feared screaming matches. Young adults from mid-range families, where even positive feelings were not overtly expressed, flower under the "love-bombing" that fills the aching void for sufficient love and acceptance. The healthy young adult would probably find the cult's brand of universal love in the confined community and hatred to those outside too extreme, somewhat absurd, and too impersonal.

In terms of task performance, expectations are clear-cut. In the cult, one is to pray or chant, do chores, and sell items to raise money for the group for a prescribed number of hours each day. This ritual is non-negotiable and some young people crave the safety of a routine, shared with many others in a patterned way after many years of having "time to kill" and feeling useless.

It is perhaps in the area of the lack of transcendental values and a sense of meaning and purpose in life that the data most clearly differentiate the vulnerable from the non-vulnerable. The non-cult group exhibited a stronger sense of personal identity and what they were about in life; they fall into the category of healthy young adults. The ex-cult members seemed to flounder about "who am I," "why am I alive," and seemed to be more susceptible to the promise of guaranteed answers to their existential questions. In addition, because of the quasi-religious nature of the cults, they hoped that their spiritual yearnings and the covert longing for a transcendental belief system would be fulfilled.

Treatment Approaches and Implications

Due to space limitations, treatment considerations can only be briefly presented. The reader is referred to earlier papers for a much fuller discussion of these approaches (Schwartz & Kaslow, 1979b, 1981), and to the work of Singer (1979b) which focuses on group therapy for ex-cult members.

While the Young Adult is Still in the Cult

While the young adult is still in the cult, some parents turn to parent networks, and groups of parents who also have had children caught in the cults. For some, this contact with other parents becomes a main source of strength. They may, if and when their child leaves the cult and is rehabilitated, remain active in the parent network, providing leadership and infusing their own lives, and perhaps their child's, with heightened meaning.

Unless the young person is successfully deprogrammed following release, he/she may still seem "possessed" by cult ideology and may manifest his/her new personality rather than partially reverting to his/her old self. If kidnapped from the cult, the youth may resent the intrusion of the parents into the new life. The young person may run away and return to the cult. Members of the cult are nearby, happy to welcome them back with open arms. Meanwhile, long smoldering family problems are likely to erupt; the parents may blame one another for their distressing plight, and a desperate atmosphere prevails.

Some bring their distress to a therapist where they attempt to sort out their hurt, confusion, guilt, fury, desperation, and anxiety. They need empathic, attentive listening, support while considering how they may have contributed to their child's vulnerability, realistic information about the specific cult their child belongs to, and assistance in determining their options and selecting a feasible course of action. The therapist may focus on problems in the family, conceptualizing the cult member as the symptom bearer, and helping the parents understand past family dynamics and functioning. Thus, while waiting for their child to be extricated from the cult, parents and siblings can be helped to deal with their dismay and to function in a healthier fashion. Themes in therapy include the pervasive sense of failure, the anguish of the parents when they realize that their child has embraced the cult as a substitute family, that he/she no longer remains in contact with them as they are considered creatures of the devil, that their hopes and dreams for this child have evaporated, and that they may never see their child again. "Therapy deals with raw emotions, the grieving process, and then mobilizing for action" (Schwartz & Kaslow, 1981).

Aftermath

When a cult member reenters the outside world, what then? If one has been deprogrammed, he/she has usually undergone a confrontive experience in which the deprogrammer has sought to counteract the mind control perpetrated by cult leaders. The deprogrammer criticizes what the cult stands for, using logic and reason to counter the internalized irrational beliefs. Family and friends may be nearby, ready to be called in to reinforce the deprogrammer's efforts and to offer support while the person's defenses are being whittled away. The emotional turmoil, disorientation, and fear of living without cult peers, coupled with a gripping awareness of the threatened penalities for defection, make this a long and difficult process (Patrick, 1976).

Family network therapy constitutes a plausible, less traumatic alternative if a family can convince their offspring to come home for a visit, and they can get permission to do so. The parents can convene the entire family and many friends. Few will refuse given the critical nature of the circumstances (Speck & Attneave, 1972; Reuveni, 1979). A team of well-qualified network therapists must be present who are familiar with the particular cult, its ethos and vocabulary. Because networks share numerous properties with cults, like the use of chanting and other rituals to enhance group solidarity, a familiar and treasured part of the cult atmosphere is utilized to show persuasively that such needs can be met in the outside world. Also, since the lead therapist is usually a powerful figure who emits a sense that he/she can heal those in his/her care and help them find the strength and motivation to make life more meaningful, feelings for the cult authority figure may be transferred to the therapist, who will utilize the positive transference to free, rather than entrap, the young person. Otherwise, networks for cult members' families proceed as do any others. In employing network therapy, one substitutes the network for the cult's mainstay of offering a group that gives unconditional love and acceptance, security and continuity. The reunited kinship-tribal group has valuable roots and much loyalty to offer emerging from family ties (Boszormenyi-Nagy & Spark, 1973). The network can be reconvened when needed, until the ex-cult member forms other solid relationships. The young person may decide, alone or with the family, to go into treatment with one of the network therapists.

Once the person is deprogrammed, it takes time for him/her to adjust to the outer world. Individual, peer group, preferably with other ex-cult members who understand the periodic "floating" and special reentry problems (Singer, 1979a) or family therapy, vocational or educational counseling; pastoral counseling, residential milieu therapy (Schwartz & Kaslow 1979; 1981); or a combination of these may constitute the most advantageous intervention. Selection should follow an assessment of the needs, developmental tasks to be accomplished, and ego strengths of the individual and his/her family, plus the tenor of the interrelationships. The therapist, regardless of treatment philosophy or modality, should be cognizant of the special syndrome of cult membership, what probably transpired and why before, during and after, the flashbacks and recriminations that occur, and any long-range after-effects of possible brainwashing.

Concluding Thoughts

In applying a family systems model to the cult phenomenon, we have utilized eight critical dimensions of family interactions where weakness or failure to function constructively may contribute to the vulnerability of young adults to seductive cult recruiting appeals. Each of these variables has been depicted in terms of healthy or optimally functioning families, average or mid-range families, and dysfunctional families. The preliminary findings of our study, discussed in some detail, are interpreted in terms of these eight characteristics as well.

Almost all of the published studies describing cult membership have omitted consideration of the background of the cult member, focusing instead only on the leader. The individual's behavior cannot be truly or effectively understood, however, without an examination of the context—in this case, intrafamilial and inter-personal relationships. Data gathered by questionnaires from ex-cult members and their parents, limited though our sample was, suggest that these family units differ in significant ways from the families of young people who never become enmeshed in a cult. These results, however, represent only a first step in understanding why bright, young adults from socioeconomically secure families succumb to the siren's call of pseudo-religious groups that provide far less materially, although on the surface they provide something quite different psychologically, than did their families of origin.

Many questions remain to be answered about the etiology, impact, and ultimate effects of cult membership on the individual and the family. Further exploration is needed to determine which characteristics of the mid-range or dysfunctional family are most critical in predisposing its young adults to cult vulnerability. In what ways can the therapist, for example, use knowledge of these characteristics to help the family modify its pattern of interaction? What are the long-range effects of such therapy? Are there clues here that could help the therapist working with a family to *prevent* vulnerability in its younger members? Is it possible that different family systems predispose their children to be responsive, i.e., vulnerable, to one cult's appeal but not another's? We hope that our impressions will lead to the development of hypotheses in these areas that can be tested empirically.

REFERENCES

Beavers, W. R. *Psychotherapy and growth: A family system perspective.* New York: Brunner/Mazel, 1977.

Beckford, James A. Cults and cures. *Japanese Journal of Religious Studies*, 1978, *5*, 225-257.

Boszormenyi-Nagy, I., & Spark, G. *Invisible loyalties.* New York: Harper and Row, 1973.

Bowen, M. Toward the differentiation of a self in one's family of origin. In F. Andres & J. Loris (Eds.), *Georgetown Family Symposium Papers I.* Washington, D.C.: Georgetown University Press, 1974.

Conway, F., & Siegelmann, J. *Snapping: America's epidemic of sudden personality change.* Philadelphia: J. B. Lippincott, 1978.

Epstein, N., Bishop, D., & Levin, S. The McMaster model of family functioning. *Journal of Marriage and Family Counseling*, 1978, *4*(4), 19-32.

Kaslow, F. W. Profile of the healthy family. *Focus pa Familie* (Norwegian Journal of Family Therapy), 1980.

Landes, M. G. Making of a Moonie. *Atlas World Press Review*, September, 1976, 20-32.

Lewis, J., Beavers, W. R., Gossett, J. T., & Phillips, V. A. *No single thread: Psychological health in the family system.* New York: Brunner/Mazel, 1976.

Lofland, J. *Doomsday cult,* enlarged edition. New York: Irvington Publishers, 1977.

Maslow, A. *Toward a psychology of being.* New York: Van Nostrand, 1962.

Minuchin, S. *Families and family therapy.* Cambridge: Harvard University Press, 1974.

Napier, A. Y., & Whitaker, C. *The family crucible.* New York: Harper and Row, 1978.

Patrick, T. (with T. Dulack). *Let our children go!* New York: E. P. Dutton, 1976.

Reuveni, U. *Networking families in crisis.* New York: Human Sciences Press, 1979.

Schwartz, L. L. Cults and family therapists. *Interaction,* 1979, *2,* 145-154.

Schwartz, L. L., Kaslow, F. W. Religious cults, the individual, and the family. *Journal of Marital and Family Therapy,* 1979, *5*(2), 15-26.

Schwartz, L. L., & Kaslow, F. W. The cult phenomenon. *Marriage and Family Review,* 1981.

Singer, M. T. Coming out of the cults. *Psychology Today,* 1979(a), *12,* (8), 72-80.

Singer, M. T. Friends Hospital Conference, Philadelphia, 1979(b).

Speck, R. V., & Attneave, C. L. Social network intervention. In C. J. Sager & H. S. Kaplan (Eds.), *Progress in group and family therapy.* New York: Brunner/Mazel, 1972.

Sprenkle, D., & Olson, D. H. Circumplex model of marital systems: An empirical study of clinic and non-clinic couples. *Journal of Marriage and Family Counseling,* 1978, *4*(2), 59-74.

Stoner, C., and Parke, J. A. *All Gods children: Salvation or slavery?* Radnor, Pa.: Chilton Publishing, 1977.

Whitaker, C. A., & Wynne, L. C. *The normal family.* Notes on the Ackerman Memorial Lecture, New York, 1974.

Wynne, L. C., Ryckoff, I., Day, J., & Hirsch, S. H. Pseudomutuality in schizophrenia. *Psychiatry,* 1958, *21,* 205-220.

Chapter 7

FAMILY THERAPY
AND SUICIDAL CRISIS
An Empirical Analysis

Anthony P. Jurich, Ph. D.

Introduction

A comprehensive review of the literature concerning the causes of suicide is beyond the scope of this chapter. They range from personal factors to social causes. Menninger, Mayman, and Pruyser (1963) posit a five-stage model outlining the course of the suicidal process. These stages are: (a): impairment of a person's coping abilities, (b) personality disorganization and the appearance of neurotic symptoms, (c) loss of control and the inability to cope with the present situation, (d) increased disorganization, regression, poor reality testing, and the romanticization of death as a relief from overwhelming emotional stress, and (e) severe depression, intense anxiety, and uncertainty.

If the stressor event is of sufficient magnitude, the person may proceed through these five stages to the final stage. It is at this point where the intrapsychic struggle is most intense and the person's self-concept becomes a crucial factor in determining the outcome. If the person's self-esteem and ego strength are high, the person may develop new coping mechanisms. Each successful resolution of a crisis is thought to produce ego growth and an enhanced self-concept (Bard, 1972). If the person has a rigid self-concept and low levels of self-esteem, however, the ego may be unable to defend against the overwhelming anxiety (Wekstein, 1979). External support systems such as family and friends have been found to play a significant role in determining whether the individual chooses life or death as an answer to the intrapsychic dilemmas (Caine, 1978; Johnson, 1978; Richman, 1979; Sargent, Jensen, Petty & Raskin, 1977; Wekstein, 1979).

Although intrapsychic forces often incubate the suicidal processes, suicidal ideations frequently include people who are closely related to the suicidal person (Wekstein, 1979). This usually includes family members. Suicidal behavior, therefore, takes place in an interpersonal context and the suicidal person can be said to be responding to the familial environment.

Although the role of the family has been acknowledged as important in the genesis of suicidal thoughts and behaviors, limited attention has been given to the systemic aspects of suicide and how suicidal gestures may serve to maintain the family's homeostasis (Richman, 1979). Frequently, the suicidal person is seen as a victim and the role as a symptom bearer in a dysfunctional family system is neglected. When family processes are addressed, however, they frequently are described in linear terms with the suicidal person's behavior usually being depicted as "caused" by other family members or simply as a "response" to them (Gould, 1965; Kolb, 1968; Rosenkrantz, 1978; Schneidman, 1976; Stone, 1973; Wekstein, 1979; Wenz, 1979).

It is hoped that the empirical findings presented below will help to foster the adoption of family therapy as a valid therapeutic approach in the treatment of suicidal individuals.

Methodology

Subjects

The data which form the basis of this report were collected from 34 patients who were referred to the writer for therapy over a six-year period. Referrals came predominantly from the university emergency crisis line of a large midwestern university.

Initial contact with the suicidal individual was made immediately following the referral. During this face-to-face encounter, an attempt was made to stabilize the person and to evaluate whether hospitalization or psychiatric referral were indicated. Regardless of the disposition, all individuals were seen for a second interview within 24 hours. The pretest was administered at that time.

In all 34 cases, the family was notified of the suicide attempt or threat within 24 hours of the initial contact. This always was done with the permission of the patient. Every effort was made to bring the patient's family into family therapy as soon as possible. Sixteen of the 34 families participated in family therapy. This involvement continued throughout the treatment process. In 18 cases, individual therapy was provided and the family was not directly involved in treatment. In the majority of cases, family members were unavailable because of work schedules or physical distance from the university. In some instances, however, the family refused to participate in the treatment process. In all cases, whether in individual or family therapy, the minimum duration of treatment was 14 weeks. Four cases extended treatment beyond six months. The majority of cases terminated treatment between five and six months.

Instrument

The research and theory outlined above stress the importance of the person's self-concept in the genesis of suicidal behavior. Therefore, each patient was given the Tennessee

Self-Concept Scale as part of the initial interview and assessment process (Fitts, 1965). This instrument is a self-administered questionnaire. The individual is asked to respond to 100 five-point Likert-type questions ranging from "strongly agree" to "strongly disagree." The instrument yields ten subscale scores: Total Self-Concept, Self-Criticism, Identity, Self-Satisfaction, Behavior, Physical Self, Moral-Ethical Self, Personal Self, Family Self and Social Self. Test-retest reliability ranged from .75 on The Self-Criticism Scale to .92 on The Total Self-Concept Scale. Fitts (1965) also reports content validity, the ability to discriminate among groups, and concurrent validity with such instruments as the MMPI and the Edwards Personal Preference Test. This scale also is reported to be sensitive to changes in self-esteem brought about by psychotherapy (Ashcraft & Fitts, 1964). In this study, the instrument was used to determine the patient's level of self-esteem and to reveal the major areas of poor self-esteem. In addition, it served as a pretest to determine the base level of self-concept so that a pretest-posttest comparison could be made to evaluate therapeutic outcome.

Treatment

Phase I: Crisis Intervention

Since this phase of therapy is a time of both physical and psychological danger with a time-limited opportunity to intervene, immediate and decisive action is essential (Puryear, 1979). The therapist must establish immediate rapport and afford the suicidal individual security from self destructive impulses by neutralizing the volatility that impels the individual to act out (Wahl, 1971). Richman (1979) has suggested that in assessing a person's suicidal potential, one should look for the following in the identified patient as well as in the people with whom he/she is most intimately involved: (a) decompensating defenses, (b) strong feelings of depression, despair and hopelessness, (c) problems in impulse control, (d) a tendency toward dissociation and altered states of consciousness, (e) psychotic features, (f) organic signs, and (g) specific suicidal ideation. In addition to these indicators, more circumstantial criteria also were considered (e.g., a well defined plan for self destruction, a recent history of genuine suicidal attempts, a clear and well defined evaluation of suicidal ideation into suicidal acts, a rejection of the therapeutic alliance in favor of a rigid and firm anticipation of hospitalization, total or extreme social isolation and extreme disappointment with the inability to get a secondary gain as a result of the suicidal threat). When the decision to hospitalize a person was uncertain, a psychiatrist was called in for consultation.

The overall goal of this phase of treatment is to restore the individual to a basic state of personal equilibrium. A major element in this process is to lessen the individual's anxiety. During this phase, the therapist encourages the person to discuss his/her plight in his/her own words. This procedure offers the suicidal person the opportunity for cathartic release and allows the therapist to gain the information needed to accurately assess the situation (Krieger, 1978; Puryear, 1979). Not all of the therapist's behaviors are passive and non directive, however, because the therapist must probe the suicidal ideation in order to assess the severity of the threat (Wekstein, 1979).

The author has found that the best results derive from an initially passive approach, followed by an active, reality based, directive style. By being active, the therapist can demonstrate that he or she is neither frightened nor seduced by the patient's suicidal attitudes and behaviors. In this way, the therapist presents an intact, well-integrated, reality-based identity (Wekstein, 1979). The therapist provides a positive model and urges the patient to focus on the realities and primary issues of the current situations. In this way, the emergency can be reduced to tangibles that can be sorted out, resolved, and explored in detail (MacKinnon & Michels,

1971). This enables the individual to enter into a therapeutic alliance and to explore expectations, formulate a plan of action, and focus on problem solving (Puryear, 1979; Wekstein, 1979). The suicidal person can then make use of his/her own resource to strengthen coping mechanisms (MacKinnon & Michels, 1971; Puryear, 1979; Wekstein, 1979). Once the therapist and the patient have entered into this very active, reality-based, problem solving alliance, the therapist can begin to help him/her move away from suicide as a course of action toward the more constructive alternative of using therapy to resolve problems. From the outset, the therapist should be "selling" therapy as a potential alternative to the suicidal solution (Wekstein, 1979).

Phase II: Family Therapy

After the initial individual session is concluded, a second appointment is scheduled for the entire family within the next 24 hour period. Families are seen either in the therapist's office or in the hospital in cases where the person needs a protective environment.

Joining with the entire family. The initial family interview begins with the therapist using the same supportive techniques applied in the first contact with the suicidal patient. This is done to help reestablish the secure, safe, and trusting relationship and to reassure the family that no one will be "blamed" for the suicidal behavior of the patient. Once the therapist has joined successfully with all family members, he/she can begin to refocus and redefine the patient's role. The therapist's goal is to have the family begin to grapple with how the patient's behavior serves a particular family function and how this behavior can be seen as a symbolic comment about the family system (Minuchin & Barcai, 1972).

Each family member is asked to discuss his/her perception of the sequence of events leading to the suicidal crisis (Malouf & Alexander, 1974). As each member speaks, other family members are asked to listen attentively and to hold their comments and responses until it is their turn. In this way, the therapist slows down the pace of the interaction, generates a clearer picture of the role that each family member plays in the genesis and maintenance of the suicidal family patterns, and lays the foundation for the idea that each family member is necessary for the maintenance of any behavior sequence. This procedure sets the ground rules for how communication will be structured during the therapy sessions. In addition, family members are instructed to talk directly to each other. This process initiates the structural changes that will take place throughout therapy and prepares the family for directives that the therapist will give later on. It also minimizes the mutual blame-avoidance patterns of symmetrical interactions which frequently are observed in such families. The therapist also helps the family members discuss their feelings about each other in a non-accusatory manner (Puryear, 1979).

Although the atmosphere is supportive, the therapist does not hinder the exchange of negative affects. As a matter of fact, disagreement and conflict may be encouraged. This is true, especially, in families where anger is not permitted expression.

Another technique that has been used with families who continually scapegoat and blame, is to positively reframe behaviors and intentions (Selvini-Palazzoli, Boscolo, Cecchin & Guiliana, 1978). This strategy helps strengthen rapport, raise self-esteem, dilute hostility, and enhance the positive atmosphere of the session. In addition to reframing, the therapist can help the family members gain more self-confidence in their ability to handle this situation by having them recall any past successes they might have had in handling family crises.

Focusing on incongruencies. Specific attention is paid to the meta communications of family members. This takes on special significance in suicidal families where the patient may experience a "conflicting message" between the verbal and nonverbal levels of the communication. The suicidal person may be responding to meta messages from family members which indicate that they would like him/her dead. A variety of strategies can be used by the therapist to establish congruent communication exchanges among family members (Haley, 1976). One technique that has been used with some success is for the therapist to openly state the verbal message and the nonverbal meta message, and then ask the sender to select the message actually intended.

Talking the family's language. By not talking down to the family members and by talking their language (Haley, 1976), the therapist can accomplish two goals simultaneously: gain their acceptance and be allowed to join the system. Gaining entrance in this manner, the therapist proceeds to push for the surfacing of family conflicts, especially conflicts between the parents in which the suicidal member is believed to have been triangulated (Minuchin & Barcai, 1972). Central to this procedure is the hypothesis that the suicidal member is acting out the repressed rage of significant family members. By doing this, the suicidal member may be thought of as protecting other family members from the explosive expression of anger. This helps maintain the family intact. By his/her actions, the suicidal individual's behavior can be seen as truly symptomatic: it protects the family's integrity while expressing the repressed rage of key family members.

Once the therapist has helped the family members express their anger, attention can be focused on restructuring the system (e.g., by rearranging the family's hierarchy, reestablishing a parental coalition, disrupting parent-child alliances, renegotiating subsystem boundaries, etc.).

Phase III: Restructuring through Contracting

This phase of treatment focuses on teaching family members to use behavioral contracting as a new method for resolving interpersonal conflicts. The model of conflict negotiation adopted for this purpose is based on the procedures outlined by Harrell and Guerney (1976). This model was chosen specifically for working with this population, because it stresses the importance of teaching empathy to all family members. The absence of empathy among families of suicidal persons has been noted by a number of clinicians (Hill, 1970; Richman, 1979). It has been suggested that the development of empathy in families where there is a suicidal member is essential for positive treatment outcome (Richman 1979).

During this contracting process, the therapist attempts to keep the discussion focused on concrete, behavioral aspects of the problem and engages in the family in the task of developing alternative response patterns. Specifically, the family is encouraged to discuss alternative solutions to the problem situation and to evaluate the efficiency of those solutions with respect to both the patient's and the family's needs. After discussing the problem from all vantage points, each family member is asked to institute a change in response to reciprocal changes by other family members. The therapist assists the family members in negotiating a behavioral exchange contract in which each member emits a behavior which would contribute to the resolution of the family's problem to the benefit of all concerned.

The therapist's goal is to help the suicidal individual and his/her family learn to use more direct and functional behavior change strategies instead of the manipulative and coercive maneuvers which are typical in such family organizations. This approach helps these families work on clearly defined tasks to achieve specific behavioral goals. The observable outcomes serve as concrete examples of the family's ability to exert power and control over what seemed to be a hopeless situation.

Once the behavioral contract is implemented, the therapist focuses on feedback from the family members in order to evaluate and, if necessary, renegotiate the contract in order to achieve maximum efficiency.

Phase IV: Termination

Termination is decided by the family members in conjunction with the therapist. A key factor in assessing the family's readiness for termination is the therapist's judgment that the family members have learned to incorporate conflict negotiation strategies and bargaining skills into their behavioral repertoires sufficiently to use them in the advent of future crises.

Results and Discussion

Pretest and posttest scores on the Tennessee Self-Concept Scale were compared for the family therapy group and the individual therapy group of suicidal patients, using a t-test to determine significant differences. The results of these analyses are presented in Table 1 for the Individual therapy group of 18 patients and in Table 2 for the Family Therapy group of 16 patients.

Significant pretest-posttest differences were found on every score for both groups. Patients in both groups significantly increased their:
1. Total Self-Concept
2. Self Criticism
3. Identity
4. Self-Satisfaction
5. Behavior
6. Physical Self
7. Moral and Ethical Self
8. Personal Self
9. Family Self
10. Social Self

Considering the extremely depressed state of the patients the day after a suicide attempt, such dramatic increases were to be expected. Whether these changes can be attributed to the treatment processes or to statistical regression is a debatable issue which cannot be resolved by the present study. In the

Table 1:   Comparisons Between Pretest and Posttest Scores on 10 Measures for those Patients Engaged in Individual Therapy.

Variable	Pre-Test		Post-Test		
	Mean	SD	Mean	SD	t-test
Total Self-Concept	233.33	38.09	279.39	44.95	6.71***
Self-Criticism	41.89	4.90	40.56	4.90	3.06**
Identity	90.33	19.75	111.33	15.57	4.77***
Self-Satisfaction	57.33	12.69	67.11	15.55	5.23***
Behavior	81.00	15.58	100.95	20.35	4.89***
Physical-Self	51.67	9.33	53.39	10.00	3.42**
Moral-Ethical Self	49.00	7.90	59.89	8.98	6.09***
Personal-Self	44.11	12.35	56.51	12.78	7.12***
Family-Self	44.61	9.25	53.56	11.39	5.11***
Social-Self	43.94	10.51	55.94	12.80	6.13***

*p.<.05
**p.<.01
***p.<.001

Table 2:   Comparisons Between Pretest and Posttest Scores on 10 Measures for those Patients Engaged in Family Therapy.

Variable	Pre-Test		Post-Test		
	Mean	SD	Mean	SD	t-test
Total Self-Concept	234.81	42.70	305.06	38.74	8.35***
Self-Criticism	41.94	3.92	39.31	4.47	3.30**
Identity	98.31	15.69	116.69	11.12	5.05***
Self-Satisfaction	56.50	14.53	82.94	16.31	8.21***
Behavior	80.00	15.80	105.44	14.43	7.33***
Physical-Self	51.88	10.58	56.06	11.19	2.78*
Moral-Ethical Self	49.19	9.12	62.38	9.85	5.46***
Personal-Self	45.56	13.16	57.88	9.99	5.51***
Family-Self	42.81	9.64	68.06	8.91	9.54***
Social-Self	45.38	11.45	61.19	10.93	7.08***

*p.<.05
**p.<.01
***p.<.001

absence of a non-treatment control group, however, it can be said that the combination of events, of which therapy was an important part, produced a significant increase in all self-concept scores. The reader will notice that the smallest increase among these ten scores, in both the individual and family therapy groups, was in the Physical Self Score. Of all the scales, this was the one that was, by and large, the least touched on in therapy. One score, Self-Criticism, showed a significant decline over the course of therapy in both groups. This could be attributed to the fact that, when pressed to the brink of suicide, the patients were overly critical of themselves. As they grew further from the suicidal crisis, they achieved more realistic self-images and became less self-critical. Therefore, in all ten areas of self-image, measured by the Tennessee Self-Concept Scale, the patients in both individual and family therapy showed improvement toward a healthier self-concept.

In order to determine if there were any significant differences in self-concept changes between individual and family therapy groups over the course of therapy, a series of t-tests were performed on the pretest-posttest differences for each of the ten self-concept scores between the two treatment groups. The results of this analysis are presented in Table 3. There were no significant differences on seven of the ten self-concept subscales. Those patients who had undergone family therapy, however, demonstrated an increase in Total Self-Concept that was significantly greater than those who had participated in individual therapy. As might be expected, the family therapy group experienced a significant increase in Family Self-Concept. In fact, for the family therapy group, the Family Self-Concept Score shifted from being the lowest of the five content self-concept scores to being the highest. A surprising finding was that the family therapy group experienced a significantly greater increase in Self-Satisfaction than the individual treatment group. The author would speculate that the family's presence and help, throughout the therapy, gave the suicidal patient a greater feeling of acceptance, which he/she translated into self-acceptance and self-satisfaction.

Several factors must be considered in comparing the individual and family therapy groups. Although every attempt was made to standardize the first phase of treatment,

Table 3:   Comparisons Between Patients Engaged in Individual Therapy
and Patients Engaged in Family Therapy on Pretest-Posttest Difference Scores.

Variable	Individual Therapy		Family Therapy		t-test
	Mean	SD	Mean	SD	
Total Self-Concept	46.06	29.11	70.25	33.67	2.23*
Self-Criticism	1.33	1.85	2.63	3.18	1.42
Identity	21.00	18.66	18.38	14.56	0.46
Self-Satisfaction	9.78	7.93	26.44	12.88	4.47**
Behavior	19.94	17.31	25.44	13.88	1.03
Physical-Self	1.72	2.14	4.19	6.03	1.55
Moral-Ethical Self	10.89	7.59	13.19	9.67	0.76
Personal-Self	12.50	7.45	12.31	8.94	0.07
Family-Self	8.94	7.42	25.25	10.59	5.14***
Social-Self	12.00	8.30	15.81	8.93	1.28

*p.<.05
**p.<.01
***p.<.001

this was difficult because of the nature of the presenting problem. The therapist, therefore, had to respond to meet the unique needs of the patient in that situation. These differences were not accounted for in the present study and are assumed to be equivalent for both groups. If there were any consistent differences, however, they might contribute to the differences observed. Another source of caution stems from the fact that, although the treatment process for those patients in family therapy was standardized, the treatments for those in individual therapy were varied and sometimes quite diverse. Although there was a conscious effort to reduce any extraneous differences between the groups, the reader should realize that the diversity of individual treatment styles must be considered an extra source of unaccounted variance. Finally, because the families who participated in treatment were volunteers, it might be argued that these families are not comparable to the families who chose not to engage in family therapy. This might account for an increase in self-concept, especially Family Self-Concept, that would be in addition to any specific effect of the family therapy. Although these possibilities must be kept in mind, they should not overshadow the fact that the family therapy group did report greater growth in Total Self-Concept, Family Self-Concept, and Self-Satisfaction than did the individual treatment group.

Conclusions

Although the research on family crisis intervention is growing, the crisis of suicide is underrepresented in the literature. The present study offers preliminary support for the use of family therapy as a treatment approach to suicide. Not only can family therapy play a significant role in the therapy of the suicidal person, but it may prove to be a more effective treatment approach than individual psychotherapy. The present study, by no means, provides conclusive evidence to be definitive. It does open the door, however, for wider use of family therapy in cases where suicide is threatened. It also can serve as a springboard for future research in the area. It is hoped that the word "suicide," although it will always arouse alarm in the therapist, also may arouse a new feeling of confidence in the therapist's ability to deal more effectively with the situation through the use of family therapy.

REFERENCES

Ashcraft, C. & Fitts, W. H. Self-concept change in psychotherapy, *Psychotherapy*, 1964, *1*, 115-118.

Bard, M. Training police as specialists in family crisis intervention. In Sager, L. J. & Kaplan, H. S. (Eds.), *Progress in group and family therapy*. New York: Brunner/Mazel, 1972.

Caine, E. Two contemporary tragedies: Adolescent suicide/adolescent alcoholism. *Journal of the National Association of Private Psychiatric Hospitals*, 1978, *9* (3), 4-11.

Fitts, W. H. *Tennessee Self-Concept Scale*. Nashville: Counselor Recordings and Tests, 1965.

Gould, R. E. Suicide problems in children and adolescents. *American Journal of Psychotherapy*, 1965, *19*, 228-246.

Haley, J. *Problem solving therapy.* San Francisco: Jossey-Bass, 1976.

Harrell, J. A. & Guerney, B. G. Training married couples in conflict negotiations skills. In Olson, D. H. (Ed.), *Treating relationships.* Lake
Mills, Iowa: Graphic Publishing, 1976.

Hill, M. N. Suicidal behavior in adolescents and its relationship to the lack
of parental empathy. *Dissertation Abstracts International,* Vol. 31
(a-A), 472, 1970.

Johnson, R. Youth in crisis: Dimensions of self-destructive conduct
among adolescent prisoners. *Adolescence,* 1978, *13,* 461-482.

Kolb, C. C. *Noyes' modern clinical psychiatry* (Seventh Edition). Philadelphia: W. B. Saunders, 1968.

Krieger, G. Common errors in the treatment of suicidal patients. *Jouranl
of Clinical Psychiatry, 1978, 39,* 649-651.

MacKinnon, R. A. & Michels, R. *The psychiatric interview in clinical practice.* Philadelphia: W. B. Saunders, 1971.

Malouf, R. E. & Alexander, J. F. Family crisis intervention. In Hardy,
R. E. & Cull, J. G. (Eds.), *Techniques and approaches in marital and
family counseling.* Springfield, Ill.: Charles C. Thomas, 1974.

Menninger, K. A., Mayman, M., & Pruyser, P. *The vital balance: The life
process in mental health and illness:* New York: Viking, 1963.

Minuchin, S. & Barcai, A. Therapeutically induced family crisis. In Sager,
C. J. & Kaplan, H. S. (Eds.), *Progress in group and family therapy.*
New York: Brunner/Mazel, 1972.

Puryear, R. A. *Helping people in crisis.* San Francisco: Jossey-Bass, 1979.

Richman, J. Family therapy of attempted suicide, *Family Process,* 1979,
18, 131-142.

Rosenkrantz, A. L. A note on adolescent suicide: Incidence, dynamics and
some suggestions for treatment. *Adolescence,* 1978, *13,* 209-214.

Sargent, D. A., Jensen, V. W., Petty, T. A., & Raskin, H. Preventing physician suicide: The Role of family, colleagues, and organized
medicine. *Journal of the American Medical Association,* 1977, *237,*
143-145.

Schneidman, E. S. (Ed.). *Suicidology: Contemporary developments.* New
York: Grune and Stratton, 1976.

Selvini-Palazzoli, M., Boscolo, L., Cecchin, G., & Guiliana, P. *Paradox
and counter-paradox.* New York: Jason Aronson, Inc., 1978.

Stone, M. H. The parental factor in adolescent suicide. *International Journal of Child Psychotherapy,* 1973, *2,* 163-201.

Wahl, C. W. The management of the presuicidal, suicidal, and postsui-
cidal patient. *Annals of Internal Medicine,* 1971, *75,* 441-458.

Wekstein, L. *Handbook of suicidology.* New York: Brunner/Mazel, 1979.

Wenz, F. V. Sociological correlates of alienation among adolescent suicide
attempts. *Adolescence,* 1979, *14,* 19-30.

FUTURE DIRECTIONS, EPISTEMOLOGICAL ISSUES, AND PHILOSOPHICAL CONCERNS

Chapter 8

FUTURE DIRECTIONS FOR FAMILY THERAPY RESEARCH

David P. Kniskern, Psy.D.
Alan S. Gurman, Ph.D.

Introduction

The field of family therapy research is exciting and rapidly changing. Research is being published at what appears to be an ever increasing rate, and new research reviews are published just as quickly in an attempt to integrate newly gained knowledge with previous research and clinical experience. In the most comprehensive review to date (Gurman & Kniskern, 1978a), we identified and evaluated more than 200 reports of family therapy research. In a more recent publication (Gurman & Kniskern, 1981a), we identify more than 35 reviews of marital-family therapy research (some summarizing reports of only one aspect of the total field.)

Considering the recency of a comprehensive review and the total number of reviews in the literature, it should be obvious that an additional review of the field cannot be justified at this time. In our opinion, what is needed in the field is a re-direction and re-focus toward identifying what needs to be studied in the future and an identification of the clinically most relevant questions requiring answers.

This re-direction and re-focusing will be the central goal of this chapter. To accomplish this task in context, however, it is necessary first to summarize what has already been learned from family therapy research in order to specify what we still do not know, and what we need to know. We also will address some crucial issues involved in how researchers might most profitably go about trying to answer the many unanswered and unaddressed questions that family therapists will face in the 1980s.

This chapter also will recognize the fact that there is no unitary theory or practice of family therapy. Rather, there are numerous family therapies, with both overlapping and clearly divergent assumptions about the nature of family process and family development, the genesis and maintenance of dysfunctional patterns, treatment goals, therapeutic techniques, and the effective routes to therapeutic change. This chapter will focus both on the issues and research questions that we believe to be of major importance to family therapy in general, and on the issues and research questions of crucial importance to one of these schools of family therapy. Since it is beyond the scope of this chapter to fully describe each school's assumptions and to suggest profitable school-specific research questions, it is our hope that by examining one model in some detail, we will stimulate other researchers and clinicians to develop focal and central empirical questions for the other major schools of family therapy.

What We Know About Family Therapy (More or Less)

The effectiveness of family therapy has been investigated predominantly by using three strategies: percentage of cases improved, comparisons of family interventions to other forms of treatment, and comparisons of family approaches to "no treatment." Each of these strategies has supported the conclusion that family therapies are valid and effective methods of intervening in family and individual problems. Results from research using each strategy will be discussed separately for non-behavioral approaches to family therapy. Results of research investigating behavioral family therapy will then be dealt with separately. Except where otherwise noted, the conclusions presented in this section of this chapter are drawn from our major review of the family therapy outcome literature (Gurman & Kniskern, 1978a)

Percent of Cases Improved

Non-behavioral marital therapies produce beneficial effects in about 61% of cases .In our review of 36 studies involving 1,528 cases, we found a 70% improvement rate for conjoint couples therapy; a 66% improvement rate for conjoint couples group therapy; a 63% improvement rate for concurrent/collaborative couples therapy; and a 48% improvement rate for individual therapy for marital problems. These studies provide a heuristically useful comparison with gross improvement rates of other types of non-maritally focused therapies (Bergin, 1971) and among types of marital interventions, yet they are methodologically crude. The typical study can be characterized as using: (a) only one evaluative perspective (usually that of therapist or patients); (b) a single change index (most often a global measure of satisfaction); (c) a change measure of undocumented validity; and, (d) treatments the nature of which are often left undescribed.

Non-behavioral family therapies produce beneficial effects in about 73% of cases. Our review of 41 studies involving 1,529 cases revealed a 71% improvement rate in studies in which a child or adolescent was the identified patient and a 65% improvement rate when adults were the identified patient. As in marital studies, single change indices, predominantly from the perspective of participants, were used in a high proportion of the studies. Few of these studies specified the exact treatment procedures carried out, although there was a greater propensity among family therapy researchers to specify some treatment operations than among the marital therapy researchers.

Non-behavioral marital and family therapies may produce negative effects as well as positive or neutral effects. This deteriorative phenomenon, well documented in individual therapy (Bergin, 1971; Lambert, Bergin & Collins, 1977) was first mentioned in the context of marital therapy by Gurman (1978). A later, more comprehensive assessment of the evidence bearing on this issue (Gurman & Kniskern, 1978b) found that among the 36 reports of non-behavioral marital and family therapy that either reported or allowed for a determination of negative treatment effects, nearly half (15 of 36, or 42%) found evidence of worsening in some family members. Roughly 5-10% of patients as individuals, or of marital/family relationships worsened over the course of treatment. Deterioration was evident on a very broad range of outcome criteria, i.e., patient self-reports of satisfaction with treatment; therapist ratings; interactional-behavioral indices; and objective indices such as school performance and alcohol consumption. Whether these individuals or relationships worsened because of treatment is less certain since most of these data are derived from uncontrolled studies, although some studies indicate a higher probability of deterioration among treated than among untreated groups of families or couples (Gurman & Kniskern, 1978b). The most striking statistical aspect of these data is what points to the rate of deterioration in individual therapy for marital problems (11.6%), in contrast to the rate for other marital therapy formats (5.6%), or that of outpatient family therapy (2.1%).

The results of several studies (Gurman & Kniskern, 1978b) suggest that a particular style of relating and intervening is associated with an increased probability of negative effects in marital-family therapy. This style is best described as one in which the therapist: (a) uses frontal confrontations of highly affective material very early in therapy rather than reflections of feelings; (b) labels unconscious motivation early in therapy rather than stimulating interaction, gathering data, or giving support; or (c) does not actively intervene to reduce negative interpersonal feedback in families in which one member has weak ego-strength.

Comparative Studies of Family Therapy

Family therapy is at least as effective and probably more effective than many commonly offered treatments for problems involving family conflict. Specifically, family therapies emerged as superior to alternative treatments in 10 of 14 comparisons. In addition, family therapy is often effective for clinical problems that are traditionally construed in terms of individual disorders, e.g., alcoholism, depression, etc.

Among the most common forms of non-behavioral marital therapy, conjoint therapy is probably the most effective. Of 44 comparisons of conjoint therapy and all other marital therapy methods, conjoint treatment emerged superior in 31 comparisons, no different in 11, and inferior in only two comparisons.

Comparisons with No Treatment

Non-behavioral family therapy, viewed generically, yields more positive change than does no treatment. Marital interventions have emerged superior in 10 of 15 (66%) of the existing comparisons, with conjoint therapy and communication approaches producing the highest number of positive comparisons. Non-behavioral family interventions emerged as superior in 8 of 13 (61%) comparisons. In only 2 of the 28 comparisons was no treatment found to be superior to a family approach. Despite the general lack of follow-up in most of these studies, the fact that predominantly positive outcomes were obtained from treatments that lasted, on the average, only ten sessions, suggests that these therapies produce real clinical changes beyond those changes that occur in everyday life.

Effectiveness of Behavioral Family Therapy

Behavioral family therapy emerges superior to no treatment in 12 of 16 studies (including analog and naturalistic studies). This rate of superiority to control conditions is similar to that of non-behavioral therapies (18 of 28). Evidence for behavioral marriage therapy is somewhat less persuasive because of too frequent use of non-clinical analog demonstrations with minimally distressed couples. In addition, behavioral family therapy has been shown to be superior to alternative treatment in 13 of 22 comparisons.

Behavioral family therapy, not unlike other approaches, at times produces deterioration in individuals of systems treated. Rates of negative effects in behavioral family therapy appear to be at least as high as and possibly somewhat higher than those reported in studies of non-behavioral therapies (Gurman & Kniskern, 1978b).

Factors Influencing Outcomes

The Therapist. More positive outcomes seem to accrue to *experienced* than to inexperienced therapists, and the latter also appear to have higher early dropout rates. Still, no one yet has examined the question of the possible differential predictive power of experience as a psychotherapist vs. experiences as a marital/family therapist. In our view, the two are *not equivalent,* since the technical, conceptual, and perceptual skills required by a family therapist often differ from those required, such as in the practice of individual psychotherapy. *Co-therapy,* while widely espoused as a training vehicle and as a therapeutic ingredient increasing the power of intervention, has never been directly tested as a factor in the outcome of marital or family therapy. There is indirect evidence, however, that co-therapists' *experience level differences* interfere with the process and, presumably, the outcome of therapy. By far, the greatest amount of empirical evidence on the impact of therapist factors centers on the *therapist's relationship skill.* Existing evidence suggests the importance of the therapist's activity and provision of structure in early interviews without quickly attacking family defenses. Moreover, there is persuasive evidence that a mastery of technical skills may be sufficient to prevent worsening or maintain pre-treatment functioning, but more refined therapist relationship skill seems necessary to yield truly positive outcomes in marital-family therapy. Finally, a minimal level of empathic ability is probably needed just to complete therapeutic tasks in even the most behavioral of such therapies.

The Family as Patient. It is curious that although family therapy is offered for families, we know very little about what family characteristics are associated with positive treatment outcomes. *Severity/chronicity* of family disorder bears an inconsistent relationship to outcome, and specific *IP diagnoses* also are weak predictively, with the exception of anorexia nervosa and a small number of other childhood psychosomatic diseases, which appear to be effectively treated with Structural Family Therapy (Minuchin, 1974). Moreover, little is known about the *family interaction* dimensions that are associated with good treatment outcomes, though a relatively cooperative, egalitarian, flexible family seems a safe bet.

Treatment Factors. The evidence to date suggests that *time-limited* marital-family therapy is not inferior to open-ended treatment. More influential of outcome appears to be the matter of *which family members are involved in treatment.* That is, in addition to the evidence we cited earlier on the outcome differences when one vs. two spouses are involved in treatment, there is consistent and analogous evidence that the involvement of the father, traditionally the "missing link" in child guidance clinics, has a very strong influence on both the family's staying in treatment and on its improvement.

Methodological Issues for all Family Therapy Researchers: Uncontrolled Studies

The scientific method is based primarily on controlled investigation. We certainly do not endorse the view that family therapy researchers should treat methodological issues casually, and, in fact, have proposed explicit guidelines for evaluating the adequacy of research in this field (Gurman & Kniskern, 1978a). We believe, however, that uncontrolled investigation still has a place in research and can be useful in reaching conclusions about the area being studied.

The results of uncontrolled studies of family therapy are illustrative of this point. The logic behind our broad conclusion of the overall efficacy of family therapy has been discussed as follows (Gurman & Kniskern, 1981a):

> First, in reaching this conclusion, we have not relied solely on the results of uncontrolled studies. Second, even the results of poorly controlled studies are *entirely consistent* with those of better quality (in keeping with the same trend in individual psychotherapy research). Third, the results of uncontrolled studies of nonbehavioral marital and family treatments suggest the same broad conclusions about both general effectiveness *and* and comparative effectiveness across the three levels (uncontrolled single group, uncontrolled comparative, and controlled studies) of design sophistication (p. 752).

Also, as we have noted elsewhere (Gurman & Kniskern, 1978a),

> largely positive results emerge on the basis of a wide variety of criteria, on change measures from a number of evaluative perspectives, for many types of marital and family problems, from therapy conducted by clinicians of all the major therapeutic disciplines, and in therapy carried out in a number of treatment settings (p. 845).

In addition to this additive purpose and use of uncontrolled studies, helping as they can to create a pattern of consistent results that illuminate convergent clinical phenomena, there is a more specific purpose to which uncontrolled studies can be put. This purpose is the "generation of hypotheses which later can be tested in controlled investigations" (Jacobson, 1978, p. 403). The important role of uncontrolled investigation in the development and refinement of therapeutic methods has been well articulated by Bergin and Strupp (1972). This type of discovery process is not well served by tightly controlled investigation, just as uncontrolled studies are often inappropriate for the verification of hypotheses. These issues are elaborated in Klein and Gurman (1980).

Controlled Group Research

The advantages of controlled group studies for investigation are so much a part of the scientific method that a listing is unnecessary. Despite the logical and pragmatic power of this approach, there are at least two problems to be considered in their use. First, although frequently described as a "no treatment" control group, in fact, untreated patients and families often seek and find help outside the research protocol. Most controlled studies are, in fact, comparative studies in which we do not know with what our formal treatment has been compared. If such informal "treatments" are effective, the chances are good that formal treatment will not be demonstrably effective by comparison. We suspect, however, that when dealing with complex interpersonal problems, the interventions made by untrained friends, bartenders, etc., are likely to exacerbate problems since they frequently involve "more of the same," such as attempts at first order change when second order change is required (Watzlawick, Weakland & Fisch, 1974).

A second matter in the use of untreated control groups raises a number of emotional, ethical, and political concerns as well as a design deficiency. The most common procedure for developing a control group involves the random (or matched random) assignment of subjects/families with whom they are "matched" and offered immediate treatment. The use of waiting list control groups also has severely limited the severity of family problems investigated. Professional ethics, if not human research subject committees, preclude the withholding of treatment for severe problems. Even voluntary consent procedures and warnings about negative effects are insufficient resolutions for these ethical dilemmas.

Recently, a viable alternative has been suggested for the development of an essentially untreated control group known as "treatment on demand" (TOD) (Gurman & Kniskern, 1981a). Although its usefulness in family research is untested, it appears to offer a partial solution to the control group ethical dilemma. Subjects assigned to a TOD control group would be able to request contact with a therapist whenever they desired. If a family requested more visits than a predetermined number set by the researchers, they would be replaced in the control group by another randomly selected family.

A study using this procedure would, thus, create four treatment conditions: (1) Family therapy group; (2) TOD remainers, for example, those families who never requested treatment; (3) TOD partial remainers, for example, those families requesting fewer sessions than the predetermined maximum; (4) TOD dropouts, for example, those families whose requests exceeded the protocol maximum. Such a procedure allows for comparisons among these four groups and offers a rich source of information about treatment effects and therapy dropouts. In addition, since every family has therapy available upon request, most of the ethical problems surrounding control groups are resolved by this procedure.

Comparative Research

The recent history of family therapy has been one of charismatic individuals who develop therapy programs and collect around themselves a dedicated band of followers and adherents. The predominant result of this process in terms of research has been the development of research projects which seek to validate a particular form of family therapy. Their stance has been a competitive and adversarial one, geared toward the establishment of a single treatment method or model as superior among family therapies. This stance has, to this point, not been overly destructive, since family therapy has been required, as are all new approaches to therapy, to establish its conceptual legitimacy in the mental health field at large. Now that family therapy has become a more or less accepted method of psychotherapy, this competitive stance has become detrimental to continuing progress because it impedes professional collaboration on empirical questions of common interest.

Comparative studies of the future need to define the patient population much more specifically than has been done in studies published to date. This can be done by identifying styles of family interaction held in common regardless of presenting complaint (Campbell, 1979), by identifying developmental or constellational similarities (Gartner, Fulmer, Weinshel & Goldklank, 1978), by limiting samples to those presenting specific complaints or symptoms (Minuchin, Rosman & Baker, 1978), or by limiting samples on the basis of traditional psychiatric nosology (American Psychiatric Association, 1980) applied to the identified patient. A combination of these approaches would obviously be most specific in identifying a similar group of families for study (such as intact families with an obese, only-child daughter requesting weight loss).

In addition to specificity of patient populations, comparative family studies are useful only to the extent to which they specify actual treatment operations used by therapists. Methodologically, researchers need to assess, rather than assume, that therapists do therapy as they say they do it. This check of procedures often can be accomplished by the random assessment of tape-recorded therapy sessions. This procedure requires a criterion for comparison, however, and, to date, few schools of family therapy have specified the nature and preferred sequence of therapist inerventions (Gurman & Kniskern, 1981b). The importance of specifying these parameters of therapy is underscored by the likelihood that, even within a given method of family therapy, ideal intervention sequences may vary as a function of different presenting problems, motivations for seeking help, etc. The development of explicit treatment manuals for therapists of differing orientations would seem to be an essential next step in the continued progress of comparative research. In addition, valid and reliable assessment instruments, which are also clinically meaningful and not cumbersome, are sorely needed.

Criterion Problems in Outcome Research

Criteria of Effectiveness

If you want to start a bitter argument among psychotherapy researchers, an effective method is the suggestion of a set of criteria for assessing the effectiveness of therapy. Effectiveness is, obviously, directly tied to the goals for therapy, and goals vary as a function of an investigator's conceptual understanding of human problems. Goals vary tremendously in terms of their specificity, focus, breadth, and depth. No single measure or set of measures will provide a satisfactory answer to the questions of effectiveness for all researchers. For the field to advance, however, we cannot tolerate a situation in which investigators use their "pet" criteria alone and ignore or criticize the criteria used by researchers of other clinical orientations. Without giving up the measures central to their conceptual vantage point, researchers could include measurement of variables that are central to other theoretical orientations. For example, Gurman (1978) has asked,

> Would it not be provocative and exciting to find, for example, that behavioral negotiation training and contracting proced-

ures (with couples) produce significant increases in differentiation of self, or that the working through of the transference in marital therapy yields significant positive changes in a couple's ability to problem-solve constructively? (p. 553).

Such findings would lead to a richer understanding of the mechanisms of therapeutic change and the further development of increasingly effective treatment.

In addition to the inclusion of measures from different clinical orientations, researchers should also distinguish among levels of treatment goals. One such distinction, suggested by Parloff (1976), is that between mediating and ultimate goals. Mediating goals are those which are understood to be stages leading toward the attainment of ultimate goals. Ultimate goals are those that are understood by the therapist to be conditions of health for all families. For example, an ultimate goal for a family might be the establishment of clear, generational boundaries, and a mediating goal for this ultimate goal might be the disentanglement of a child from a marital conflict. The failure to distinguish these goals as being of different logical types leads to confusion and inappropriate or meaningless comparisons.

When keeping the distinction between mediating and ultimate goals in mind, however, investigators must not conclude that the achievement of one class of goals allows for the assumption that the linked goal of the other class was met or will automatically follow. This caveat is bidirectional in that the achievement of a mediating goal does not dictate that the logically linked ultimate goal will necessarily be reached, and the achievement of a specific ultimate goal does not allow the inference that one understands the necessary intermediate steps. Moreover, if one adopts a developmental viewpoint about families, these steps would have to be known and addressed in order for treatment to be consistent with theory. Goals of both types need to be assessed and the measurement of ultimate goals may require multiple follow-ups beyond the termination of treatment.

Units for Assessment

In our view, since family therapy frequently seeks to improve the functioning of all family members and their intrafamily interactions, it is imperative that change be assessed routinely at the individual, dyadic, and system levels. Since it will often not be practical to measure change in all possible family subunits, priorities must be established to guide the selection of subunits to be assessed. We have proposed a tentative model (Gurman & Kniskern, 1978a), shown in Table 1, that we believe provides these needed guidelines.

We believe that family units I, II, and III, the Identified Patient, the Marriage, and the Total System, which in some cases is equivalent to the marriage, are the minimal units for assessment and must be examined in any marital/family therapy outcome study, regardless of the family constellation of treatment context. This schema is based on our belief that families have strong morphostatic characteristics that will tend to negate symptom change, and produce symptoms in other family members or relationships other than those identified as "problemed."

Units IV to VII represent other family units on two dimensions: same versus other generation relative to the identified patient, and individual versus relationship functioning. These four family units are listed in order of their importance for the assessment of change in marital/family therapy, from unit IV (Same Generation of IP: Individual), which we consider most important, to unit VII (Cross-Generation of IP: Relationship), which we consider least important. Our rationale for this order of importance is discussed elsewhere (Gurman & Kniskern, 1978a, 1981a).

Vantage Points for Change Assessment

Just as multi-dimensional criteria are a necessity in studying the outcomes of the family therapies (Gurman & Kniskern, 1978a, 1978b; Wells & Dezen, 1978), assessmesnt of change from multiple perspectives also is required. It is increasingly being recognized that it is difficult to achieve consensus on outcome measures deriving from different vantage points. Fiske (1975) has argued persuasively that since a source of data is not a measuring instrument, attempts to eliminate disagreement among rating sources, and reduce what is usually considered error, are futile. Fiske (1975) notes that, "instead of seeking to minimize (differences in perceptions), researchers should seek to identify the unique components of the perceptions and judgments from each source" (p. 23).

We suggest that in deciding on the perspective from which change in marital/family therapy should be assessed, researchers must consider two dimensions: the perceiver's "insideness-outsideness" (Olson, 1974) relative to the treatment system and the degree of inference involved in making a given judgment. In decreasing order of insideness, we see the following potential evaluative sources: family members, therapist(s), therapy supervisors, significant others, trained judges making inferential assessments (for example, family members' individuation), objective observers recording non-inferential public events (for example, smiles, self-reference statements) and computers and machines doing likewise (for example, voice-activated apparatus to record speech duration). Not only must the degree of perceiver insideness-outsideness to the treatment system be considered, but also the level of inference involved in making given evaluative judgments. Table 2, from Gurman and Kniskern (1981a), defines the nature of information obtained at various inferential levels of assessing therapeutic change in family therapy, and suggests the ideal judges for each level of inference.

The degree of inference involved in a given judgment increases from simple behavior counts (Level I) to system properties and individual psychodynamics (Level VI). Not all levels are meaningfully or economically assessed by all possible sources. For example, highly inferential dimensions are best judged by the therapist providing treatment or by expert

Table 1: A Priority Sequence for Assessing Therapeutic Change in Couples and Families.

	Treatment Context and Family Constellation				
	FAMILY THERAPY I: Child as Identified Patient		FAMILY THERAPY II: Parent as Identified Patient	MARITAL THERAPY: Spouse/Parent as Identified Patient	
Familial Unit of Assessment	Family with More than One Child	One-Child Family		Marriage with Child(ren)	Childless Marriage
I. Identified Patient (IP)	IP child	IP child	IP parent	IP spouse	IP spouse
II. Marriage	Marriage	Marriage	Marriage	Marriage	Marriage
III. Total system	Family	Family	Family	Family	(Marriage)
IV. Same generation of IP: individual	IP's siblings	--	Non-IP spouse	Non-IP spouse	spouse
V. Cross-generation of IP: relationship	Each parent	Each parent	Each child	Each child	--
VI. Same generation of IP: relationship	IP child and non-IP child(ren)	--	(Marriage)	(Marriage)	(Marriage)
VII. Cross-generation of IP: relationship	Parents and IP child: child 1 = IP	Parents and IP child	Child(ren) and IP parent	(Parents and child(ren), i.e., Family)	--
	Parents and non-IP child(ren)	(Parents and IP child)	Children and non-IP parent	(As above)	--

Note: Parentheses indicate that this familial unit has already been accounted for at earlier level of assessment priority. Blank spaces indicate that assessment of this familial unit is logically impossible.

Table 2:   Levels of Inference in Assessing Family Therapy Outcome.

Level	Information Obtained	Illustration	Best Judge/Source
Ia.	Simple behavior counts	Frequency of interruptions, verbal assents, topic shifts	Machine or trained objective observers
b.	Performance on clinically relevent, nonfamilial objective criteria	School grades, hospitalization, police arrest history	Institutional records
II.	Perceived family interaction patterns	Reciprocity, conflict-resolution, decision-making	Trained observers
III.	Behavioral self-reports, individual or interactionally focused	Sexual Interaction Inventory, Spouse Observation Checklist	Family members
IV.	Nonbehavioral self-report, intrapersonally focused	MMPI, Eysenck Personality Inventory	Family members
V.	Nonbehavioral report of self in relationship to others (and/or vice versa	Marital satisfaction, various communication inventories)	Family members
VIa.	Individual psychodynamics or personality structure	Rorschach, TAT	Expert judge
b.	Family psychodynamics	Collusion	Therapist or expert
c.	Inferred family system properties	Enmeshment pseudomutuality	(professional) judge

professional judges, whereas simple behavior counts could be accomplished by a variety of people, but to use the therapist for this purpose would be, at least financially, wasteful. Finally, it should be obvious that it is much more difficult to measure validly and reliably Level VI variables than variables at lower levels of inference.

Crucial Questions for Family Therapy

The field of family therapy research has progressed and been reviewed as a unitary body of knowledge and practice. Differences among "schools" and orientations, for the most past, have been ignored as researchers have demonstrated the overall effectiveness of "the family approach" to treatment. A few questions may remain that can be profitably studied in this general manner, but the future of research in the field must become largely "orientation-specific," as noted above in our discussion of comparative outcome studies.

In our *Handbook of Family Therapy*, (Gurman & Kniskern, 1981b) we identify six major conceptual approaches to family therapy: Behavioral, Structural, Strategic, Multigenerational-Bowenite, Experiential, and Psychodynamic-object-relational. Others may quarrel with this particular division of the field or believe that some important orientation is not represented, but we believe the importance of the empirical study of "school specific" assumptions can be stated without risk of controversy.

Each school of family therapy should attend to at least the following, clinically relevant, comparative studies. First, what elements within the treatment influence the rate of dropouts or of premature termination? Gurman and Kniskern (1978a) have identified several factors that seem to operate across treatment methods, but little is known about factors influencing this phenomenon within different treatment methods. Second, the practice of co-therapy has been widely espoused as a superior method of therapy, although often not practical. Little empirical support for this position exists, yet it remains an important part of family therapy lore. It seems likely that co-therapy will be differentially useful for various schools. The question of which school for what problem is one of great importance. Third, a high priority should be given to the comparison of specific family treatment methods with reliably effective methods of individually focused therapies. Finally, and perhaps most importantly, we suggest the component analysis of effective and essential treatment ingredients of each school of family therapy. Every school's approach to therapy is a combination of specific techniques, tactics, and non-specific therapist behavior. For example, the Structural Family Therapy for anorexia nervosa routinely involves operant strategies, structural techniques and interpretation, and often includes paradoxical techniques as well. The overall effectiveness of this approach is widely accepted (Gurman & Kniskern, 1978a), but which techniques are essential or important have not yet been investigated.

Structural-Strategic Family Therapy: An Illustration of a Clinically Meaningful Research Approach

Theoretical Orientation. Our choice of the school of family therapy we term Structural Strategic (Andolfi, 1979; Stanton, 1981) will serve as a model for developing school-specific research questions. The selection is not an endorsement of the model but rather is reflective of the school's importance and relatively sophisticated research history (Stanton, 1981). Furthermore, the school's theoretical framework is as well, if not better, articulated as any other school of family therapy. Although any school might serve as the example we seek, and although we plan to articulate research questions, structural-strategic family therapy seems to be an appropriate choice for our purposes.

Many family therapists consider the structural and strategic approaches to be of separate schools. For the purpose of suggesting important research questions, however, strategic and structural family therapy may be considered as technical variations of a single school of family therapy. Strategic therapy has been associated particularly with "paradoxical" techniques, and structural therapy with the direct change of system properties (such as boundaries, alliances, power hierarchies) of a family. The overlap between them in their assumptions, stance of the therapist, goals for change, and many of their techniques is great enough to allow consideration of them as a single school.

Structural-Strategic Family Therapy has been defined as therapy in which the therapist initiates what happens during treatment and designs a particular approach for each problem. Prominent figures in the school are Haley, Minuchin, Watzlawick, and Palazzoli. *Strategic therapists regard all individual problems as manifestations of disturbances in the family.* Stanton (1981) summarizes the strategic view of dysfunction as follows:

> 1. "symptoms" can be viewed simply as particular types of behavior functioning as homeostatic mechanisms which regulate family transactions (Jackson, 1957, 1965); 2. problems in an identified patient cannot be considered apart from the context in which they occur and the functions which they serve; 3. an individual cannot be expected to change unless his family system changes (Haley, 1962); 4. "insight" per se is not a prerequisite for change. (p. 365).

Structural-strategic therapists maneuver to get covert control of the therapy session and the family, but do so within the probem framework as defined by the family. The therapist insists, however, that goals for change be put in behavioral terms. Once defined, the meeting of goals becomes the responsibility of the therapist as change agent. If treatment fails, the structural-strategic therapist accepts the fault as his/her own. On the other hand, if the treatment succeeds, the therapist does not accept credit for it because this would purportedly inhibit generalization and durability of change (Stanton, 1981).

Structural-strategic therapists also assume responsibility for determining the structure of the therapy process. In general, all systems of importance are included in therapy; this could include grandparents, teachers, etc. No hard and fast rules exist, however, and structural-strategic therapists will see individuals, parents, couples as the situation demands, although they will continue to conceptualize the problem in large system terms (Madanes & Haley, 1977).

Most structural-strategic therapists limit the number of sessions offered to any particular family. The absolute number appears to be contingent on the problem but, in general, varies from 10-30 sessions (Aponte & Van Deusen, 1981; Stanton, 1981).

Structural-strategic therapists are marked by their pragmatism, adopting any techniques that work including those that do not derive conceptually from structural-strategic models (Aponte & Van Deusen, 1981). Still, certain techniques and beliefs have become a "standard" part of the school's belief system and certain approaches are considered to be unwise or destructive of progress.

One emphasis is on tasks and directives. These tasks are designed to be carried out either between sessions or within sessions and seek to create a structural change in the system. It is hypothesized that extra-session tasks shorten the process of therapy. At times, these tasks and directives are of a paradoxical nature. Hare-Mustin (1976) has described paradoxical interventions as "those which appear absurd because they exhibit an apparently contradictory nature, such as requiring clients to do what in fact they have been doing, rather than requiring that they change, which is what everyone else is demanding" (p. 128). When the therapist, thus, prescribes the system, the family is in a bind; resistance moves them toward improvement, which if they comply, makes them relinquish control to the therapist.

Interpretation, particularly genetic interpretation, is seen as a universal technique since "awareness" of a problem is frequently seen as engendering resistance. A focus on interpretation also may distract the therapist from his/her goals of initiating change in the present. Interpretation, when used, is not concerned with unconscious processes but is aimed at reframing the meaning of a situation.

Research Questions. The most pressing broad question needing investigation within the structural-strategic school concerns the generalization of treatment effects within the family system. Because of the theoretical primacy of the presenting problem, virtually all research projects have assessed change within the identified patient. It has been rare, however, for researchers to investigate change within other individuals or within relationships as suggested by our priority sequence for outcome in Table 1. Suggesting the need for this type of research is not meant to minimize the impressive results reported by structural-strategic researchers (Gurman & Kniskern, 1978a; Stanton, 1981). Assessing change in relationships and individuals would, if found to be in expected directions, support the mechanisms of change suggested by their therapy.

Another important question involves the relative power of and indications for the use of extra-session tasks as compared to the use of tasks within sessions, or enactments (Aponte & Van Deusen, 1981). At present, no empirical evidence exists to suggest that assigning homework procedures changes or speeds up therapy, or the conditions under which tasks of either sort are productive. These interventions are extremely important for the approach in question, and their differential efficacy should be tested. In addition to efficacy, the frequency and timing of family tasks need to be investigated. Moreover, extra-therapy tasks are assigned not only on the assumption that the length of treatment will be affected, but also on the basis that producing such out-of-therapy change during treatment will foster both the generalization and durability of therapeutic effects. Since both structural and strategic therapists do little explicit teaching of interpersonal skills (Apointe & Van Deusen, 1981; Stanton, 1981), as do, say, behavioral family therapists (Gordon & Davidson, 1981; Jacobson, 1981), there is, in our view, good reason to be suspect regarding the durability and generalization of clinical changes achieved during structural-strategic family therapy. In any case, empirical scrutiny in this area seems clearly called for, and, even more specifically, we would like to see addressed the question of whether the use of more educational-instructional interventions increases the durability and generalization of systemic change, once it has been produced by "traditional" methods of restructuring family interactions.

As a major case in point, the usefulness of paradoxical techniques as an alternative to more direct change procedures such as interpretation, skill training, etc., needs to be studied empirically: With what type of families should they be used? Should direct approaches be tried first? Do some families worsen as the result of paradoxical directions as a function, for example, of their openness to change, degree of family disorganization, severity of distress, etc.? A reliance on therapist judgment in the final analysis may be necessitated, but guidelines could be developed to facilitate judgment. For example, Papp (1979), Haley (1976), and Stanton (1981) have suggested some explicit guidelines for the application of paradoxical injunctions, but which dimensions of these guidelines are always necessary to follow, which are more "elective," and which, if not followed, may be harmful, remains to be evaluated. The development of such empirically based guidelines is particularly important if paradoxical directives are as "powerful" as they are considered by most structural-strategic therapists. Moreover, special attention needs to be paid to different categories of paradoxical intervention, for example, paradoxical *instruction*, which calls for specific patient behavior, and paradoxical *observation*, such as the use of "positive connotation," "ascribing noble intention," etc. (Stanton, 1981). It is possible that behaviorally focused versus cognitively focused uses of paradox exert different effects and are potent under different clinical conditions.

Structural-strategic therapists have been second only to the behaviorists in their reliance on technique and their minimal attention to therapist relationship factors. The relative importance of relationship skills versus technical competence has not been investigated. Recent evidence has indicated that therapist relationship factors play an important role in behavioral family therapy (Alexander, Barton, Schiavo & Parsons, 1976). Findings related to relationship skills of structural-strategic therapists might have consequences for training future therapists.

A priority for all schools, as stated previously, is the delineation of the essential ingredients for effective treatment. Perhaps for no school, however, is this as important as for the structural-strategic school. The structural-strategic school explicitly and openly utilizes techniques commonly thought of as behavioral, experiential, communicational, as well as many non-specific techniques utilized by psychotherapists in general. Which of these components reliably produce change, and in what combinations, is a question of crucial importance to further development in the field.

Conclusions

In the last 20 years, the growth of marriage and family therapy has been astounding, in terms of the numbers of its adherents and practitioners, the numbers of its journals and other professional publications and its influence on health delivery systems. There now exists an impressive array of clearly articulated conceptual models of family and marital process and therapy (Gurman & Kniskern, 1981b) each of which has a sizeable and identifiable following. Research on the process (Pinsof, 1981) and outcome (Gurman & Kniskern, 1978a, 1978b, 1981a) of the family therapies has increased perceptibly in both quality and quantity during the last decade. Unfortunately, as has happened so often when other major therapeutic models have been put forth that challenge the psychodynamic tradition in the mental health fields (such as, client-centered therapy, behavior therapy), these newer models seem to require about two to three decades of independent growth before they can begin to reconcile their differences with the models against which they have been in competition. But family therapy comes packaged in many more "brand names" than, say, behavior therapy. Thus, the "good guys-bad guys," "we-they" phenomenon in family therapy incorporates both traditional psychotherapists and many family therapists as "outsiders." This unfortunate political development, due in no small measure to the charisma of many first generation family therapists, has created serious blocks to the emergence of family therapy research which adequately reflects the wealth of clinical and experiential understanding of families that has developed recently (Gurman & Kniskern, 1981b).

There are many reasons for family therapists to be concerned about the near future of family therapy research, not the least of which involves serious fiscal considerations. But beyond this, if family therapy is to broaden its scope of applicability to health delivery systems in general, and its respectability to policy makers in mental health delivery systems, its empircal base and sophistication must progress almost as rapidly as has its theoretical base. In our view, the major route to such progress will come from the scientific study of family therapy that is well informed and influenced by clear-headed clinical understanding.

References

Alexander, J., Barton, C., Schiavo, R., & Parsons, B. Therapist characteristics, family behavior and outcome. *Journal of Consulting and Clinical Psychology*, 1976, *44*, 656-664.

American Psychiatric Association. *Diagnostic and statistical manual (DSM-III)*. Washington, D.C.: APA, 1980.

Andolfi, M. *Family therapy: An interactional approach*. New York: Plenum, 1979.

Aponte, H., & Van Deusen, J. Structural family therapy. In A.S. Gurman & D.P. Kniskern (Eds.), *Handbook of family therapy*. New York: Brunner/Mazel, 1981.

Bergin, A.E. The evaluation of therapeutic outcomes. In A.E. Bergin & S. Garfield (Eds.), *Handbook of psychotherapy and behavior change*. New York: John Wiley and Sons, 1971.

Bergin, A.E., & Strupp, H.H. *Changing frontiers in the science of psychotherapy*. Chicago: Aldine, 1972.

Campbell, D. Personal communication, Spring, 1979.

Fiske, D.W. A source of data is not a measuring instrument. *Journal of Abnormal Psychology.* 1975, *84*, 20-23.

Gartner, R., Fulmer, R., Weinshel, M., & Goldklank, S. The family life cycle: Developmental crises and their structural impact on families in a community mental health center. *Family Process,* 1978, *17*, 47-58.

Gordon, S., & Davidson, N. Behavioral parent training. In A.S. Gurman & D.P. Kniskern (Eds.), *Handbook of family therapy.* New York: Brunner/Mazel, 1981.

Gurman, A. Contemporary marital therapies. A critique and comparative analysis of psychoanalytic, systems and behavioral approaches. In T. Paolino & B. McCrady (Eds.), *Marriage and marital therapy.* New York: Brunner/Mazel, 1978.

Gurman, A., & Kniskern, D. Research on marital and family therapy: Progress, perspective, and prospect. In S. Garfield & A.E. Bergin (Eds.). *Handbook of psychotherapy and behavior change.* Second ed. New York: John Wiley and Sons, 1978a.

Gurman, A., & Kniskern, D. Deterioration in marital and family therapy: Empirical, clinical, and conceptual issues. *Family Process,* 1978b. *17*, 3-20.

Gurman, A., & Kniskern, D. Family therapy outcome research: Knowns and unknowns. In A. Gurman & D. Kniskern (Eds.), *Handbook of family therapy.* New York: Brunner/Mazel, 1981a.

Gurman, A., & Kniskern, D. (Eds.). *Handbook of family therapy.* New York: Brunner/Mazel, 1981b.

Haley, J. Whither family therapy. *Family Process,* 1962, *1*, 69-100.

Haley, J. *Problem solving therapy.* San Francisco: Jossey-Bass, 1976.

Hare-Mustin, R. Paradoxical tasks in family therapy: Who can resist? *Psychotherapy: Theory, Research, and Practice,* 1976, *13*, 128-130.

Jackson, D. The question of family homeostasis. *Psychiatric Quarterly Supplement,* 1957, *31*, 79-90.

Jackson, D. The study of the family. *Family Process,* 1965, *4*, 1-20.

Jacobson, N. A review of research on the effectiveness of marital therapy. In T. Paolino & B. McCrady (Eds.), *Marriage and marital therapy.* New York: Brunner/Mazel, 1978.

Jacobson, N.S. Behavioral marriage therapy. In A.S. Gurman & D.P. Kniskern (Eds.), *Handbook of family therapy.* New York: Brunner/Mazel, 1981.

Klein, M.H., & Gurman, A.S. Ritual and reality: Some clinical implications of research designs. In L.P. Rehm (Eds.), *Behavior therapy for depression.* New York: Academic Press, 1980.

Lambert, M., Bergin, A. & Collins, J. Therapist-induced deterioration in psychotherapy. In A. Gurman & A. Razin (Eds.), *Effective psychotherapy: A handbook of research.* Elmsford, N.Y.: Pergamon Press, 1977.

Madanes, C., & Haley, J. Dimensions of family therapy. *Journal of Nervous and Mental Disease,* 1977, *165,* 88-98.

Minuchin, S. *Families and family therapy,* Cambridge, Mass.: Harvard University Press, 1974.

Minuchin, S., Rosman, B.L., & Baker, L. *Psychosomatic families,* Cambridge, Mass.: Harvard University Press, 1978.

Olson, D.H. *Insiders and outsiders view of relationships: Research strategies.* Paper presented at the Symposium on Close Relationships. University of Massachusetts, 1974.

Papp, P. Paradoxical strategies and countertransference. *American Journal of Family Therapy,* 1979, *7,* 11-12.

Parloff, M.D. The narcissism of small differences—and some big ones. *International Journal of Group Psychotherapy,* 1976, *26,* 311-319.

Pinsof, W. Family therapy process research. In A.S. Gurman & D.P. Kniskern (Eds.), *Handbook of family therapy.* New York: Brunner/Mazel, 1981.

Stanton, M.D. Strategic approaches to family therapy. In A. Gurman & D. Kniskern (Eds.), *Handbook of family therapy.* New York: Brunner/Mazel, 1981.

Wells, R., & Dezen, A. The results of family therapy revisited: The nonbehavioral methods. *Family Process,* 1978, *17,* 251-274.

Watzlawick, P., Weakland, J., & Fisch, R. *Change. Principles of problem foundation and problem resolution.* New York: W. W. Norton and Co., 1974.

Chapter 9

RESEARCHING THE FAMILY THEORIES
OF SCHIZOPHRENIA:
An Exercise In Epistemological
Confusion

Paul F. Dell Ph.D

Introduction

The research to date that has sought to investigate the family theories of schizophrenia has suffered from a major deficiency that has been largely overlooked in the empirical literature. The family versus gene debate about the origin of schizophrenia arose in the 1950s and it has left a lasting mark on all later research in the field. In particular, research in this area has built on earlier investigations of the cognitive and communicative characteristics of schizophrenics. Accordingly, similar research was directed toward other members of schizophrenic families. Such family research benefited from the prior research, but in the process lost much of what is, or should be, unique to the family positions.

This loss was abetted in the mid 1950s by family theories of schizophrenia (and other types of psychopathology) that were in a seminal stage. These theories were an admixture of family theory and individual theory that indiscriminately mixed two epistemologies: one based on force, quantity, and characteristics—the other based on pattern, relationship, and differences (Bateson, 1979). The epistemology of pattern constitutes that which is most truly creative and original in the family theories of psychopathology, but it has been repeatedly ignored and misunderstood. As a consequence, investigators have proceeded on the assumption that family theories of schizophrenia differ from other theories merely in that they posit a different set of etiological factors. This, however, is not the case. The family theories of schizophrenia properly present a different epistemology of schizophrenia and of other forms of mental disorder.

Family Theories of Schizophrenia

Clinical and theoretical interest in the familial roots of schizophrenia was galvanized by Fromm-Reichmann's (1948) classic paper wherein she described the schizophrenogenic mother. Following a latency period of eight years, Bateson, Jackson, Haley, and Weakland (1956) advanced the concept of the *double bind.* Two years later Lidz, Cornelison, Terry and Fleck (1958) described schizophrenic families in terms of the *transmission of irrationality.* Wynne, Ryckoff, Day, and Hirsch (1958) described them in terms of *pseudomutuality* involving transactional thought disorder (Wynne & Singer, 1963). The work of these three groups has been almost solely responsible for generating the now existing body of research on the family theories of schizophrenia. Other clinical theorists (Bowen, 1960, 1978; Haley, 1959; Laing & Esterson, 1964; Laing, 1965; Palazzoli, Boscolo, Cecchin, & Prata, 1978; Scheflen, 1978; Searles, 1959; Whitaker, 1978), have described family interactional bases of schizophrenia. Nevertheless, these theorists have generated almost no research.

Synopsizing the theories of Bateson, Lidz, and Wynne is made difficult by the fact that each theory has evolved and become more comprehensive, such that the three theories now appear more similar than did the original versions (Mishler & Waxler, 1965). As presently constituted, the theories of Bateson, Lidz and Wynne *all* deem language or communication in the family to be of primary significance in the appearance of schizophrenic phenomena within the family.

The emphasis on language and communication is relatively recent for Lidz. In his early thinking, he emphasized the blurring of age and boundaries, and the presence of behavior that is inappropriate to the parents' ages and sex roles. Initially, Lidz spoke of the transmission of irrationality wherein the child learned culturally atypical views about mothers, fathers, families, and the outside world. More recently, Lidz (1972) has strongly emphasized the role of *language* and *categories* as a means of conceptualizing and categorizing experience. He believes that schizophrenic families foster the existence of inappropriately defined *categories* for making sense of one's experience. He considers the impetus for this defective language to lie in the egocentricity of parents who need to maintain their distorted views about themselves and the world. Lidz maintains that the ability of the preschizophrenic to become psychotic is founded on a faulty categorization of experience that further deteriorates when faced with the cognitive egocentrism of adolescence that accompanies Piaget's stage of formal operations (Inhelder & Piaget, 1958). This, together with continued family input and all the developmental crises of adolescence for which the preschizophrenic individual is so ill-prepared, precipitates a psychotic break. In short, Lidz' position on schizophrenia is an elaboration of the ways in which neurotic, narcissistic parents sacrifice their children in the service of maintaining their own precarious adjustment. As such, Lidz has much in common with Fromm-Reichmann's original thinking regarding the schizophrenogenic mother.

At first glance, double bind theory appears to be similar to the positions of Fromm-Reichmann and Lidz. Bateson et al. (1956) described the double bind as a situation wherein the child is subjected to incongruent messages that require him/her to systematically distort and deny important aspects of his/her self and perceptions. Bateson et al. (1956) specified six necessary ingredients of the double bind: (a) two or more persons; (b) repeated experience so that the double bind situation comes to be an habitual expectation; (c) a primary negative injunction of "Do not (or do) do so and so, or I shall punish you"; (d) a secondary injunction conflicting with the first at a more abstract level (also enforced by threats of punishment); (e) a tertiary negative injunction that prevents the victim from fleeing the field and commenting on the paradox; and, (f) once the victim has learned to perceive his universe in double bind patterns, the entire set of ingredients is no longer necessary to precipitate the victim's experience of panic or confusion.

This initial conception of the double bind and his victim was subsequently retraced and re-explained (Bateson et al., 1963; Jackson, 1965; Watzlawick, 1963; Weakland, 1960). The victimizer-victim portrayal violates the systemic epistemology toward which Bateson and his colleagues were striving. The essential concept here is that the double binding behavior of a schizophrenic's mother can only be understood in its context—as a reaction to previous events that constitute the existing relationship. Double binding sequences ensnare both victim and victimizer in the same net. Jackson (1965) pointed out that "there is no possible response to a double bind except an equally or more paradoxical message, so if neither can escape the relationship it can be expected to go on and on until it matters little how it got started" (p. 5).

Double bind theory is not so much a theory as it is an epistemology (Bateson, 1966, 1979) or a language (Weakland, 1974). It is a radically different way of viewing or categorizing the world that focuses on pattern of interaction rather than on single events, discrete elements, or individuals. In this sense, it is not the diagnosed individual who is schizophrenic, but the interaction pattern or relationship in which he/she participates. Similarly, parents do not *cause* schizophrenia with double binds. Rather, all parties behave as they do because within a double bind interaction pattern there is no other way to behave. Thus, Bateson (1960) once suggested that the patient was overtly schizophrenic and the rest of the family was covertly schizophrenic. In short, double bind theory entails an epistemology of organized pattern such that one cannot talk of discrete elements exerting force on one another in a Newtonian cause-and-effect fashion. It is a systemic epistemology that subordinates "elements" to the organization of the whole (pattern).

Wynne et al. (1958) described schizophrenic families as being characterized by *pseudomutuality*, a brittle persistence in maintaining the concept—inaccurate as it may be—that everyone in the family shares the same expectations. In order to preserve this illusion, no divergent or independent expectations are tolerated. The family is set into a rigid mold that does not yield before the vagaries of time and circumstance —even though old expectations and roles may become obsolescent or invalid. The family has a "predominant absorption with fitting together."

The pseudomutuality is maintained, or more accurately, constituted by the transactional thought disorder: "those dawning perceptions and incipient communications which might lead to an articulation of divergent expectations, interests, or individuality are, instead, diffused, doubled, blurred, or distorted" (Wynne et al. 1958, p. 210). Wynne and Singer (1963) emphasize that "the degree of disturbance in family interactions is greater and qualitatively different from that found in the contributions of any individual member" (p. 194). That is, while the isolated statements of any individual member may appear to be normal, when the communicational transaction is considered as a whole, it becomes apparent that there is little maintained focus or direction to what was discussed. Point and meaning get lost, are only fuzzily achieved, or are badly distorted.

Singer and Wynne (1965a) maintain that there is a relationship between parents' styles of handling attention and meaning and the thinking-communication defects found in their schizophrenic children. Along with genetic factors, these parental styles are seen as codeterminants of schizophrenia. Furthermore, Singer and Wynne (1965a) contend that there is a specific fit between the parents' styles of communicating and thinking and those of their offspring:

> ...we have assumed that styles of attending, perceiving, thinking, communicating, and relating used in family transactions are likely to have promoted the cognitive development of the offspring in certain directions, either by serving as models for identification or by eliciting complementary behaviors. It would follow that once an offspring has grown up within a given kind of family, his styles of behaving and experiencing will "fit" into the particular family which, transactionally, has produced him and which he has helped produce (p. 190).

Note that, like Bateson and his colleagues, Wynne and Singer are describing schizophrenia in terms of how it fits within a pattern of communication rather than as being *caused by* certain types of communication (Singer & Wynne, 1965a, 1965b). This distinction is vital to the differences between the epistemologies involved in individual versus family theories of psychopathology, early family theories and later family theories, and inadequate and adequate research of the family theories of schizophrenia.

Researching the Familial Basis of Schizophrenia

The family theories of schizophrenia spawned a first decade of research that can be divided into three groups: parental thought disorders, deviant family communication patterns or styles, and double bind research. This research will not be extensively reviewed, but instead will be placed in its context. The historical meaning, heritage, general outcome, and epistemological underpinnings of these areas of investigation will be explored.

The most traditional of the three areas of research looked for thought disorder in parents of schizophrenics by using concepts and instruments that had already borne results in past research on schizophrenics themselves. Following the early indications of impairment of abstract conceptualization in schizophrenics (Bolles & Goldstein, 1938; Vigotsky, 1934), investigators measured the incidence of conceptual impairment as manifested in overinclusive and underinclusive thinking in parents of schizophrenics. In general, the literature seems to indicate the presence of such thought disorder in parents of schiozphrenics, but the results are fuzzy. Many studies do not show significant thought disorder in these parents; instead, statistical results indicate only strong trends in that direction. The most compelling finding is that very few studies have reported a clear absence of thought disorder in parents of schizophrenics. Lidz was one of the serious researchers in this area of investigation (Lidz, Wild, Schaefer, Rosman & Fleck, 1963; Rosman, Wild, Ricci, Fleck & Lidz, 1964).

The second major area of schizophrenic family research is founded on Wynne and Singer's hypothesis of family communication disorder. Singer and Wynne (1965a) maintain that families have enduring styles of focusing attention, thinking, and relating such that family members fit together in their styles of communication. Singer and Wynne showed that parents' communication style on projective tests could be used to blindly pair parents' test protocols with the projective test protocols of their schizophrenic offspring (Singer & Wynne, 1965b) and that offspring could be diagnosed solely from the test protocols of their parents (Singer & Wynne, 1963, 1965b). Research in this area has shown, with striking consistency, that parents of schizophrenics demonstrate communication deviance. The few failures to replicate these results (Hirsch & Leff, 1971; Wender, Rosenthal, Zahn & Kety, 1971) may be due to some investigators' inability to match Singer's diagnostic acumen (Gunderson, Autry, Mosher & Buchsbaum, 1974; Lidz, 1973).

The third major area of research on schizophrenic families focused on the double bind. This, unquestionably, is the most confused and unproductive of the three areas. Not only is there little apparent empirical support for the double bind hypothesis, but each of the major reviews of this research has either decried the slipperiness of the concept or even contended that the double bind simply does not exist (Abeles, 1976; Gootnick, 1973; Olson, 1972; Pease, 1970; Schuham, 1967; Vetter, 1969). The broadest difficulty is that researchers have continued to argue about what constitutes a double bind and, therefore, what sort of research can be considered to be a valid test of the double bind hypothesis.

The source of this confusion is the persistent failure of most researchers to grasp the epistemological shift inherent in the concept of the double bind (Abeles, 1976; Bateson, 1966; 1979; Weakland, 1974). Granted, there are few tasks—perhaps no task—more difficult than making a complete epistemological shift of perspective. Nevertheless, the task of double bind researchers has been made still more difficult by the inadequate, "too concretistic," and misleading portrayal of this epistemology in the original double bind paper. In particular, Bateson et al. (1956) delineated a recipe for double binding "victims" that dualistically violated the systemic epistemology toward which they were striving. The double bind is not done to someone, it resides in the "interaction-over-time" whereby "important basic relationships are chronically subjected to invalidation through paradoxical interaction" (Abeles, 1976). The correction of this error by Bateson and his colleagues has been largely ignored or misapprehended by subsequent researchers. Typically, the double bind has been interpreted to be a particularly noxious maneuver that may (or may not) drive people away.

During the 1960s, the mounting research evidence of cognitive and communication impairment in parents of schizophrenics was claimed by both family theorists and geneticists as proof of their respective theories of the etiology of schizophrenia. In its most unsophisticated form, the argument of the family theorists contended that parental impairment caused schizophrenia, while others suggested the opposite: schizophrenic family members caused impairment in their parents. Mishler and Waxler (1968) introduced some order into the flurry of claims, refutations, and counterclaims by defining four alternative explanations of the causal relationship between the behavior of a schizophrenic and that of his family.

The etiological explanation is the naive or unsophisticated family theory of schizophrenia. In this view, the interaction patterns observed in the families of schizophrenics are understood to exist prior to the onset of schizophrenia and are directly causal of the patient's illness. The *responsive explanation* is the naive, genetic position. It contends that the distinctive patterns of interaction in schizophrenic families developed along with or in direct response to the onset of schizophrenia. The *situational explanation* suggests that the fact of having a child who is diagnosed as schizophrenic and has been hospitalized affects the family such that they react with different expectations and orientations in a research situation. The *transactional explanation* is the sophisticated family position. It contends that causality must be understood in terms of complex feedback models and sets of interdependent forces. In this view, "attempts to isolate one factor such as prior family relationships as an etiological agent in schizophrenia are viewed as naive and unlikely to be productive" (Mishler & Waxler, 1968, p. 215). The transactional explanation encompasses the epistemological shift inherent in double bind theory. Wender, Rosenthal, Kety, Schulsinger and Welner (1974) provided a fifth explanation of the family data that might be called the sophisticated *genetic explanation*:

> the attributes designated as schizophrenogenic are concomitant, not causal, personality characteristics associated with a parent's being in the schizophrenic spectrum, i.e., the biological parents carry some of the same genetic load as their offspring and that as one manifestation of this load they are cold, rejecting ambivalent, double-binding, etc. (p. 127).

Mishler and Waxler's (1968) analysis of the debate between geneticists and family theorists should have clarified two issues. First, there are at least two identifiable family theories of schizophrenia: *etiological and transactional.* Lidz clearly exemplifies the etiological position, whereas Bateson and Wynne opt for the transactional position and explicitly reject the etiological position (Bateson et al., 1963; Jackson, 1965; Singer & Wynne, 1965b). Although this distinction should have been taken into consideration in designing additional studies, the epistemology of the transactional position continued to baffle investigators who persisted in interpreting the work of Bateson and Wynne as if it represented the etiological position.

Second, in order to maintain credibility, proponents of the etiological position, for example, Lidz and wrongly, Bateson and Wynne, must move beyond correlational data (that shows parents of schizophrenics do have thought and communication disorders) to experimental data that *demonstrate* some deleterious effects of parents on their schizophrenic offspring. This was a timely and reasonable request to impose on advocates of the etiological position. It left untouched, however, the more sophisticated—and more elusive—transactional position.

Two clusters of studies remain to be covered in this review of research on the familial basis of schizophrenia: attempts to directly test the etiological hypothesis and a series of studies by Reiss that stand as the best example of genuine transactional research. These two areas make up most of the second decade of effort to investigate the family theories.

A handful of studies have sought to directly test the effects of parents and schizophrenics on one another. Of these, three used an artificial family design wherein parents of schizophrenics interacted with normals from another family (Haley, 1968; Liem, 1974; Waxler, 1974); in two studies, parents of normals interacted with schizophrenics from another family (Liem, 1974; Waxler, 1974). A fourth study attempted to directly assess the ongoing impact of schizophrenics on their own parents, and vice versa (Dell, 1977).

These studies had no success in demonstrating support for *any* of the hypotheses tested: etiological, responsive, or transactional. In none of these studies were parents of schizophrenics demonstrated to adversely affect the communication or quality of problem-solving of their own schizophrenic offspring or offspring from another family. Similarly, no study was able to demonstrate that schizophrenics adversely affected the communication or quality of problem-solving of their own parents or parents from another family. Inasmuch as these studies could demonstrate no cause to explain the impairment of schizophrenics or their parents, one could conceivably argue that these studies support the sophisticated genetic hypothesis. That is, there are, in fact, no familial causes of the impairment; the deficits are biological. Nevertheless, hidden in the welter of data compiled in these studies are three incidental, anomalous findings.

First, Waxler (1974) found that when tested alone, parents of schizophrenics solved problems as well as parents of normals. Second, following interacting with normal parents, schizophrenics significantly *improved* the quality of their thinking in problem solving as compared to their performance following interaction with schizophrenic parents (Waxler, 1974). Third, in a problem-solving task, parents of schizophrenics tended to make fewer errors when responding to a schizophrenic stranger than when responding to their own schizophrenic families—which is evident in the transactional studies of Reiss.

Reiss' research strategy allowed him to measure the relative contributions of individual and family performance to the completion of experimental tasks (Reiss, 1967a). In contrast to previous researchers who assessed problem-solving when parents gave directions to offspring, Reiss examined the specific impact of family interaction upon the ongoing functioning of its members. Based on this research, Reiss described schizophrenic families as being *consensus-sensitive*, a concept that has much in common with pseudo-mutuality (Wynne et al. 1958):

> In this kind of family there is a joint perception that the analysis and solution of the problems are simply a means to maintain a close and uninterrupted agreement at all times. Even transient dissent is not tolerated.... Family members will quickly surrender their ideas or have others accept them without reference to the externally given cues concerning problem solution.... The family reaches its hastily forged consensus early in the task. If cues and information continue to be provided, the family distorts or oversimplifies them in order to justify its initial collective solution.... (Each individual's) sense of regularity and structure will be derived from the predictability of his family's responses to each new piece of information, not from his own scheme for ordering and patterning the cues themselves (pp. 6-7).

What this means in practice is that, when pretested alone on a task, individual members of schizophrenic families (the patient included) did as well as those of normal families (Reiss, 1967b). Consensus-sensitivity emerged during the subsequent family problem solving session and its effects were measurable when members were later individually retested; members of normal families substantially improved their performance from pretest, but members of schizophrenic families either did not improve or even deteriorated in their performance compared to pretest (Reiss, 1967b). In such problem solving, it makes a difference whether the information necessary to solve the task comes from outside or inside the family. When the information must come from within the family, schizophrenic families perform well (Reiss, 1969); when it must come from outside, they do poorly (Reiss, 1967b, 1968, 1971c, 1971d) unless family members are performing alone (Reiss, 1967b, 1971a, 1971c, 1971d). Perhaps the most dramatic demonstration of consensus-sensitivity is the finding that a schizophrenic family may collectively engage in very poor quality problem-solving despite the fact that its individual members could each do far better when left alone (Reiss, 1971c, 1971d)! It seems that the old adage about committee decisions must be turned on its head when the committee is a schizophrenic family.

In summary, there are five things that can be said about the effort to research the family theories of schizophrenia. First, for the most part the research is naive and epistemologically confused, if not misguided. Few researchers have realized that some of the family theories (Bateson, Wynne and Singer) propose *not* a different etiology of schizophrenia, but a redefinition of what schizophrenia *is*. Under this new definition, the psychotic phenomena that result in the patient being diagnosed as schizophrenic are considered inseparable from the synchronic/diachronic pattern in which they are embedded. The behavior and communication of the rest of the family are all part of this pattern. And, inasmuch as the pattern is a whole, it is no more epistemologiclly correct to isolate from it the cognitive impairment of the parents than it is to isolate the schizophrenic patient from the pattern. Yet, research on parental thought disorder does precisely that.

Second, in accordance with the wholism of such a systemic epistemology, no part of the pattern can be dualistically understood as causing another part of the pattern. The behaviors of family members which together constitute the various aspects of the pattern are not linearly causal of one another, but are co-evolutionary. Bateson (1960) and Singer and Wynne (1965a) speak not of causation but of how the family as a whole fits together. Thus, etiological constructions of the family theory of schizophrenia (e.g., Fromm-Reichmann, Lidz), as embodied in most research to date, neither grasp nor adequately test the transactional position.

Third, the work of Singer and Wynne on communication deviance is seldom correctly understood. Communication deviance is not a characteristic of individual family members that can be equated with traits such as thought disorder. Rather, it is an emergent property of interaction: "the degree of disturbance in family interactions is greater and qualitatively different from that found in the contributions of any individual member" (Wynne & Singer, 1963, p. 194). For example, Wynne (1970) has described a sample of parents of schizophrenics who showed high communication deviance scores, but no "diagnosable psychopathology beyond ordinary neurotic levels." Attempts to test the etiological hypothesis using Wynne and Singer's concept of communication deviance are, in some sense, therefore, double in error. Such research violates at once the epistemology and the construct as defined by its authors.

Fourth, probably the only valid transactional research is that conducted by Singer and Wynne and Reiss. Both series of investigations addressed themselves to family interaction without seeking dualistic, linear causal effects in the family. Wynne and Singer demonstrated transactional fit by diagnosing offspring solely from the communication patterns of their parents. They successfully matched parents and offspring from transcripts of projective test protocols. Reiss was able to demonstrate dramatic family transactional phenomena by comparing the problem-solving performance of members of schizophrenic families when with the family versus when alone. Note, however, that while these researchers investigated transactional phenomena, neither sought to demonstrate that family interaction *causes* schizophrenia.

Fifth, the transactional hypothesis may not be testable. How can one evaluate whether family interaction causes schizophrenia within a theory that specifically denies the validity of such dualistic causality? Co-evolutionary processes simply cannot be construed to be causal. This perspective, of course, is a consequence of the epistemology of pattern which accords importance to the relationships among, rather than to, the components themselves. In addition, the wholism of the pattern precludes the reductionism that has come to be considered almost synonymous with the experimental method. That is, a pattern cannot be examined by the traditional approach of holding all factors constant except the variable being investigated. The self-recursiveness of the patterned field of interaction frustrates attempts to provide such experimental control by immediately changing the very pattern that one is trying to investigate. In fact, part of the problem is that attempts to investigate schizophrenia—and attempts to diagnose and treat it—are actually integral features of the schizophrenic pattern itself.

Schizophrenia and the Epistemology of Pattern

Western thinking is primarily dominated by an Aristotelian/Cartesian/Newtonian epistemology. In this view, what is real is what can be weighed and measured. Objects and things are accorded the status of primary reality. The word "real," reflects this epistemology. It comes from the Latin word *res* which means "thing." Things are considered to be imbued with absolute characteristics that constitute the nature of the object. Such characteristics include weight, size, energy (e.g. heat or velocity), hardness, and so on. Thus, any object can be assessed on a variety of *quantitative* dimensions. The nature of the object is understood to be specified by the quantity that it has on each relevant dimension. This perspective underlies the successes of Newtonian physics in that it allows one to calculate the behavior of physical objects such as falling bodies, billiard balls, and so on. This classical mechanics portrays a deterministic, cause-and-effect world where the outcome of any set of events can be analyzed and predicted, if only one knows beforehand the quantified characteristics of the objects involved. The world described by this epistemology is one where change is reversible. For example, the ball in a six-cushion billiard shot can be returned to its original position by applying to it the same quantity of force in the opposite direction.

The epistemology of pattern (in Western thinking) comes from Pythagoras, Plato, and Gnosticism. In contrast to the Aristotelian orientation to things with quantified characteristics, the epistemology of patterns orients to shapes, forms and relations. It looks not at objects themselves, but at the "pattern which connects" them (Bateson, 1979). It is a relational reality wherein the actuality of any "object" is inseparable from the pattern in which it is embedded. The pattern or context is primary; the object within it is secondary. Patterns are assessed in terms of *quality* rather than quantity. That is, patterns are discontinuous. A pattern derives its quality from its specified form. If the form is altered in any way, so too is the pattern altered. There is no way for the quality of the pattern to become "more" or "less" without changing the quality (and the pattern). Thus, whereas change in the Aristotelian/Newtonian sense is continuous and reversible, change in pattern is always discontinuous and irreversible. The epistemology, or perhaps more accurately, the metaphysics of pattern does not afford the ability to analyze and manipulate by design. One can intervene in a pattern at the level of objects, but one cannot intervene at the level of the pattern itself. The "pattern which connects" is not accessible to conscious design; it may only be impacted in a stochastic fashion. That is, one can only intervene at the level of objects and, thereby, bring about a change in the pattern, but the exact nature of the change can be neither predicted nor designed. In short, patterns can be changed by disrupting them, but they cannot be sculpted to a planned design.

Modern psychiatric thinking is essentially Aristotelian. People are considered to have quantities of various properties (i.e., personality) which determine their behavior. The personalities of parents and their children are understood to be related to one another in a Newtonian fashion. That is, the parents are believed to have certain fixed characteristics which act as forces on their children with more or less predictable causal effects—a sort of billiard ball physics of human interaction. When it comes to schizophrenia, even this Newtonian form of human interaction is abandoned. Schizophrenics are understood to be impaired by their very nature (i.e., biologically and genetically). Clinically, the relevant characteristic of any given schizophrenic is his/her degree (quantity) of impairment. The patient is assessed in terms of quantity of social skills, thought disorder, aggressiveness, and so on. Similarly, changes in the patient are measured in a quantitative fashion: he/she is "more assertive," "less aggressive," "more socially appropriate," and even "less crazy." Therapeutic interventions seek to reverse the patient from schizophrenic or psychotic to normal.

The epistemology of pattern which underlies family therapy contends that classical deterministic physics is not a useful model or metaphor for human interaction. According to this view, there is no calculus of human interaction to apply to a great, interpersonal billiard table. Similarly, individuals do not have quantities of inherent characteristics. Instead, humans behave with some regularity because of the patterns in which they participate. The pattern, itself, is primary and cannot be reduced for experimental analysis. As Abeles has noted, "it is not possible to isolate the participants and components and events and history and context of a pattern and still have that pattern" (1976, p. 147). The same is true of the schizophrenic and context. It is not possible to isolate the schizophrenic and family and their interaction and their history and the patient's diagnosis and hospitalization and the context of the patient in the family and the context of schizophrenia in psychiatry today and still have the pattern that Bateson and Wynne and Singer call schizophrenia.

Isolating these components from one another, which is done in the daily treatment of schizophrenics, obscures the pattern and mystifies those who are part of it. The Aristotelian act of according independent, self-sufficient status to each of these components is the praxis which actually *constitutes* and drives the pattern. That is, the family's isolation of the patient as deviant, their ways of handling deviance (i.e., schizophrenia), medicine's way of handling such deviance (i.e., hospitalization, diagnosis, drugs), and the patient's response to all of the foregoing constitutes the pattern. Thus, medicine's "schizophrenia" is but an *aspect* of the pattern that is called "schizophrenia" by family epistemology.

Family epistemology and the medical model are looking at two different schizophrenias. The medical model focuses on a schizophrenia, tied to cognitive disorder, which is always present in the individual. Family theory focuses on a schizophrenia, tied to social interaction, which assists an individual to be generally incompetent and periodically psychotic. The essential difference is that family theory may concede the validity of a subtle, inherent impairment, but does not agree that such impairment is relevant to interactional schizophrenia.

Family epistemology contends that psychiatry's difficulty in treating schizophrenics stems from the medical model's incompatability with, and unwitting participation in, the schizophrenic pattern. This inability of the participants (patient, family, therapists, etc.) to extract themselves from or even perceive the epistemological web in which they are embedded has been aptly termed *metabinding* by Wynne (1978). Such metabinding not only operates in trying to treat schizophrenics, but also in attempts to grasp the family theories of schizophrenia. That is, the epistemology of pattern simply cannot be adequately described or interpreted from within the Aristotelian/Newtonian epistemology that pervades modern psychiatry and psychology. Unfortunately, this is what has happened. Family epistemology has been reduced to a simplistic and inaccurate view by those who have sought to test it experimentally: "Parents drive their offspring crazy." Accordingly, a great deal of research has subjected to microscopic analysis the thinking and communication of schizophrenic families. Yet, as noted above, thought disorder is largely irrelevant to the family epistemology of schizophrenia. In fact, epistemological consideration aside, it can even be shown, solely in terms of the socially relevant aspects of schizophrenia, that thought disorder is a poor choice of phenomenon to study.

True, thought disorder is what usually causes an individual to be diagnosed "schizophrenic." But once having diagnosed "schizophrenia" in an individual, what has one accomplished? To be sure, one eventually succeeds in defining a population of individuals with something in common: a thought disorder, a diagnosis of schizophrenia, perhaps even a common biolgical-genetic defect. Continued research on this population will accumulate knowledge about thought disorder and biological defects. Nevertheless, such a research strategy contributes little to a social understanding of schizophrenia. Remember, schizophrenia is first, and foremost, a *social* phenomenon.

There are many schizophrenics with thought disorders who have never been hospitalized. Furthermore, those who have been hospitalized have not been institutionalized because of their thought disorder, but because they were disruptive to the point where their environment refused to tolerate them (Gruenberg, 1967; Langsley & Kaplan, 1968). The law implicitly recognizes this same distinction. People are not committed because they have a thought disorder, but because they are also judged a danger to themselves or others. In short, it is not possible to talk about schizophrenia without talking about deviance and how it is managed by particular families and society in general.

Erikson has suggested that all social systems induce deviant behavior and that the volume of deviance induced is directly correlated with the amount of concern expended to control it (Dentler & Erikson, 1959; Erikson, 1966). Waxler (1975) applied this thinking to family systems and noted that:

> we would expect that the volume of deviance in a family is directly related to the family's concern with and capacity to sanction deviance. How much time and effort the family is willing to put into rewarding and punishing members to keep them in line will determine how much behavior they are willing to call "deviant" (p. 44)

It must be added, of course, that such deviance control is part of a self-recursive creative spiral wherein control begets deviance, which begets control, new kinds of deviance, and sudden transformations in control/deviance (violence, psychotic behavior, imprisonment, hospitalization, etc.).

Schizophrenic families are highly concerned with the management of deviance. They have been described as "pseudomutual," "consensus-sensitive," "highly reactive," and having a "predominant absorption with fitting together." Both research and clinical data concur in describing this concern with the management of deviance as being family-wide, rather than specifically directed at the patient. Deviance control, thus, seems to be part of the greater pattern within which the patient exists. In this sense, chicken or egg questions regarding the time of onset of the patient's psychosis vis-a-vis the family's consensus-sensitivity are irrelevant in that, either way, both psychosis and deviance control are part of the pattern. It may be that those people with thought disorders who never present for treatment do so because their deviance has not been amplified by pseudomutuality and consensus-sensitivity. Presently, however, the only available data pertain to those patients who *have* presented for treatment; *their* families are pseudomutual. Only epidemiological field work could answer the question as to whether thought disordered nonpatients live in families that are not consensus-sensitive. Nevertheless, there is some very suggestive analogous data on cerebral palsied children. Schaffer (1964) described a phenomenon similar to consensus-sensitivity in a subset of parents of cerebral palsied children. These families were "too cohesive." Specifically, they became insular as the parents dropped relationships with friends and relatives and reduced job time and community participation in order to devote themselves to the care of their cerebral palsied child. This high concern for the child's deviant (sick) role resulted in a sharp increase in deviance in the child compared to other cerebral palsied children from families that were not "too cohesive." In particular, children from too cohesive families were more helpless, emotionally dependent, egocentric, and uncooperative. This finding bears out Erikson's contention that increased concern with managing deviance begets greater deviance. It would seem reasonable, therefore, to assume that the social and interactional aspects of schizophrenia can be considerable.

Those who hold conventional views of schizophrenia typically concede the validity of the social elements of psychotic episodes and hospitalization, but consider them to be simply "noise" variables. That is, psychiatrists usually admit that environmental factors play a role in worsening the patient's condition and in complicating his/her treatment, but not a role in the schizophrenia itself. In short, such concessions do not deter psychiatry from its hubris of assuming that it knows already the nature of the "disease" and, therefore, pronouncing social and environmental factors to be irrelevant to the reality of schizophrenia. This assumption is a major impetus behind the attempts of DSM III to narrow the definition of schizophrenia to the point where "extraneous" factors can be proved to play no role in the "disease." In this sense, Psychiatry is engaged in a Platonic search for the good or real schizophrenic. The only good schizophrenic, of course, is one that is self-sufficient—one who is able to become schizophrenic without the taint of environmental variables.

Family theories of psychopathology are inescapably social in both their ideology and epistemology. It is fair to say that it is of little importance to family theorists that there exists a population of people, both diagnosed and undiagnosed, with thought disorders. What matters is that there is a population of people who are engaged in an interactional process involving their family, the legal system, and medical establishment that culminates in irrational behavior, incarceration, labeling, and general personal incompetence. In particular, the active psychotic state that causes people to be hospitalized is considered by family theory to be the outcome of an escalating interactional process between patient and family. Through this process, the patient is defined as incompetent and maintained in that role by the manner in which patient and family provoke each other to react. Or, to state this another way, psychosis is both a disordered state and a social role, and family theory accords extreme importance to the latter. The process that keeps the patient in the role of incompetent is considered to periodically escalate into the disordered state of active psychosis. Hospitalizing the patient is, thus, seen to be a most powerful component of this process that reaffirms the patient in his role of incompetence! In short, family theories would say that schizophrenia *is* the process that brings people to hospitals as opposed to schizophrenia being thought disorders, cognitive defects, ego weaknesses, and a set personality organization.

From this frame of reference, studies that investigate communication and thinking in schizophrenic families are anachronistic and epistemologically confused. Such investigation focuses attention on an overly narrow feature of families with schizophrenia and helps to preserve an illusion that family theories stand or fall on the question of parental thought and communication disorder. Research that is germane to the interactional view of schizophrenia would investigate the interaction involved in perpetual incompetence and psychotic episodes, rather than the subtleties of cognitive disorder.

REFERENCES

Abeles, G. Researching the unresearchable: Experimentation on the double bind. In C. E. Sluzki, & D. C. Ransom (Eds.), *Double bind.* New York: Grune & Stratton, 1976.

Bateson, G. Minimal requirements for a theory of schizophrenia. *Archives of General Psychiatry*, 1960, *2*, 477-491.

Bateson, G. Slippery theories. Comment on "Family interaction and schizophrenia: A review of current theories," by E. G. Mishler & N. E. Waxler. *International Journal of Psychiatry*, 1966, *2*, 415-417.

Bateson, G. *Mind and nature: A necessary unity.* New York: Dutton, 1979.

Bateson, G., Jackson, D. D., Haley, J., & Weakland, J. H. Toward a theory of schizophrenia. *Behavioral Science*, 1956, *1*, 251-264.

Bateson, G., Jackson, D. D., Haley, J., & Weakland, J. H. A note on the double bind—1962. *Family Process*, 1963, *2*, 154-161.

Bolles, M., & Goldstein, K. A study of impairment of "abstract behavior" in schizophrenic patients. *Psychiatric Quarterly*, 1938, *12*, 42-65.

Bowen, M. A family concept of schizophrenia. In D. D. Jackson (Ed.), *The etiology of schizophrenia.* New York: Basic Books, 1960.

Bowen, M. Schizophrenia as a multi-generational phenomenon. In M. M. Berger (Ed.), *Beyond the double bind.* New York: Brunner/Mazel, 1978.

Dell, P. F. *The relationship between the communication of parents and sons in schizophrenic and normal families.* Unpublished doctoral dissertation, University of Texas at Austin, 1977.

Dentler, R. A., & Erikson, K. The functions of deviance in groups. *Social Problems*, 1959, *7*, 98-107.

Erikson, K. *Wayward puritans.* New York: John Wiley and Sons, 1966.

Fromm-Reichmann, F. Notes on the development of treatment of schizophrenics by psychoanalytic psychotherapy. *Psychiatry*, 1948, *11*, 263-273.

Gootnick, A. T. Double bind hypothesis: A conceptual and empirical review. *Journal Supplement Abstract Service Catalog of Selected Documents in Psychology*, 1973, *3*, 86, Manuscript 417.

Gruenberg, E. M. The social breakdown syndrome—some origins. *American Journal of Psychiatry*, 1967, *123*, 1481-1489.

Gunderson, J. G., Autry, J. H., Mosher, L. R., & Buchsbaum, S. Special report: Schizophrenia, 1974. *Schizophrenia Bulletin*, 1974, *9*, 16-54.

Haley, J. The family of the schizophrenic: a model system. *Journal of Nervous and Mental Disease*, 1959, *129*, 357-374.

Haley, J. Testing parental instructions to schizophrenic and normal children: A pilot study, *Journal of Abnormal Psychology*, 1968, *73*, 559-565.

Hirsch, S.R., & Leff, J.P. Parental abnormalities of verbal communication in the transmission of schizophrenia. *Psychological Medicine, 1971, 1,* 118-127.

Inhelder, B., & Piaget, J. *The growth of logical thinking: From childhood to adolescence.* New York: Basic Books, 1958.

Jackson, D. D. The study of the family. *Family Process, 1965, 4,* 1-20.

Laing, R.D. Mystification, confusion, and conflict. In I. Boszormenyi-Nagy & J.L. Framo (Eds.) *Intensive family therapy.* New York: Harper & Row, 1965.

Laing, R. D., & Esterson, A. *Sanity, madness and the family.* Baltimore: Penguin Books, 1964.

Langsley, D. G., & Kaplan, D. M. *The treatment of families in crisis.* New York: Grune and Stratton, 1968.

Lidz, T. Egocentric cognitive regression and a theory of schizophrenia. Proceedings of the Fifth World Congress on Psychiatry, Amsterdam: Excerpta Media, 1972.

Lidz, T. *The origin and treatment of schizophrenic disorders.* New York: Basic Books, Inc., 1973.

Lidz, T., Cornelison, A., Terry, D., & Fleck, S. Intrafamilial environment of the schizophrenic patient: VI: The transmission of irrationality. A.M.A. Archives of Neurology and Psychiatry, 1958, *79,* 305-316.

Lidz, T., Wild, C., Schaefer, S., Rosman, B., & Fleck, S. Thought disorders in the parents of schizophrenic patients: A study utilizing the Object Sorting Test. *Journal of Psychiatric Research,* 1963, *1,* 193-200.

Liem, J. H. Effects of verbal communications of parents and children: A comparison of normal and schizophrenic families. *Journal of Consulting and Clinical Psychology,* 1974, *42,* 438-450.

Mishler, E. G., & Waxler, N. E. Family interaction processes and schizophrenia: A review of current theories. *Merrill-Palmer Quarterly,* 1965, *11,* 269-315.

Mishler, E., & Waxler, N. Family interaction and schizophrenia: Alternative frameworks of interpretation. *Journal of Psychiatric Research,* 1968, *6,* 213-222.

Olson, D. H. Empirically unbinding the double bind: A review of research and conceptual reformulations, *Family Process,* 1972, *11,* 69-94.

Palazzoli, M. S., Boscolo, L., Cecchin, G., & Prata, G. *Paradox and counterparadox.* New York: Jason Aronson, 1978.

Pease, K. Is the "double bind" a myth? *New Society,* 1970, *16,* 538-539.

Reiss, D. Individual thinking and family interaction: I. Introduction to an experimental study of problem solving in families of normals, character disorders and schizophrenics. *Archives of General Psychiatry,* 1967(a), *16,* 80-93.

Reiss, D. Individual thinking and family interaction: II. A study of pattern recognition and hypothesis testing in families of normals, character disorders, and schizophrenics. *Journal of Psychiatric Research*, 1967(b), *5*, 193-211.

Reiss, D. Individual thinking and family interaction: III. An experimental study of categorization performance in families of normals, those with character disorders and schizophrenics. *Journal of Nervous and Mental Disease*, 1968.

Reiss, D. Individual thinking and family interaction: IV. A study of information exchange in families of normals, those with character disorders and schizophrenics. *Journal of Nervous and Mental Disease*, 1969, *149*, 473-490.

Reiss, D. Intimacy and problem-solving: An automated procedure for testing a theory of consensual experience in families. *Archives of General Psychiatry*, 1971(a), *25*, 442-455.

Reiss, D. Varieties of consensual experience: I. A theory for relating family interaction to individual thinking. *Family Process*, 1971(b), *10*, 1-28.

Reiss, D. Varieties of consensual experience: II. Dimensions of a family's experience of its environment. *Family Process*, 1971(c), *10*, 28-35.

Reiss, D. Varieties of consensual experience: III. Contrast between families of normals, delinquents, and schizophrenics. *Journal of Nervous and Mental Disease*, 1971(d), *152*, 73-95.

Rosman, B., Wild, C., Ricci, J., Fleck, S., & Lidz, T. Thought disorders in the parents of schizophrenic patients: A further study utilizing the Object of Sorting Test. *Journal of Psychiatric Research*, 1964, *2*, 211-221.

Schaffer, H. R. The too-cohesive family: A form of group pathology. *International Journal of Social Psychiatry*, 1964, *10*, 266-275.

Scheflen, A. Communicational concepts of schizophrenia. In M. M. Berger (Ed.), *Beyond the double bind*. New York: Brunner/Mazel, 1978.

Schuham, A. I. The double bind hypothesis a decade later. *Psychological Bulletin*, 1967, *68*, 409-416.

Searles, J. F. The effort to drive the other person crazy—an element in the etiology and psychotherapy of schizophrenia. *British Journal of Medical Psychology*, 1959, *32*, 1-18.

Singer, M. T., & Wynne, L. C. Differentiating characteristics of parents of childhood schizophrenics, childhood neurotics, and young adult schizophrenics. *American Journal of Psychiatry*, 1963, *120*, 234-243.

Singer, M. T., & Wynne, L. C. Thought disorder and family relations of schizophrenics: III. Methodology using projective techniques. *Archives of General Psychiatry*, 1965a, *12*, 187-200(a).

Singer, M. T., & Wynne, L. C. Thought disorder and family relations of schizophrenics: IV. Results and implications. *Archives of General Psychiatry,* 1965b, *12,* 201-212(b).

Vetter, H. *Language, behavior and psychopathology.* Chicago: Rand McNally, 1969.

Vigotsky, L. S. Thought in Schizophrenia, *Archives of Neurology and Psychiatry,* 1934, 31, 1063-1077.

Watzlawick, P. Patterns of psychotic communication. In P. Doucet & C. Laurin (Eds.), *Problems of psychosis,* Amsterdam: Excerpta Medica, 1963.

Waxler, N. E. Parent and child effects on cognitive performance: An experimental approach to the etiological and responsive theories of schizophrenia. *Family Process,* 1974, *13,* 1-22.

Waxler, N. E. The normality of deviance: An alternate explanation of schizophrenia in the family. *Schizophrenia Bulletin,* 1975, *14,* 38-47.

Weakland, J. H. The "double-bind" hypothesis of schizophrenia and three-party interaction. In D. D. Jackson (Ed.), *The etiology of schizophrenia.* New York: Basic Books, Inc., 1960.

Weakland, J. H. The "double-bind" theory by self-reflexive hindsight. *Family Process,* 1974, *13,* 269-277.

Wender, P. H., Rosenthal, D., Kety, S. S., Schulsinger, F. & Welner, J. Cross-fostering: A research strategy for clarifying the role of genetic and experiential factors in the etiology of schizophrenia. *Archives of General Psychiatry,* 1974, *31,* 121-128.

Wender, P., Rosenthal, D., Zahn, T., & Kety, S. The psychiatric adjustment of the adopting parents of schizophrenics. *American Journal of Psychiatry,* 1971, *127,* 1013-1018.

Whitaker, C. Co-therapy of chronic schizophrenia. In M. M. Berger (Ed.), *Beyond the double bind.* New York: Brunner/Mazel, 1978.

Wynne, L. C. Communication disorders and the quest for relatedness in families of schizophrenics. *American Journal of Psychoanalysis,* 1970, *30,* 100-114.

Wynne, L. Knotted relationships, communication deviances, and meta-binding. In M. M. Berger (Ed.), *Beyond the double bind.* New York: Brunner/Mazel, 1978.

Wynne, L. C., Ryckoff, I. M., Day, J. & Hirsch, S. I. Pseudomutuality in the family relations of schizophrenics, *Psychiatry,* 1958, *21,* 205-220.

Wynne, L. C., & Singer, M. D. Thought disorder and family relations of schizophrenics. I. A research strategy. *Archives of General Psychiatry,* 1963, *9,* 191-198.

Chapter 10

An Anthropological View
of Family Therapy

Howard F. Stein Ph.D.

Introduction

Clinical Ethnography: A Vignette

During a consultation with family practice residents, one resident asked me to come into his examination room and see a 16-year-old patient with her mother. He told me only that he had been working with Karen for nearly a year on her obesity problem using a variety of behavioral, self-monitoring and record-keeping techniques. These just had not worked. Karen was also hypertensive, and somewhat on the depressed side, he said. I asked if the mother sat in on every encounter with the patient. Yes, she not only brings her five children, ranging from ages four through 20, but comes into the examining room and office with each of them, staying through their appointment. I asked what the other children looked like. All obese. And the mother: very slim, in her late thirties, craggy and weather worn, many diffuse physical problems of her own. At this point, I know no "history" whatsoever.

Although this physician and I had collaborated on a number of family sessions, home visits, and individual cases, I wanted to make certain that we agreed on my role before we went into the examining room. In this first encounter, we agreed that I would mostly observe. I suggested to him that at some time during the session he might ask Karen what she would fantasize doing if she were not obese. So far everything had focused on her obesity. Even attempts at improving her self-esteem were based on the self-defeating assumption: "You should really start feeling good about yourself even though you are fat." He first asked them in private if it was all right for me to sit in. They agreed.

I entered the room, finding Karen sitting on the end of the examining table, bent slightly forward, eyes mostly on the floor. The physician sat on a stool to her left. Her mother, Joyce K., sat in a corner to Karen's right, about ten feet away. I pulled up a chair in the corner midway between the mother, daughter, and physician. To my surprise, the physician began with my question, directed to Karen. Karen looked up briefly, smiled, looked to her mother, gave a brief reply, and again slouched forward. As the physician asked a variety of questions, the sequence was repeated each time. Sometimes the mother would answer for Karen. Sometimes the daughter's glance would seem to be a go-ahead signal for mother to intervene. On one occasion, Joyce answered for Karen; Karen told her to shut up; after the physician's next question, Karen looked again to her mother, engaging re-entry.

The physician asked Karen how her left forearm was doing, the one she had burned about two weeks earlier while making french fries! The mother immediately intervened: "It still hurts. She probably needs something to put on it." Further confirmation of an hypothesis: mother-daughter inseparability. I wondered, but did not ask, whether Mrs. K. had always been so slim, and what in the world Karen had been doing making french fries at home in the first place, if the mother's purpose in coming to the treatment room was to help her daughter lose weight. The physician suggested that Karen buy a paperback book, *Think Yourself Thin*.

I decided to voice an observation, directed to Karen: "Karen, I noticed that every time the doctor asks you a question, you look to your mother, almost like you are asking her to answer for you. I wonder if you can answer on your own." Karen burst into tears, sobbing, burying herself in her hands —the first eruption of feeling beyond her usual apathy in a year of treatment. Joyce immediately instructed her not to cry, but the physician countered that it was all right for her to express her feelings. Karen composed herself, and said, looking at her mother, "I know what my mother went through, and I'm scared to go through it."

This provided the leverage needed to defocus from the daughter, and focus at least momentarily on the mother. Joyce recounted briefly that when she was small she had been fat, ridiculed, and isolated. "When I was 16, a junior in high school (precisely Karen's age and class), I took one look in the mirror and didn't like what I saw. I resolved to lose weight, and I did." Shortly thereafter, the session terminated. At least temporarily, the dam had broken, and this only by paying attention to the relationship from which Karen's obesity cannot be separated.

Within 15 minutes, a family pattern had become clear. The hefty charts on all members of the family—except the father, who almost predictably is never sick—further corroborated the impression of what can variously be called an enmeshed family (Minuchin, 1974) or a family projection process (Bowen, 1978), and the like. In a subsequent session with Joyce and Karen, I learned that not only did each member contribute to the family-owned retail business, but each was literally the business of every other family member; that no family member could think of a personal distinct interest or hobby apart from the family, and that home and business were both contiguous to and extensions of one another, spatially and relationally. Certainly, obesity has a number of medically pathological sequelae. But for this family, obesity meant something more. It was a way of life. Karen's obesity was an identified issue for constant family discussion. Yet, their labeling of it and focusing on it was their way of not identifying other facts and problems that had to do with each and all.

In this family medicine setting I was doing little different from what I had been doing for nearly a decade with first, second, third, and fourth-generation Slovak- and Ruthene-American families: observing family dynamics and attempting to bridge the methodological/ideological chasm between the levels of individual psychodynamics, family process, and culture (Stein, 1973, 1974, 1976a, 1978a, 1978b; Stein & Hill, 1977). The major difference is that now I try to engage my subjects, whether they be families in illness or physicians in training, in their own self-corrective ethnography. What I call clinical ethnography consists not only in observing as an anthropologist what the natives are doing and saying, but serving as the didactic and therapeutic observing ego who provides feedback to those observed on what has been observed.

Anthropology, the Family, and Family Therapy

What would be an anthropological view of family therapy? Certainly there is hardly any more unanimity of theory and method in anthropology than there is in family therapy. Nonetheless, an anthropological approach would stress the ubiquity and nature of the human family and would view family therapy as a recent, culturally innovative way of describing, conceptualizing, explaining, and treating illness. The value of an anthropological perspective is that it offers the evolutionary depth, and cross-cultural breadth, to provide a comprehensive context for explaining human nature, diversities, and universals alike. Anthropologists are interested in systems of relationships, and the meanings given to them, which, in turn, perpetuate or modify those relationships.

The anthropological approach is distinguishable conceptually from other behavioral sciences by its holism and methodologically by its commitment to naturalistic observation. It is precisely the open endedness of free-floating attention that allowed me to decipher quickly the family-culture pattern of this family group. At its best, the ethnographic method is a mode of inquiry that does not mutilate and, thus, distort its object of study with compulsively sanitized criterial preselections (La Barre, 1978). The reason is simple: preoccupation with method has the consequence, if not intent, of excluding the unanticipatably significant in the service of confirming the expected (Devereux, 1967). Devereux notes that "theories are 'proven' by studying subjects educated to behave in conformity with these theories." (p. 195), an education that lamentably applies as often to researchers as to their official subjects.

I shall argue that:(a) the human family is rooted in the invariants of a distinctive human biology; (b) family/group therapies of all varieties can be found universally; and (c) family therapy as a set of distinct, often competing, theoretical propositions, observational perspectives, and treatment modes is rooted in the American present. I first briefly address this latter issue: Why family therapy now?

Two complementary points of view come to mind. On the one hand, family therapy is clearly a social movement (Blumer, 1969), specifically, a revitalization movement (Wallace, 1956) expressing a wider cultural concern for the rescue and rehabilitation of the family unit from the narcissistic excesses of rabid individualism. As social thought has turned increasingly toward group identity and away from the individual identity, attempts are being made to strengthen family, ethnic, racial, neighborhood, religious, and regional units (Stein & Hill, 1977).

At the same time, family theory/therapy are strikingly lineal descendants of individual oriented psychoanalytic investigation, this despite the ideological chasm between them. Family theory/therapy is continuous, rather than discontinuous with investigations of human behavior begun by Freud and his colleagues (Sander, 1978). It is a matter of the expansion and inclusion of contexts. Classical psychoanalysis was based on the reconstruction of childhood conflicts from adult memory, based on the transference, resistances, and free association. Subsequent research-clinicians sought to understand normal and pathological development from the child's point of view: such as play therapy with children (Erikson, 1963) and the observation of early mother-infant interaction (Caudill, 1973; Mahler, Bergman & Pine, 1975). The observation of interaction patterns, verbal and nonverbal, in whole families with psychotic or psychosomatic members (Bowen, 1978; Henry, 1967; Minuchin, 1974) is an essential extension of the earliest investigation. In family therapy, one is able both to observe intrafamilial transference and to experience how the family tries to engage the therapist in its conflict structure.

A crucial difference, however, remains in that the theoretical, clinical, and research focus of family therapy is the distinct personality of the family system, while traditional psychiatry has drawn its professional boundary around the individual character of the identified patient (Sander, 1978). The difference lies in the choice of data that is regarded as valid and in what is done with that data (Eisenberg, 1977; Stein & Kayzakian-Rowe, 1978). An anthropological perspective on treatment modes suggests that this apparent dichotomy is, in fact, an illusion.

From an evolutionary perspective, the family is inextricably part of our species-specific human biology, as much a part of our adaptive specialization as is the enlarged pelvis for bipedal walking. The mother/father/child trinity of the nuclear family is the biologically basic social unity. This unit may be expressed by different forms of marriage and by greater or lesser extensions both laterally and generationally, but it remains the molecule from which larger social forms are built (La Barre, 1968).

The dizzying variety of alternate family lifestyles does not impugn the immutability of this norm, but, rather, attests to it by self-conscious negation. As Spiro (1979) observes in his restudy of the Israeli kibbutz a quarter-century after his initial study, the communal form of life is becoming a kin-based society with an instrumental and affective division of labor based on sex whose origin is not the European Jewish shtetl but the hunter-gatherer band. The family is, mutatis mutandis, quite a stabile unity throughout history.

What might be called family or communal therapy figures prominently throughout the preliterate world. As Turner (1975) notes, in so-called primitive diagnosis, divination is a process in which the group attempts to discover the pathology in the identified patient's social field. Illness is perceived as a symptom of the disruption of the social and natural order, an order the entire family and community have a stake in restoring. Without doing injustice to the immense variation in theories of disease etiology cross-culturally, one can generalize that primitive illness is commonly traced to some interpersonal cause of imbalance, some affront to the harmony of interpersonal relations including ancestors, ghosts, spirits, if not the cosmos.

Once the etiology (explanation) is determined and the diagnosis made, the appropriate treatment follows. The same deductive model applies, incidentally, to the range of modern pychotherapies as well. Primitive therapies involve public rituals that include not only the immediate extended family, but often the entire kin group or village (Foster & Anderson, 1978; Turner, 1969, 1975). Family, group, or societal therapy can be mobilized not only in the service of the patient's support, recovery, and reintegration in the social order, but just as often, in the service of isolating, extruding, pronouncing socially dead, or killing the one who has been diagnosed as deviant from the norm.

In all cases, the ritual which manifestly concerns itself with the prognosis and disposition of the identified patient, latently expresses the wish of the group for the restoration of the status quo ante (Hallowell, 1955; Wallace, 1966). Here, the patient is the group's delegate (Stierlin, 1973), its temporary homeostat, and an excellent measure of the group's conflicts (Hay, 1971). By defocusing on the identified patient, we come to know the basis for the family or group's stability and upset. Thus, in the opening vignette, to focus on obese Karen as the problem patient is to use the cultural medical model to confirm a tacit family rule: the denial that Karen's obesity is a systemic pathology.

In much of primitive therapy, the patient's illness is experienced as the family's or community's dysfunction (Foster & Anderson, 1978). One could not speak of a more enmeshed, symbiotic family. Yet, despite the magical thinking involved in the interpretation and treatment of disease, this is unmistakably family or macrosystems therapy. Disorders, which we so neatly parse into mental, physical, behavioral, and psychosomatic, are seen as various metaphors of some systemic disturbance. There is the conviction that the disturbance pervades a relationship system.

To summarize: from evolutionary and cross-cultural consideration, we conclude that:(a) the homeostatic model is virtually universal; (b) primitive therapy accepts that the social milieu is part of the disturbing or disturbed system, and likewise part of the system for restoring equilibrium; and (c) an understanding of pathogenesis and treatment for human malaises calls for a truly relational biology. By the latter, I mean that relationships both impinge on the organism and, through internalization, are experienced as being inside.

Anthropological Contributions and Pitfalls

Anthropology has tended to draw an invidious distinction between non-Western and Western medicine, arguing that non-Western conceptualizations of illness and treatment are holistic rather than atomistic or mechanistic. That is, in primitive therapy, the diseased part is not artificially separated from the whole person and the whole social situation (Ackerknecht, 1971; Turner, 1969). Our romantic oversimplification and dichotomization cozens us such that we fail to discern that the nature of the illness is misdefined, while the therapy which is expected to cure or alleviate the illness is a ritual act, the enactment of symbolic statements that mask, rather than clarify, reality. A careful examination of therapeutic symbolism and ritualism both in much of traditional folk medicine and modern neoprimitive cults of holistic medicine suggests that the cure is part of the disease. Primitive theory and therapy are based on the correct assumption that people can make other people sick and crazy. The incorrect assumption has to do with how this takes place: a fallacious epistemology based on developmentally primitive cognitive and regressed affective structure (La Barre, 1975).

I distinguish tribalist therapies from scientific therapies on the basis of whether they are self-indulgent or self-critical, closed or open. In every therapeutic situation, patient, or patient-and-family, and therapist(s) bring expectations and wishes, some of which can be articulated, others of which are out-of-awareness (Hall, 1977). The issue is not whether expectations and wishes will be brought, but what the therapist will do with them. It is one matter for the patient to believe he has been invaded by a foreign body, and for the therapist to comply with a reciprocal therapeusis by sucking out the disease; or for the clincian to draw in sand a representation of the malady, erase the picture, and declare his patient cured (La Barre, 1975). It is quite another thing to accept and utilize the patient or family's symbolic system as an opening therapeutic gambit toward discovering and dealing with what the myths and representations signify (Stein, 1979a).

In an era of increasing demands on therapists of all persuasions, increasing dependency on medical technology and mistrust of it, how might we repersonalize the therapeutic experience without reintroducing the very magical cures—exorcisms—our patients seem to request? It will be important to assess the degree to which family theory/therapy correspond to tribal pseudoholism or genuine scientific holism.

Anthropologists have recognized the key role played by the family in health maintenance, illness definition, and treatment of illness episodes. The family is one of the first and most compelling consultants/diagnosticians of any significant deviation from its norm. The family defines not only the nature of the condition, but its etiology, what should be done, by whom, and its probable course. The family often determines the reason for which that help is sought, where to seek help, whether to comply, or decides against outside assistance altogether (Kleinman, 1978). The member of the family feeling ill or different may take the initiative and consult with family members, friends, peers, superiors, and the like to confirm or disconfirm by consensus his or her initial self-assessment. Conversely, the identified deviant may not be consulted at all by family, peers, or elders, but is labeled by a consensus that does not include him or her. In any case, the illness or altered condition is often negotiated through the family long before "professional" help is sought. In this context, recall again the introductory vignette in which Mrs. K.

dutifully accompanies her obese daughter to their family physician to help Karen lose weight, yet tacitly assumes that Karen cannot slim down, thus, undermining the overt therapeutic goal both in the doctor's office and at home.

From the observer's or metacultural viewpoint, the distinction between health and illness, normal and abnormal, is one of degree, rather than kind (Devereux, 1956; Mead, 1947). The family or cultural group, however, dichotomizes affect-laden distinctions concerning states of health or spirit, so that the identified afflicted individual can be clearly distinguished from them as different (DeVos, 1975; Stein, 1976a).

The anthropological literature is rich on family rules and structures of reciprocal obligations, rights, inheritance, descent, division of labor, artifact use, marriage exchange, child socialization (Goodenough, 1970; Levi-Strauss, 1969; Murdock, 1949; Schusky, 1965). Anthropologists, however, have specialized in instrumental, to the neglect of expressive, aspects of familial roles (Spiegel, 1971). That the deviant individual is acting out repressed wishes with tacit approval, or is a safety valve for the group-homeostasis, is rarely discussed.

Kinship studies have underestimated the role of the emotional economy in task performance, assignment, and choice, and the family as a possible unit of morphostatic dysfunction (Speer, 1970) has been virtually absent in ethnographic observation. Anthropologists have unwittingly conferred on rules, roles, and myths the very sanctity and mystique that the social group attempts to project and protect. Within the family of anthropologists, there is a forceful, yet tacit rule, rationalized by the crypto-Rousseauan idology of cultural relativism, not to notice pathogenesis in a shared, normative system (Stein, 1979b).

A regnant myth in anthropology is that the mere existence, let alone perdurability, of a social system attests culture is necessary to specify both the role of the symptomatic member and of the pathogenic family in the emotional homeostasis of the society.

Family Therapy and Holism

The promise of family therapy lies in its holism. Holism is nothing more mysterious than the functional or dysfunctional relatedness of interpersonal, psychological, behavioral, and psychosomatic systems. As a clinical method, family theory/therapy has cast an ever widening net: schizophrenia, addiction, delinquency, asthma, anorexia nervosa, obesity, heart disease, chronic illness, disability, depression, to name but the most common. At its best, family theory/therapy is an ethnographic mode of observing the family in order to assist the family out of its self-maintaining vicious cycles. As clinical ethnography, family therapy discovers those repetitive, patterned interaction sequences in which verbal statements, voice inflection, body posture, and spatial and temporal arrangements punctuate or qualify one another. From observed sequences of metacommunication, underlying relationship rules, conflicts, values, expectations, and roles are inferred.

Psychoanalysts listen primarily to verbal content. Family therapists observe speech content in context, as with the brief vignette of Karen in the introduction. Unfortunately, the term context is slippery, elusive. Its variable, pragmatic usage reflects the domains which family therapists consider admissable data or evidence. A rigorous holism, to be comprehensive, must be intensive or deep, as well as extensive or broad. Otherwise, incomplete, hence spurious, inferences will be made (Devereux, 1967) and family theory will fossilize as a once promising part-theory.

This highlights the universal fact that theories of behavior and deviance predetermine what type of data is acceptable. Models become self-perpetuating, error-activated, closed systems. Therapeutic plans are not only determined by

prima facie to its adaptiveness. One consequence
unself-critical appraisal of family and cultural tradi
that many anthropologists have insisted that Weste
non-Western therapies are equivalent, or that 1
therapies are superior because of their purportive "h
(Torrey, 1972). Out of an admirable zeal not to be eth
tric, anthropologists often commit the opposite ei
inverted ethnocentrism, gauzily overvaluing everythin
Western. Here, family therapists have often been the si
ethnographers, recognizing that highly dysfunction;
terns not only endure, but thrive over generations as
traditions enshrouded in sanctity. They know that the i
unobservant therapist can play into family patholc
accepting the family's definition of the deviant's pi
(Ferreira, 1963).

To discern symptoms as stabilizing simultaneou
interpersonal and intrapsychic environment, is to im
the officially normal in the pathological. It is to say tl
ostensibly well are merely sick differently (for example
defenses patterned differently) from those who are moi
spicuously deviant or who are so labeled. It is to expa
unit of pathogenesis not only to the family system, but
culture system as well. As La Barre (1956) remarks,
must consider more deeply the problem of the dynam
the 'abnormal' milieu, in which the abnormal individu;
home" (p. 545), and likewise that milieu in which the st;
of the home is purchased at the price of the perpetual a
mality of designated members of the system. And Schai
(1973) writes: "Nearly everyone who has studied famil
persons labeled schizophrenic agrees that the irrational
the schizophrenic finds its rationality in the context (
first family. In what context does that family context fi
rationality?" (p. 84). Family therapy has supplemente
dividual psychosocial or psychosomatic diagnosis with f
diagnosis. Diagnosis and explanation at the level of sl

the method of observation, but by the kind of information one is looking for derived from assumptions underlying that methodology. It has been the fate of scientific reformations to forget that what is now doctrine once began as fresh insight and observation. There is the danger that family therapy, in defocusing, will overfocus and exclude sources of data that now conflict with a central dogma (for example, the site of pathology consists of a suprapersonal system). For example, infantile sexuality, primal scenes, incest fantasies, castration fears, separation anxiety, and oedipal resolutions cannot be excluded from family dynamics without our understanding of family motivation and conflict perpetuation becoming not only impoverished but distorted. After all, an essential member of the family division of labor is the neotenous infant who specializes in infancy, just as the parents reexperience their own childhood reawakened by their child (La Barre, 1968, 1972; Parsons, 1969).

Family theory/therapy shares with biology and psychoanalysis a concern for pathological versus healthy equilibrium: indeed, a homeostatic model is central to family theory/therapy (Beavers, 1976; Jackson, 1957). Among the shared assumptions of family therapy, many violate our cultural canons of common sense. Some examples would be:

1 Disease as a way of communicating with the family.
2 Disease as a symptom of an underlying interpersonal dysfunction, of which the identified patient is a metaphor.
3 Pathology as a way of not communicating about something and someone that is more disturbing.
4 The familiar family theme of, "The harder we try, the sicker he/she gets," irrespective of the type of pathology.
5 The powerful role of the ostensibly powerless victim in stabilizing the family structure.
6 The normative stability, or at least facade normalcy, of the identified healthy members as based on the pathology

of an identified sick member.

7 The rigidity of interaction sequences and responses to typical or new situations in pathological families.

8 Morphostasis as preventing adaptation or adaptability in closed system families (Speer, 1970).

9 Family myths (Ferreira, 1963) as interpersonal self-representations that function as group defenses to prevent the eruption of conflict.

10 Covert coalitions, often intergenerational, that regulate power and access (Haley, 1969).

11 Therapy as based on a renunciation of the illusion of alternatives (Watzlawick, Weakland, & Fisch, 1974) whose choices are based on the repetition of pathogenic premises.

12 Therapy as consisting of a reframing of the problem such as to allow second order change, i. e., a change in the premises themselves.

13 Therapy as consisting of a repunctuation of the interactional syntac.

14 The therapist as remaining largely outside of the family transference system, serving as a facilitator of change.

15 Improvement in one member of the family system, if treatment occurs independent of that system, will result in systemic pressure for restoration of status quo ante, decompensation of other family member(s) whose defensive system has failed, or commonly both.

Despite their diversity, family systems theorists have demonstrated the utter inappropriateness of the question which every society poses, i. e., "Who has the real problem?" The unity of illness is simultaneously the organism, individual, family, and the culture.

Illness and Levels of Analysis

Let us explore a familiar problem: How do we characterize a heart attack in American society? We first note that heart attack is a folk medical term used to subsume a variety of cardiovascular pathologies discretely defined in scientific medicine. In both models, however, a specific organ system is identified as the site and cause of the disease. So there is medical and lay consensus that a heart attack is a coronary event. Although evidence strongly suggests that heart attacks are associated with stress (Alexander, 1950; Byrne, 1978; Friedman & Rosenman, 1974; Rowland & Sokol, 1977), often the treatment is strictly biomedical, emergency medicine, acute care, coupled with the afterthought to "take life a little easier...or else."

Meanwhile, there has accumulated literature on the Type A Personality who is premorbidly more vulnerable to heart attacks (Dembroski et al., 1978; Friedman & Rosenman, 1974): one who is especially ambitious, time-conscious, aggressive, driven, mobile, eager for higher and higher rungs of success, competitive, and industrious. This personality will press onward, allowing no obstacle to hinder him or her in pursuit of a goal. The stress is largely self-induced.

A Type B Personality also has been diagnosed, a veritable mirror image of the Type A (Friedman & Rosenman, 1974; Jackson, 1966): relatively easy-going, soft-spoken, ready to delegate work, etc. On closer inspection, as Jackson notes (1966), one finds that Type As and Type Bs are complementary in a mutually reinforcing system. Each, in fact, recruits the other into his or her interpersonal network that is, seeks those who will reinforce Type A or Type B behavior. Each needs the other. They constitute a relationship system, an interpersonal organ system or complementary neurosis (Sander, 1978) of which the cardiovascular system is both metaphor and microcosm. Yet, if one inquires into the heart attack patient's family system or work situation, one will most often be offered the smokescreen of family myth or group fantasy wherein everything is fine, there are really no insurmountable problems, "It's just my heart." The heart attack is, thus, a metaphor for pathological communication (Van Egeren, 1979).

Medical metaphor, personality profile, and family/occupation dynamic, however, must be further supplemented by what Fine (1977) terms a culturally sanctioned adjustment neurosis. Family myth receives additional support from cultural myth and value system: that of individualism, exclusive self-reliance, achievement, meriting one's status, and the like (Erikson, 1963; Hsu, 1972). A family symbiosis, which supplements individual defenses, is further supplemented by a cultural symbiosis where the ruggedly driven individualist is far from a loner, but is an actor performing for a societal audience of competitors and cheerleaders.

Why, however, do people invest so heavily, and at such high risks, in particular cultural values, attitudes, and institutions? This tenacious investment serves to defend the individual against early experiences associated with the fear of abandonment, maternal intrusiveness, repressed rage, and the fear of failure (Erikson, 1963). Worthwhileness is sustained by doing. The anlagen for cardiovascular decompensation are established in the process of culturally normative development. From the point of view of a holistic family theory/therapy, the real problem cannot be heuristically isolated or even spatially localized in the patient with the heart attack. The "real" problem extends to the societal division of labor in which only some will become debilitated in a socially or familially official way.

A central tenet of holistic family theory is that one could perform a systemic analysis for any disease entity or social problem, identical to the present one on cardiovascular disease. This paradigm renders precise the concept of relational biology introduced earlier. When we approach the division of labor by affect rather than by manifest instrumental role, we discover that those who are, in family and society, labeled as well, purchase their stability and well-being at the price of the sick members of the system. They are not normal; they are simply sick differently. Even the victim or scapegoat does not suffer passively (though this may be his private or even group myth). The victim as much sustains the remainder of the system as the others in it enlist him for heroic sacrifice.

One needs to ask not only why a given individual is sick, and sick now, but for whom else he or she is ill. What greater disturbance does the symptomatically disturbed member keep under control, undisturbed? Returning to the opening vignette, what would happen to Karen's mother were Karen to obey her mother's overt wish to lose weight, instead of complying with her tacit injunction to stay fat? One need hardly speculate: the mother's self-hate, now dissociated to Karen, would no longer have an external object and would return with a vengence. In all likelihood, the mother would again become obese and depressed.

Here again, the perspective of levels of analysis is crucial in the emotional economy of the family. Frequently when the identified sick member recovers, the family must find another outlet for its sickness in the florid pathology of a new member. Likewise at the level of the psychosomatic patient, "Improvement of the organic symptoms...often presents a new problem for the ego: to find a new outlet for the tendencies heretofore relieved by the organic symptoms" (Alexander, 1950, p. 269). In the first instance, the pathological individual is designated to embody the deviance from the family norm; in the second instance, psychosomatic pathology gives expression to ego-alien tendencies. It is a matter of recognizing that one is describing the same thing from different levels (Spiro, 1951).

In family therapy, however, not unlike other treatment modes, clinicians often have become selectively perceptive of one domain of data to the exclusion of others. Theory and therapy, instead of being holistically inclusive, may become reductionistically exclusive, a trend well under way. For instance, one therapist will be exquisitely attuned to his family's use of space and time as metacommunications about their relationship in his presence (Minuchin, 1974); another will pay close attention to his patient's emotional relationship systems several generations upward (Bowen, 1978); another will focus on the imprisoning paradoxes which the family uses to deal with the most trifling matter (Watzlawick, Beavin & Jackson, 1967); still another will limit what is admissible in family therapy to solving problems of living together (Bell, 1974); and so on. Instead of seeing each of these as complementary frames of reference, as different levels of the family's reality, a single context is chosen as truth and the royal road to family health. The heart attack patient's problem is neither all in his cardiovascular system nor in his family, but both. And Karen's obesity is neither her personal problem nor that of her family, but both.

Arbitrariness of Boundaries

At some point, the most structuralist, behavioralist, or paradoxicalist family therapy draws an arbitrary boundary around what is manageable, assuming internalized process and intrapsychic motivation. One can never assemble the entire family, living and deceased, in the conference room. One can never visit every relative whose relationship function in the family has impinged on one's development. One can never entirely eliminate the powerful effect of the transference, even though one has vowed to stay out of it, if not ignore it.

The very willingness of family members to participate in therapy, to be relationally engineered or sculpted, make emotionally difficult or financially costly visits to relatives or comply with programmed tasks, assumes a prepotent internal readiness for change in the direction the therapist directs them to go. It appears that the family therapist must tacitly accept that family members not only respond to the relational context, but participate in its creation and in the maintenance of patterned sequences for reasons of their own. The therapist who defines himself or herself as consultant, sculptor, or engineer must keenly take into consideration the unconscious meanings of family interaction in order that a spatial rearrangement, task, or interpretation be timed so as to meet the abilities and needs of the family.

Subtle attentiveness to unconscious forces in the intra- and interpersonal defense system may facilitate the acceptability and, hence, the outcome of therapeutic management. The context cannot be manipulated toward genuine change, that is, second order change, a change in assumptions or premises, (Watzlawick, Weakland & Fisch, 1974) unless the context is ready for that change and the therapist engineers the change precisely when the first condition prevails. The parallel with insight-interpretation in psychoanalysis is obvious.

Even the most directive therapy must obey the paradoxical rule of leading by following if the therapist is to use the personality or family system as the basis for changing itself. People can be engineered only when they are first engineerable. The relationship of the therapist to the patient or family is a decisive ingredient in that engineerability. The much maligned placebo effect of the therapeutic relationship is a nuisance and embarrassment only because we compulsively insist on the purity of our method, and fear its contamination by the most effective therapeutic agent: the meaning of that relationship for the patients (Balint, 1957; Devereux, 1967; La Barre, 1978; Rogers, 1951). To borrow from Buber (1958), you cannot foster in your patient the emergence of "Thou" by treating him/her as an "It."

If techniques of child-rearing are inseparable from the affective communication in which they are embedded (Erikson, 1963; Hartmann, Kris & Lowenstein, 1970; Mead, 1954; Sperling, 1974; Stein, 1978a), what would make therapeutic communication (Reusch, 1973) operate according to other rules? Perhaps only our culturally shared worldview.

Family Therapy, American Culture, and Metacultural Therapy

To what extent can we say that the goals of family therapy are culture-bound? To what degree do they help the individual and family to transcend his or her family biog raphy, to foster the capacity for mature love, separation-individuation, differentiation, reality testing, morphogenesis, and adaptability? To the extent that family therapy accepts the depersonalizing cultural totems and metaphors of machine and computer as the basis for its worldview and view of human nature, its goals and means are culture-bound (Weizenbaum, 1976).

Family therapy, certainly, is native to American culture. One should question the extent to which family therapy, like any indigenous healing paradigm, is fixed by cultural premises or transcends them. American culture has largely indigenized much of the Western scientific and medical tradition. As a consequence, such dominant value-orientations as efficiency, quick solutions to problems, easy mastery of obstacles, an empiricism which accepts as valid data only what the eye and its technological extensions can see, and the like influence the proccess of diagnosis, deter-mining etiology, making treatment plans and prognosis. We conduct endless clinical trials based on an empiricism whose cultural premises we do not challenge. Machine and com-puter are our totem; and affect, our taboo (Stein & Kayzakian-Row, 1978). Treatment consists of an impersonal repair of a malfunctioning device, the correction of informa-tion flow. In medicine, one rigorously rules out physical or somatic or organismic pathology before dubiously ruling in psychiatric or social considerations.

The very language of much of family therapy expresses the imagery of mechanics and cybernetics, behavioral modifica-tion, engineering, structural change, positive feedback loops, etc. This is to impugn neither industrialization nor computerized data processing, but to recognize that cultural patterns and metaphors spread inappropriately and indiscriminately. An ethos tends to be used as an article of faith, not an hypothesis. One could profitably see in cultural metaphors symptoms of what people try to avoid speaking about, yet which they reveal in the act of concealing.

Consider again the principle of homeostasis. The homeostat does not exist as a force external to the system which uses it. Rather, it is a mutually negotiated and constantly renegotiated tacit division of labor within the family. Although it is an extremely useful metaphor for the equilibration of the family and social system, it does not operate independent of how family members regulate it to regulate themselves; nor does it explain why it is kept.

If pathology is error-activated behavior, why are the same errors so recursively reactivated (Devereux, 1956)? If, as Minuchin (1974) argues in his widely adopted structural theory, man is not himself without his situations, still we must account for the fact that man recreates his unhappy situations throughout life, finding partners who will enable him to reenact personal dramas he cannot relinquish—just as they find in him the partner and audience with and for whom to perform. Is it not necessary to infer, at least hypothesize, an internal environment that is the building block of human situations? As Hallowell (1955) suggests, human societies consist of a "culturally constituted behavioral environment," an outer situation to which people adapt, yet which they have played a considerable role in creating. The very environment that is perceived as a given is first an assumption.

Family therapy, in my opinion, may fall into the same culture-bound trap as have ecological and community psychiatry and psychology, namely operating on the transculturally false assumption that the mere manipulation of the environment, say, the modification of interaction patterns, results in permanent change and, hence, resolution of the presenting problem. We may become more attentive to, and captivated by, our metaphors than by our patients. As wardens of our own conceptual prisons, we may conduct our therapy and measure the outcome of our interventions by an empiricism of whose premises and myths we, like our patients, are only dimly aware (Devereux, 1967; La Barre, 1978). I say this as a word of warning and foreboding, for I discern in family theory/therapy at its core, rather than in its cultural trappings, a metacultural revolutionary potential which it may unwittingly subvert. In my view, a family therapy unencumbered by cultural blinders should be valid transculturally, since it would be grounded in the species specific biology of the human family.

As psychoanalysis, it would have to accept the family/-patient symbol and relationship system in order to be accepted by it as an agent of change. This is only to say that initially family therapy does not so much execute as observe, awaiting those openings in which change is appropriately induced.

The family therapist should expect to modify his or her technique to the extent of preparing the family patient for therapy, for making the patient what Devereux (1969) calls in another context therapeutizable. The goal of family therapy should not vary one whit from culture to culture—unless we buy into the culture-relativistic argument that therapy is designed to help the individual or family readjust or conform to the very cultural system that was the pathway to madness.

Families of diverse cultures will certainly bring different expectations. But this should no more dissuade us than the fact that culturally familiar families expect us to conform to and validate their myths. Membership in a different culture means only that the family myth may be different, not that theirs is more sacred. Clinically, if we keep in mind the universal human family with its species-specific conflicts (such as separation/individuation, Oedipus, adolescence), we will find differences only in their emphasis and expression. This is precisely why Freud (in the Schreber case, 1911) could develop a paradigm of paranoia on the basis of a single case, and why, today, family therapists can develop universally valid models of psychosomatic disorder based not on sample size but on the quality of observation in very few families (Minuchin, 1975).

Perhaps ironically, family theorists/therapists most solidly based in human biology and psychodynamics stand the best chance for avoiding the lures of resocializing their families to American culture, or any ethnic culture for that matter. Instead, they help them discover for themselves those values and rules that foster the developmental potential and functional autonomy of each member within the relationship. Ideally, the family in its life cycle becomes freed to mature as it frees the one or ones in whom it had a stake in developmental arrest. Once growth can be diagnostically distinguished from mere change, and normal individuation from normative individualism, the family therapist has transcended culture-bound folk-scientific therapy.

The holistic direction of family therapy would seem to be at odds with the closed systems model that various schools have adopted. Much of family therapy tends to discourage consideration both in theory and therapy of:(a) intrapsychic development and psychodynamics, and (b) suprafamilial social units from neighborhood to culture. Frequently such concepts as symbiosis, enmeshment, fusion, togetherness, dependency are virtually depsychologized and either pseudo-biologized or made into structural principles which appear to govern relationships independent of those who adopt and use them.

We need to ask again what relationships are about, why particular norms and structures of relationships are invested in, and what is the source of their tenacity. Pathological communication, for example the double bind, is a vehicle for the expression and mystification of internalized conflict or ambivalence. By themselves, communication structure, feedback, power alliances, and covert cross-generational coalitions do not explain what all the strife, loyalty, anguish, secrecy, or acting out are about. Boszormenyi-Nagy (1966), for instance, is correct in calling for a psychology of relationships. If family therapy is to be holistic, it would need to incorporate concepts of personality change and growth (Boszormenyi-Nagy, 1966). One would need to know the object relations which facilitate or inhibit the psychobiologically built-in developmental epigenesis (Erikson, 1963); and, furthermore, specify the developmental stages in which they are experienced and become self-representations.

Family Systems and Social Systems

This discussion of family theory/therapy as a systemic approach to pathology would, in my opinion, be incomplete without at least brief mention of how society might be conceptualized in the anthropological framework utilized here. Society can, not by analogy but homology, be considered as family writ large or as a widely expanded extended family. Cultural myths and group fantasies serve the identical homeostatic/morphostatic function at the level of society that family myths serve at the level of the family. The dynamic is the same; only the scale is different. In cultural groups, as in families, one finds members or subgroups being delegated roles and statuses in accordance with an unconscious, affective division of labor. Group-shared double binds and covert coalitions are designed to appoint, label, and perpetuate deviant pariah groups who bear the burden of the normals' outrage, anxiety, vicarious enjoyment, and unconscionable wishes. At the same time, from the point of view of either family or society, the officially labeled symptomatic deviant or subgroup is not the only casualty of the system. The social system that needs its casualties is, likewise, the casualty of its own failures of integration, differentiation, and morphogenesis.

One must be careful to note that the hypernormal as well as the officially abnormal are group-delegated and self-appointed victims of the social drama in which they participate. I refer not only to those negative or stigmatized departures from the norm, but those as well who seem to be its cynosure (La Barre, 1956) and suffer its consequences as well: for instance, the Type A aggressive achiever as opposed to the refractorily overweight Karen in the opening vignette. Culture hero and villain, alike, openly display what the normal represses, or at most, expresses in a more modulated, private form (Devereux, 1956). One can easily enumerate those motley social diagnoses that denote the more familiar deviants, such as criminals, the mentally ill, homosexuals, ethnic minorities, etc. These cognitive categories, tied with affective conflict, are never a matter of indifference (DeVos, 1975). Physical and linguistic boundaries place and identify these threats to inner homeostasis outside the group self—to segregate them as different while needing that very difference. Hollywood and the ghetto are simply two opposite ends of the social spectrum. Members of these groups, the admired and condemned, are kept safely at arm's length, but, nonetheless, kept. The culturally normal community needs them to be abnormal for itself. Those differences which society's normals regard as intrinsic to the abnormals and hypernormals are perceived as such precisely to the degree to which the normals need to externalize these attributes from themselves. A vicious circle is, thus, created. For instance, neither criminals nor the insane can be truly rehabilitated and integrated into the community mainstream so long as the normals need them to act out their pathology.

On a societal level, one hears the familiar familial rules: Once an "X," always an "X," and so forth. The various deviants and deviant groups function to bind the larger group-anxiety in the same way that the identified sick member of the family is both delegated and internalized the role of homeostat for the family. All attempts at social change, without a change in the unconscious premises, lead only to "more of the same"—for which the deviant is then blamed, for example, the failed War on Poverty in the 1960s, and the subsequent blame aimed at blacks for not bettering themselves. This author certainly does not advocate the discontinuance of therapy with identified deviants, to help them develop the autonomy to withstand and keep out of the societal transference. Those equally in need of treatment, however, are those whom we have mistaken to be normal. We must begin conceptually to defocus on the deviant population, and direct greater research and therapeutic atention to that wider population who are dependent on their deviants.

We must also take a more careful look at processes of social change, for example, the alleged current decline or demise of the family. Much of social change, even ostensibly radical change, possesses a "more-of-the-same" quality to it that we see in families whose homeostasis has been upset and which search frenetically for a new basis for equilibrium (Stein, 1976b, 1978c). Commonly, a revolutionary inversion of the previous social order masks continuity with the past with official ideological and behavioral upheavals. The French Revolution deposed the King, only to make way for Emperor Napoleon; Czar Nicholas II was "succeeded" in the Russian Revolution by Stalin as "our dear little father." Nowhere is the symbiosis more strong than where the repudiation is most strident (Stein, 1976c, 1978c). Hardly surprising to the jaded observer, those who at first glance seemed most deviant came to represent and enforce the new status quo. Massive social turnarounds generate their own morphostasis in new ideological guise.

Summary and Implications

This chapter has offered an anthropological perspective on the nature of the family and family therapy. The opening vignette stated a premise that wove a continuous strand throughout the chapter, namely, that the promise of family therapy as a holistic treatment approach lies in the therapist's learning how to observe, not what to choose. This author emphasized that major breakthroughs in family therapy have come from clinician-researchers who have conducted naturalistic observation of pathological families in the treatment setting. Thus the author concludes that the basis for good therapy is good clinical ethnography. Moreover, the perceptive observation of the family must be based in an understanding of the psychobiological nature of the human family.

The greatest obstacles to family therapy's realizing its holistic potential were shown to lie:(a) in its reliance on the culture-bound metaphors of the machine and the computer, and (b) its tendency to reify the family into a closed unit, organism, and level of abstraction separate from the people who constitute it and who assign its relationship meanings. The author has argued that one must approach family and social homeostasis and change from multiple levels of analysis, otherwise, family therapy will become yet another reductionism.

The author proposes that the open-ended ethnographic framework allows the family therapist to discover something genuinely new, not simply translate novelty into expectation. Specifically, the author suggests that the ethnographic method allows the clinical investigator, unmediated by biasing instruments, to discover the extent and type of change that takes place in family therapy. Furthermore, the author proposes the intensive ethnographic study of therapy in vivo, followed by a similar long term ethnographic study of these families after termination of treatment, as a means of evaluating outcome. The author hopes that family therapy will not be content to commit the dynamically naive error that has plagued anthropological studies of medical systems: namely, awe over the immediate results of spectacular curing rites. The rite and the cure still need to be explained, and the patient or family followed over time so that one can determine how, who, and if the treatment succeeded or failed.

Finally, there remains the question of the goal of family therapy. If the goal is not readjusting the family to a cultural norm, then to what norm is our therapy directed? Normality, individual and familial, is metacultural, beyond the culture principle. Yet, neither are self-mystifying family norms to be taken as sacred. Normality, at the level of the family, lies in the absence of the need for pathological communication and for those family myths that safeguard family pathology. The measure of family normality or health lies in a relational biology in which, as the poet Rilke (1962) so hauntingly put it, "two solitudes protect and border and salute each other" (p. 59). To be able to enter into a genuine "we," one must be able to utter, and mean, I.

REFERENCES

Ackerknecht, E.H. *Medicine and ethnology.* Baltimore: Johns Hopkins Press, 1971.

Alexander, F. *Psychosomatic medicine.* New York: Norton, 1950.

Balint, M. *The doctor, his patient and the illness.* New York: International Universities Press, 1957.

Beavers, W.R. A theoretical basis for family evaluation. In J.M. Lewis, W.R. Beavers, J.T. Gossett, & V.A. Phillips (Eds.). *No single thread: Psychological health in family systems.* New York: Brunner/Mazel, 1976.

Bell, J.E. *Family therapy.* New York: Jason Aronson, 1974.

Blumer, H. Social movements. In B. McLaughlin (Ed.), *Studies in social movements.* New York: The Free Press, 1969, 8-29.

Boszormenyi-Nagy, I. From family therapy to a psychology of relationships: Fictions of the individual and fictions of the family. *Comprehensive Psychiatry,* 1966, *7,* 408-423.

Bowen, M. *Family therapy in clinical practice.* New York: Jason Aronson, 1978.

Buber, M. *I and thou.* New York: Charles Scribner's and Sons, 1958.

Byrne, D.G. Personality, stress, and coronary heart disease. *Medical Journal of Australia*, 1978, 10, 469-470.

Caudill, W. Psychiatry and anthropology: The individual and his nexus. In L. Nader, & T.W. Maretzki (Eds.), *Cultural Illness and Health*. Washington, D.C.: American Anthropological Association, 1973.

Dembroski, T.M. et al. (Eds.). *Coronary-prone behavior*. New York: Springer, 1978.

Devereux, G. Normal and abnormal: The key problem of psychiatric anthropology. In *Some uses of anthropology: theoretical and applied*. Washington, D.C.: The Anthropological Society of Washington, 1956.

Devereux, G. *From anxiety to method in the behavioral sciences*. The Hague: Mouton, 1967.

Devereux, G. *Reality and dream: Psychotherapy of a Plains Indian*. New York: New York University Press, 1969.

DeVos, G. The dangers of pure theory in social anthropology. *Ethos*, 1975, *3*, 77-91.

Eisenberg, L. Disease and illness: Distinctions between professional and popular ideas of sickness. *Cultural, Medical Psychiatry*, 1977, *1*, 9-24.

Erikson, E.H. *Childhood and society*. (revised ed.) New York: Norton, 1963.

Ferreira, A.J. Family myths and homeostasis. *Archives of General Psychiatry*, 1963, *9*, 56-61.

Fine, R. Psychoanalysis as a philosophical system: The basis for integrating the social sciences. *Journal of Psychohistory*, 1977, *5*, 1-66.

Foster, G.M., & Anderson, B.G. *Medical anthropology*. New York: John Wiley and Sons, 1978.

Freud, S. *Psychoanalytic notes on an autobiographical account of a case of paranoia*. (Standard ed., 12) London: Hogarth Press, 1911.

Friedman, M., & Rosenman, R.H. *Type A behavior and your heart*. New York: Alfred A. Knopf, 1974.

Goodenough, W.H. *Description and comparison in cultural anthropology*. Chicago: Aldine, 1970.

Haley, J. Whither family therapy. In *The power tactics of Jesus Christ, and other essays*. New York: Avon, 1969.

Hall, E. *Beyond Culture*. Garden City, N.Y.: Doubleday/Anchor, 1977.

Hallowell, A.I. *Culture and experience*. Philadelphia: University of Pennsylvania Press, 1955.

Hartmann, H., Kris, E., & Loewenstein, R.W. Some psychoanalytic comments on culture and personality. In W. Muensterberger (Ed.),

Man and his culture: Psychoanalytic anthropology after 'totem and taboo.' New York: Taplinger, 1970.

Hay, T. The Windigo psychosis: Psychodynamic, cultural, and social factors in aberrant behavior. *American Anthropology,* 1971, *73,* 1-19.

Henry, J. My life with the families of psychotic children. In G. Handel, (Ed.), *The psychosocial interior of the family.* Chicago: Aldine, 1967.

Hsu, F.L.K. American core value and national character. In F.L.K. Hsu (Ed.), *Psychological anthropology: Approaches to culture and personality.* Homewood, Ill.: Dorsey Press, 1972.

Jackson, D.D. The question of family homeostasis. *Psychiatric Quarterly Supplement,* 1957, *31* (part 1), 79-90.

Jackson, D.D. Family practice: A comprehensive medical approach. *Comprehensive Psychiatry,* 1966, *7,* 338-344.

Kleinman, A. International health care planning from an ethnomedical perspective: Critique and recommendations for change. *Medical Anthropology,* 1978, *2,* 71-96.

La Barre, W. Social cynosure and social structure. In D. Haring (Ed.), *Personal character and cultural milieu.* Syracuse, N.Y.: Syracuse University Press, 1956,

La Barre W. *The human animal.* Chicago: University of Chicago Press, 1968.

La Barre, M. *The ghost dance: The origins of religion.* New York: Dell, 1972.

La Barre, W. Anthropological perspectives on hallucination and hallucinogens. In R.K. Siegal, & L.J. West (Eds.), *Hallucinations: Behavior, experience and theory.* New York: John Wiley and Sons, 1975.

La Barre, W. The clinic and the field. In G.D. Spindler (Ed.), *The making of psychological anthropology.* Berkeley: University of California Press, 1978.

Levi-Strauss, C. *The elementary structures of kinship.* Boston: Beacon Press, 1969.

Mahler, M., Bergman, A., & Pine, F. *The psychological birth of the human infant: Symbiosis and individuation.* New York: Basic Books, 1975.

Mead, M. The concept of culture and the psychosomatic approach. *Psychiatry,* 1947, *10,* 57-76.

Mead, M. The swaddling hypothesis: its reception. *American Anthropology,* 1954, *56,* 395-409.

Minuchin, S. *Families and family therapy.* Cambridge: Harvard University Press, 1974.

Minuchin S. A conceptual model of psychosomatic illness in children. *Archives of General Psychiatry,* 1975, *32,* 1031-1038.

Murdock, G.P. *Social structure*. New York: MacMillan, 1949.

Parsons, A. Is the oedipus complex universal? The Jones-Malinowski debate revisited and a South Italian nuclear complex. In W. Muensterberger (Ed.), *Man and his culture: Psychoanalytic anthropology after 'totem and taboo.'* New York: Taplinger, 1969.

Rilke, R.M. *Letters to a young poet*. M.D.H. Norton (Trans.), New York: W.W. Norton, Co., 1962.

Rogers, C.K. *Client-centered therapy*. Boston: Houghton-Mifflin Co. 1951.

Rowland, K.F., & Sokol, B. A review of research examining the coronary-prone behavior pattern. *Journal of Human Stress*, 1977, *3*, 26-33.

Ruesch, J. *Therapeutic communication*. New York: Norton, 1973.

Sander, F.M. Marriage and the family in Freud's writings. *Journal of American Academy of Psychoanalysis*, 1978, 6, 157-174.

Schatzman, M. Paranoia or persecution: The case of Schreber. *History of Childhood Quarterly*, 1973, *1*, 62-88.

Schusky, E.L. *Manual for kinship analysis*. New York: Holt, Rinehart and Winston, 1965.

Speer, D.C. Family systems: Morphostasis and morphogenesis, or is homeostasis enough? *Family Process*, 1970, *9*, 259-278.

Sperling, M. *The major neuroses and behavior disorders in children*. New York: Jason Aronson, 1974.

Spiegel, J. *Transactions: The interplay between individual, family, and society*. New York: Science House, 1971.

Spiro, M.E. Personality and culture: The natural history of a false dichotomy. *Psychiatry*, 1951, *14*, 19-46.

Spiro, M.E. *Gender and culture: Kibbutz women revisited*. Durham, N.C.: Duke University Press, 1979.

Stein, H.F. Cultural specificity in patterns of mental illness and health: A Slovak-American case study. *Family Process*, 1973, *12*, 69-82.

Stein, H.F. Envy and the Evil Eye among Slovak-Americans: An essay in the psychological ontogeny of belief and ritual. *Ethos*, Spring 1974, *2*, 15-46.

Stein, H.F. A dilectical model of health and illness attitudes and behavior among Slovak-Americans. *International Journal of Mental Health*, 1976(a), *5*, 117-137.

Stein, H.F. *Peter and the Wolf*, a musical tale of individuation and imagery of the new Soviet man: A psychoanalytic perspective on Russian culture history. In W. Muensterberger, A. Esman, & L.B. Boyer (Eds.), *The Psychoanalytic Study of Society*. New Haven: Yale University Press, 1976(b), 31-63.

Stein, H.F. Russian nationalism and the divided soul of the westernizers and slavophiles. *Ethos,* Winter 1976(c), *4,* 403-438.

Stein, H.F. The Slovak-American swaddling ethos: Homeostat for family dynamics and cultural continuity. *Family Process,* 1978(a), *17,* 31-45.

Stein, H.F. Aging and death among Slovak-Americans: A study in the thematic unity of the life cycle. *Journal of Psychological Anthropology,* 1978(b), *1,* 297-320.

Stein, H.F. Judaism and the group-fantasy of martyrdom. *Journal of Psychohistory,* 1978(c), *6,* 115-210.

Stein, H.F. The salience of ethno-psychology for medical education and practice. *Social Science and Medicine,* 1979(a), *3,* 199-210.

Stein, H.F. Rehabilitation and chronic illness in American culture: The cultural psychodynamics of a medical and social problem. *Journal of Psychological Anthropology,* 1979(b), *2,* 78-97.

Stein, H.F., & Hill, R.F. *The ethnic imperative: Exploring the new white ethnic movement.* University Park, Pa.: The Pennsylvania State University Press, 1977.

Stein, H.F. & Kayzakian-Rowe, S. Hypertension, biofeedback, and the myth of the machine: A psychoanalytic-cultural exploration. *Psychoanalysis and Contemporary Thought,* 1978, *1,* 119-156.

Stierlin, H. Group fantasies and myths: Some theoretical and practical aspects. *Family Process,* 1973, *12,* 111-125.

Torrey, E.F. *The mind game: Witch doctors and psychiatrists.* New York: Emerson Hall Publishers, 1972.

Turner, V. *The ritual process,* Ithaca, N.Y.: Cornell University Press, 1969.

Turner, V. *Revelation and divination in Ndembu ritual.* Ithaca, N.Y.: Cornell University Press, 1975.

Van Egeren, L.F. Social interactions, communications, and the coronary-prone behavior pattern: A psychophysiological study. *Psychosomatic Medicine,* February 1979, *41*(1), 2-18.

Wallace, A.F.C. Revitalization Movements. *American Anthropology,* 1956, *58,* 264-281.

Wallace, A.F.C. *Religion: An anthropological view.* New York: Random House, 1966.

Watzlawick, P., Beavin, J., & Jackson, D. *Pragmatics of Human Communication.* New York: W.W. Norton & Co., 1967.

Watzlawick, P., Weakland, J., & Fisch, R. *Change: Principles of problem formation and problem resolution.* New York: W.W. Norton, 1974.

Weizenbaum, J. *Computer power and human reason: From judgment to calculations.* San Francisco: W.H. Freeman and Co., 1976.

INDEX

Abeles, G., 243, 252
Ackerknecht, E.H., 270
Adaptability dimension, 26
  balanced relationships, 29;
  changes in, 29, 30, 32; studies
  measuring, 33, 38, 39; *See*
  Cohesion dimension; Family
  adaptability indicators
Alexander, F., 277, 279
Alexander, J.F., 196, 232
Anderson, B.G., 269
Andolfi, M., 227
Anthropological framework of
  society, 286-288
Aponte, H., 229, 230
Ashcraft, C., 194
Assertiveness. *See* Family
  adaptability indicators
Assessment tools
  Beavers-Timberlawn Family
  Evaluation Scale, 140-142,
  155; Bowerman and Bahr
  Identification Scale, 33;
  Coping Health Inventory for
  Parents (CHIP), 113, 114;
  Edwards Personal Preference
  Test, 194; Family Adaptability
  and Cohesion Evaluation Scale
  (FACES), 33, 35, 36, 39-41;
  Family Bond Inventory (FBI),

140; Genogram, 140, 152, 154;
  Global Health-Pathology
  Scale, 141, 155; Inventory of
  Parent-Adolescent Conflict,
  33, 35; Kveback Family
  Sculpture Test, 33; Lock-
  Wallace Short Marital
  Adjustment Scale, 83; Moos
  Family Environment Scale
  (FES), 36-38, 114, 115, 118,
  129; Simulated Family Activity
  Measure (SIMFAM), 33, 34;
  Spousal Inventory of Desired
  Changes and Relationship
  Barriers (SIDCARB), 85-88,
  91, 93, 94, 96, 97, 101, 102;
  Tennessee Self-Concept Scale,
  194, 200, 202
Attneave, C.L., 187
autonomy, 148-150, 155
See Family, dimensions of
Autry, J.H., 243
Azrin, N.H., 95

Bagarozzi, D.A., 69, 70, 79, 80,
  82, 88, 92, 101
Bagarozzi, J.I., 101
Baker, L., 219
Balint, M., 281
Bank, S., 92

295

Date Due